Crusades for Freedom

Crusades for Freedom

Memphis and the Political Transformation
of the American South

G. Wayne Dowdy

University Press of Mississippi   Jackson

www.upress.state.ms.us

The University Press of Mississippi is a member
of the Association of American University Presses.

Copyright © 2010 by University Press of Mississippi
All rights reserved
Manufactured in the United States of America

First printing 2010

∞

Library of Congress Cataloging-in-Publication Data
Dowdy, G. Wayne.
  Crusades for freedom : Memphis and the political transformation of the American South / G. Wayne Dowdy.
  p. cm.
  Includes bibliographical references and index.
  ISBN 978-1-60473-423-2 (cloth : alk. paper) 1. Memphis (Tenn.)—Politics and government—20th century. 2. African Americans—Tennessee—Memphis—Politics and government—20th century. 3. Memphis (Tenn.)—Race relations—History—20th century. 4. Crump, Edward Hull, 1874–1954. 5. Democratic Party (Shelby County, Tenn.)—History—20th century. I. Title.
  F444.M557D69 2010
  976.8'19053—dc22   2009023095

British Library Cataloging-in-Publication Data available

Contents

Preface　vii

Acknowledgments　ix

1. "We Are Living in a Different Day"　3
2. "My Family Ties in the South"　19
3. "All the Cooperation We Can Muster"　33
4. "Why Didn't Someone Tell Us This Before?"　47
5. "To Compel the White Race"　66
6. "Please Don't Do That"　86
7. "A Great Movement Here in Memphis"　108

Afterword　139

Appendix A. Memphis City Government, 1948–1968　143

Appendix B. Election Returns　145

Notes　149

Bibliography　173

Index　179

Preface

This volume is a sequel of sorts to my first book, *Mayor Crump Don't Like It: Machine Politics in Memphis* (University Press of Mississippi, 2006). While that book traced the early career of legendary boss Edward Hull Crump and his construction of a biracial, multiethnic political machine in the segregated South, this volume chronicles the demise of that organization and the corresponding rise to power of the South's two minorities, African Americans and Republicans, between the years 1948 and 1968. During that time Memphis emerged as a small, but nevertheless consequential, battleground in the struggle to create a strong two-party South and, for the first time in its history, both Republican and Democratic presidential candidates campaigned vigorously for the Bluff City's votes.

Closely tied to these changing political fortunes was the struggle of African Americans to overturn two centuries of discrimination and exploitation which had begun decades before but reached its zenith during the years chronicled in this book. Memphis was by no means at the forefront of the black freedom movement but neither was it a civil rights backwater. In the 1950s the local branch of the National Association for the Advancement of Colored People joined with black political organizations in conducting voter registration drives while also initiating legal action to desegregate public accommodations in the Bluff City. During the 1960s legal and political action was augmented by nonviolent protests which ultimately forced city government to integrate its libraries, parks, restaurants, and other public places.

Along with this social revolution a corresponding political realignment was taking place in Memphis and across the American South. Until Franklin Roosevelt's reelection in 1936 the majority of African Americans who were eligible to vote cast ballots for the GOP. But during that watershed campaign many blacks turned their backs on the party of Lincoln and joined with farmers, industrial workers, and progressive liberals to create the Democratic-New Deal coalition which dominated American political life for a generation. Conditions began to change, however, in the late 1940s as African Americans, emboldened by their participation in the New Deal and service in World War II, enlarged their involvement in political affairs by challenging legalized segregation and electing black candidates to public office. At the same time "lily-white" Republicans, who for decades had been trying to purge their party of black influence, severed their longstanding "black-and-tan" alliance with African Americans and recast their party into a conservative, anti–civil rights faction. The victory of the lily-whites over the black-and-tans was hailed by many white southerners who were disenchanted with the liberal wing of the Democratic Party. At the same time this alienated black Republicans who had worked tirelessly to make the GOP live up to its historic commitment to equality.

While this combination political realignment/social revolution was taking place, Memphis was being directed by an outmoded form of government which placed executive and legislative authority in the hands of a five-man commission. During this twenty-year period those paying attention to public affairs were often distracted by a series of petty squabbles which convinced many that Memphis needed a more modern political structure to meet the challenges of the 1950s and 1960s. To that end a group of local reformers persuaded Memphians to scrap the city commission and replace it with a mayor–city council governmental structure. By 1968 the segregated social order had collapsed, black politicians were firmly entrenched within the Democratic Party, southern whites had swelled the ranks of the GOP, and Memphis had adopted a new city charter.

But all of that was in the future. As our story opens, the city of Memphis is governed by the Shelby County Democratic Party headed by Edward Hull Crump, whom *Time* magazine described as "the most absolute political boss in the U.S." As mentioned previously, Crump's organization was a broad-based coalition made up of nearly every major voting bloc in the city, including African Americans and Republicans. Both minorities participated in the electoral process, but neither could field their own candidates nor were they members of the organization's inner circle. Forced to sit on the sidelines, both groups seethed as Crump's Democratic organization controlled the machinery of government. But, as we have seen, all of this was about to change. Unbeknownst to Crump and his lieutenants, a different day was about to dawn in Memphis and all across the American South.

Acknowledgments

My colleagues in the History and Social Sciences Department at the Benjamin L. Hooks Central Library—Betty Blaylock, Andy Carter, Joan Cannon, Gina Cordell, Laura Cunningham, Jasmine Holland, Verjeana Hunt, Dr. James R. Johnson, Thomas W. Jones, Patricia M. LaPointe, Gregg L. Newby, Patrick W. O'Daniel, Belmar Toney, and Marilyn Umfrees—encouraged me and patiently supported my research. In particular my colleague and friend Gina Cordell and her husband, Paul Gahn, kindly listened to countless tales of Memphis politics when they would have rather talked about their Boston terrier, Violet.

My Kia Kima/TSB Brudder Carey D. White was perhaps more interested in the subject than Gina and Paul, but he, too, endured hours of local history discussions while always chiding me to write in the past tense rather than the present.

On a cold Saturday in January 2007 I traveled to the Hollywood Branch Library to visit with my friend Johnnie Mosley and attend a meeting of the Renaissance Men's Book Club. Johnnie and the other members graciously critiqued my book *Mayor Crump Don't Like It: Machine Politics in Memphis* and offered suggestions which made this present volume a far better book than it otherwise would have been.

Library volunteer and retired educator Hugh Higginbotham, Jr., shared his memories of working on the Kefauver, Gore, and Orgill campaigns; this was invaluable in helping me to understand the significance of those elections.

My editor at the University Press of Mississippi, Craig W. Gill, has encouraged me in my writing over the years and was unfailingly helpful throughout the publishing process. The noted historian Dr. Kenneth W. Goings read the entire manuscript and offered insightful comments which greatly improved the finished manuscript.

As with everything else, I could not have completed this work without the love and generosity of my family. I dedicate this book to my parents, Gerald McLain and Barbara Ann Nance Dowdy, my grandparents, John McLain and Ivy Lucile Heckle Dowdy and William Herbert and Lurline Belle Griffin Nance, my brother and sister-in-law, William Johnathan "Bud" and Robin Paige Clement Dowdy, my niece, Britney Amber Dowdy, my nephews, Cody Austin Dowdy and Brandon Ryan Dowdy, Uncle J. B. and

Aunt Carole Nance, Uncle Larry H. Nance, Uncle Ron G. and Aunt Donna Nance, Aunt Viola Heckle, and my cousins, Justin, Clay, and Clint Nance, Lisa Nance Brooks, Mike and Forrest Brooks, Chris, Heather, and Haleigh Nance, Gene and Jean Hair Miller, Laura Leigh Miller Traylor, John, Olivia Belle, and Conrad Traylor, Eddie, Rachel, Alex, and Stuart Miller, Faye Stabler, Kim Hair Sox, Donald, Corey, and Luke Sox, Kerri Hair Brittingham, Emily, Jim, Trent, and Grant Brittingham, Lynn and Debbie Hair, and W. D. Hair.

Crusades for Freedom

1

"We Are Living in a Different Day"

E. H. Crump was cold and wet. On January 1, 1948, he attended the Delta Bowl football game between Texas Christian and the University of Mississippi. As he sat in the stands he was buffeted by high winds and stinging rain that had blanketed Memphis. The night before, on New Year's Eve, a tornado had touched down in rural Shelby County, killing three people and injuring eighteen.[1] Meanwhile, nine hundred miles away in the nation's capital, President Harry Truman was dealing with another type of storm that threatened to rip the nation asunder. As the new year dawned, neither leader had any way of knowing that in 1948 Republicans would establish a toehold in the Democratic South while the first cracks would begin to appear in the fortresses of white supremacy and Jim Crow segregation.

In September 1946 a delegation of African American leaders, including NAACP executive director Walter White, met with Truman in the White House to discuss the rise of racial violence then occurring across the American South. The president was particularly shocked by the brutal attack upon an African American soldier in South Carolina. Honorably discharged from the army in February 1946, Sergeant Isaac Woodard was traveling by bus through South Carolina when, during an unscheduled stop, he asked the white driver if he could use the restroom. The driver refused permission and cursed Woodard, who responded in kind. When the bus arrived in Batesburg, the driver informed police chief Lynwood Lanier Shull that Woodard had been unruly during the trip. Boarding the bus, the police chief arrested Woodard for disturbing the peace. When he protested that he had done nothing wrong, Shull savagely beat the discharged sergeant, blinding him in both eyes.[2]

"My God!" the president exclaimed. "I had no idea it was as terrible as that! We've got to do something."[3] Under the president's direction, the Justice Department prosecuted Shull for violating Woodard's civil rights, but an all-white jury found him not guilty.[4] In December 1946, one month after Schull's acquittal, Truman issued an executive order creating the President's Committee on Civil Rights to investigate civil rights abuses and propose federal statutes that would prevent them in the future. As the committee began its work, Truman continued to call for an end to racial discrimination. On June 29, 1947, the president spoke at the annual meeting of the National Association for the Advancement of Colored People, the first chief executive to ever do so. Standing on the steps of the Lincoln Memorial, Truman committed the federal government to insuring equal rights for African Americans. Four months later the president was given the tools to make his commitment real when his civil rights committee presented him with its 178-page report on October 29 1947. Entitled *To Secure These Rights*, the report not only catalogued egregious abuses of civil rights, but also recommended measures "to extend full and equal rights of citizenship to all Americans." The list included recommendations to end segregation in education, employment, and housing.[5]

If Truman had wanted merely to appease northern black voters and thus keep Roosevelt's New Deal coalition intact, he would have acknowledged the panel's recommendations and then done nothing. To be sure the president was a professional politician who wanted a united Democratic Party to assist in the 1948 campaign, but the available evidence suggests that civil rights was more than a political expedient to Harry Truman. During a White House luncheon a Democratic national committee member from Alabama asked the president for a statement on his civil rights views for the upcoming campaign. "Can I tell them you're not ramming miscegenation down our throats? That you're for all the people, not just the North?" Truman dramatically reached into his coat and pulled out a copy of the Bill of Rights, which he proceeded to read to the astonished audience. When finished, Truman declared, "I'm everybody's president."[6]

The president seemed to have concluded that some southern Democrats would remain loyal to the party, if not to him, and that a civil rights program would solidify northern liberal and black votes for his reelection bid. Consequently, the president sent a special message to Congress on February 2, 1948, proposing a set of laws designed to secure some measure of equality for African Americans. The president's program included the creation of a civil rights commission and a Justice Department civil rights division to investigate and prosecute violations of civil liberties, establishment of a federal commission to prevent discrimination in the workplace and ensure fair employment practices, antilynching legislation, the outlawing of segregation in facilities servicing interstate transportation, and further protection for the right to vote.[7]

A "stab in the back by the so-called Democratic Party" was how Mississippi governor Fielding L. Wright described the president's message.[8]

Wright emerged as the most vocal critic of the civil rights program, urging southern Democrats to break with their party.[9] Truman's pronouncement came just before a scheduled meeting of the Southern Governors' Conference. Meeting in Tallahassee, Florida, the assembled state executives publicly deplored the president's proposals but refused to endorse Wright's call for revolt.[10] Although they refused to formally break with their party, the executives adopted a resolution proposed by South Carolina's Strom Thurmond to reconvene in forty days if the party refused to abandon its "attacks on white supremacy."[11]

While the southern governors met in Florida, E. H. Crump vacationed in Hot Springs, Arkansas. Upon his return to Memphis, he weighed the growing controversy. Privately, Crump felt that black southerners were being manipulated by "northerners" who were "making them believe they should accept nothing as a substitute but demand equal rights and eventually complete social equality."[12] In Memphis, segregated access to city services such as parks, and improved black schools, were considered acceptable substitutes for equality by the majority of white Memphians. There was another factor that influenced Crump's future actions. Truman despised the Memphis leader. During a 1946 conversation with Alabama senator Lister Hill, the president referred to him as "old man hypocrite Crump."[13] A combination of personal animosity for the president and his commitment to white supremacy led Crump to break his silence.

On March 1, the Memphis leader publicly declared: "I will vote for a Democrat next November but it will not be Truman."[14] Charging that the president was attempting to "reduce the South to a country of crawling cowards," Crump predicted that "the F.E.P.C. [Fair Employment Practices Committee] will create bitter feeling . . . and the white people of the South will never accept it." Letters poured into Crump's office from throughout the United States praising his position. An engineer from Las Vegas wrote: "I am in full sympathy with the Southern states in their present fight against the traitorism of the North,"[15] while a businessman in Nashville encouraged Crump to form a "Southern Democratic Party."[16] Crump agreed, writing to a Middle Tennessee banker that if Truman was nominated "the South should put up their own candidates and vote for them, win, lose or draw."[17] As spring came to the Volunteer State, Crump hoped to block Truman's nomination by denying him Tennessee's votes at the national convention.

His chance came in mid-April when twenty-five hundred Tennessee Democrats met in Nashville to choose delegates to the national convention in Philadelphia and instruct them on whom to support. Crump hoped to convince his fellow delegates to reject Truman and support a southern alternative. Presumably on Crump's order, Shelby County delegate Roane Waring introduced a resolution that stated: "We shall never cast our votes for him, Truman, but on the contrary, will vote for a true Democrat, representing the best interests of the public of Tennessee, the South and the nation."[18] As Waring finished his introduction, several speakers rushed to the platform to challenge the resolution. A delegate from Nashville, Cecil Sims, denounced the step as being "conceived in hatred and animosity and which I believe carries in it the seeds of destruction."[19] The majority of delegates agreed, rejecting the Shelby resolution. This was a bitter, personal defeat for Crump. The anti-Truman resolution was clearly his idea. One cannot help but notice that the wording of the resolution echoed Crump's statement of March 1. He was far from crippled, however. Recognizing this, the convention chose Crump a member of the Philadelphia delegation. It remained to be seen what Crump would do.

Meanwhile, on May 10, one thousand southern Democrats met in Jackson, Mississippi, to force the national party to reject President Truman's civil rights program. Governors Wright, Thurmond, and Ben Laney of Arkansas dominated the proceedings, which called for the national party to reject Truman, nominate a presidential candidate who had an "unshakable belief and abiding faith in states' rights," and defeat any candidate that failed to repute civil rights.[20] If these demands were not met, the conference agreed to reconvene in Birmingham, Alabama, after the Democratic convention to discuss additional resistance.[21] Crump did not attend the meeting, but he did send Memphis mayor James Pleasants and former American Legion national commander Roane Waring to represent the Shelby County organization.[22] Despite their fervor, Crump was convinced they could not influence the party's choice. Still smarting from his Nashville defeat and believing that Truman's nomination was inevitable, Crump refused to attend the convention. During a press interview a reporter asked Crump, "Why don't you all go up there and walk out of the convention just to show your opposition to President Truman's nomination?" He replied, "We'll be walking out in spirit if not in our shoes."[23]

When the convention opened in Philadelphia, Democratic national chairman J. Howard McGrath proposed a compromise. The convention would approve a vaguely worded civil rights plank while also adopting a section that would reinforce the party's commitment to states' rights. In exchange the southern delegations would accept Truman's nomination. Southern firebrands were far from mollified, however. Governor Laney explained that "I doubt if even adoption of our plank could stop the walkout. These folks won't vote for Harry Truman." Liberals, led by Minneapolis mayor Hubert Humphrey, were just as adamant that the civil rights plank incorporate Truman's proposals "right down the line." If not, Humphrey declared that "we will fight it out before the entire conclave."[24] Unbeknownst to Humphrey and the liberals, Truman had already sent word to the platform committee to avoid mentioning his civil rights proposals and adopt an ambiguously worded plank in hopes the southern delegates would stay in line.[25]

After four hours of raucous debate, which at one point had to be controlled by the Philadelphia police, the resolutions committee adopted a civil rights plank that promised merely to continue "its effort to eradicate all racial, religious and economic discrimination." This might have been acceptable to the southern caucus if the pro–states' rights plank had also been adopted, but the resolutions committee flatly rejected the measure.[26] Humphrey was no more sanguine than the southerners, so he secured the support of several key northern delegations to replace the compromise plank with the president's proposed civil rights legislation. Humphrey's maneuver surprised the majority of delegates when the convention reconvened the following day. Receiving support from the most populous northern states, the liberal platform was adopted over the strenuous objections of moderate northern delegates and the unreconstructed southern delegations.

When Truman was nominated, along with Kentucky senator Alben W. Barkley for vice president, Governor Fielding Wright led his fellow Mississippi delegates out of the convention hall vowing to nominate a states' rights candidate for president.[27] Six thousand delegates convened in Birmingham on July 17 to offer a southern alternative to Harry Truman. Strom Thurmond was nominated to head the States' Rights Democratic Party (dubbed Dixiecrats by the press) presidential campaign, while Mississippi's Fielding Wright ran for vice president.[28] Eight days after their gathering, Truman defied them by issuing two executive orders that weakened the bonds of legalized segregation. Executive Order 9980 required all federal departments to insure equal employment opportunities for all applicants regardless of race, color, religion, or national origin and established a Fair Employment Board to oversee compliance.[29] The second executive order, 9981, was even more radical.

For decades one of the most segregated institutions in the country was the United States military. Denied opportunities to advance, most black servicemen were prevented from service in combat units and were allowed only to engage in menial activities. In the marines, for example, blacks could only enlist as kitchen personnel, while in the army only one African American in seventy was a commissioned officer. Appalled by this, Truman ordered military commanders to integrate the armed forces. High-ranking military leaders, most notably army chief of staff General Omar Bradley, bitterly denounced the plan, but again Truman refused to back down.[30] Truman's executive orders were in fact brave acts that furthered the cause of civil rights, but political calculation was also at work. In addition to the Dixiecrats and the GOP, the president was opposed by former vice president Henry Wallace, who was running for chief executive on the ultraliberal Progressive Party ticket. No doubt Truman hoped to siphon some liberal votes, particularly those upset over the civil rights platform plank, away from Wallace and the Progressives.

As we have seen, Crump's sympathy was clearly with the Dixiecrats, but he did not attend the Birmingham meeting nor did he send any representatives, a fact that led the *New York Times* to speculate that he would join with other southern leaders to crush the Dixiecrat insurgency. Although uncertain of how much support he should offer, he had no desire to stop Thurmond's campaign. Crump's unease came mostly because his political organization was attempting to elect friendly candidates in the August Democratic primary. Fear that a close association with the Dixiecrats might alienate local voters led Crump, for the moment, to distance his organization from the states' rights banner.

The Republicans, paying close attention to the faltering Democrats, began their national campaign to unseat Truman. In late June they convened in Philadelphia to choose their party's standard bearers. Several candidates, including New York governor Thomas E. Dewey, Ohio senator Robert Taft, Harold Stassen, governor of Minnesota, and California governor Earl Warren, traveled to Philadelphia in late June in hopes of securing the nomination. Dewey was the favorite largely because he had been the party's nominee in 1944, but Taft and Stassen had strong support as well.[31] The chairman of the convention was East Tennessee congressman Carroll B. Reese, who supported Taft as did the majority of delegates from the Volunteer State. Several Memphians were members of the Tennessee delegation, including businessman C. Arthur Bruce, attorney George Klepper, and an African American, George W. Lee.[32] All were black-and-tan regulars who had for decades successfully marginalized the lily-whites in Tennessee.

George W. Lee was one of the most remarkable Memphians of his day.

Born in Indianola, Mississippi, in 1894, Lee attended Alcorn A&M College and after graduation joined the United States Army. Commissioned a lieutenant, one of the few black soldiers to achieve that distinction, Lee was sent to France and participated in the Meuse-Argonne offensive, where he was awarded a medal for bravery by the French government. After the war Lee returned to Memphis and opened an insurance business on famed Beale Street. Fascinated by the city, Lee wrote three books about Beale Street, including the novel *River George*, which was a featured selection of the Book-of-the-Month Club. Lee was also fascinated by politics. Joining the GOP, he quickly became indispensable to Robert Church, Jr., one of the most respected Republican leaders in the United States.[33] Church and Lee often cooperated with the Crump organization; for example, in 1927 they endorsed the Crump ticket, which played an important role in the machine's ultimate victory.[34] When Church was forced to relocate to Chicago, Lee became the undisputed black leader of the Shelby County GOP.[35]

Traditionally, convention delegations would nominate a respected citizen from their state, called favorite sons, on the first ballot in honor of their prominence. In 1948 the Tennessee delegation nominated Reese, and Lee was asked to second his nomination, a singular honor for an African American and a nod of recognition to black Memphians.[36] As in Tennessee, the black-and-tan coalition remained a powerful force within the national GOP and influenced the writing of the party's platform. As a result of black-and-tan influence, the national Republicans supported legislation to abolish poll taxes, make lynching a federal crime, and endorsed the president's desegregation of the armed forces.[37] Although the majority of Tennessee delegates supported Taft, when Dewey inched closer to victory, they switched their votes to the New York governor, who secured the nomination on the third ballot. Earl Warren was chosen the vice presidential nominee.[38]

Meanwhile, in Memphis, fallout from their association with the Dixiecrats was but one problem facing the Shelby County organization in 1948. Although it was not apparent in the summer, Crump had made a fatal mistake the previous September when he decided to withdraw his support from Senator Tom Stewart, who was up for reelection in 1948.[39] Crump had previously supported Stewart, who was best known for prosecuting Dayton science teacher John Scopes in the 1925 "monkey" trial. But from Crump's point of view Stewart presented something of a problem. "Tom Stewart is a very nice, pleasant gentleman, but he is no ball of fire . . . ," Crump wrote to a political supporter of Stewart.[40] But there was more to it than that. In the 1942 election Stewart had failed to carry his own county and had only won because of the large turnout in Memphis. There was also some unease because Stewart was not an enthusiastic supporter of the Tennessee Valley Authority.[41] For these reasons Crump decided to sever his connection to the incumbent senator.

Stewart did not accept Crump's decision, however, and made plans to run independently for a third term. Shortly after Stewart lost Crump's patronage, Chattanooga congressman Estes Kefauver announced his candidacy for the Senate seat in November 1947.[42] Although a liberal Democrat who opposed the House Un-American Activities Committee, Kefauver shared Crump's opposition to civil rights and was a strong supporter of the Tennessee Valley Authority.[43]

These similarities should have been enough for Crump to support the Chattanooga congressman, but they were not. Suspicious of the liberal wing of the Democratic Party, Crump implied in a newspaper statement that Kefauver's candidacy was Communist inspired.[44] Crump shared the view of Memphis congressman Clifford Davis that Kefauver had "radical and ultraliberal tendencies."[45] In addition to Kefauver, Cookeville circuit judge John A. Mitchell also announced his candidacy, making the campaign a three-way race. The Memphis leader knew little of Mitchell: "I have never met Judge Mitchell—don't know what he looks like, but from what I've heard I thought that he would measure up head and shoulders above Stewart and Kefauver...," he surprisingly revealed.[46] Two factors influenced Crump's decision to endorse Mitchell. First, he had little choice but to endorse someone if he wanted to maintain his political influence, and he had previously ruled out supporting Stewart and Kefauver. Second, he strongly believed that the votes of military veterans were crucial in the coming election. Mitchell was a veteran of both world wars, while neither Stewart nor Kefauver had served in the military.

Crump's endorsement of Mitchell appeared to give him the edge. Kefauver confided to his congressional colleague Clifford Davis that he was "discouraged" by political conditions in the state.[47] But this discouragement did not last long. Despite being urged to "[c]arry the fight to them,"[48] Mitchell made little headway with Tennessee voters.[49] In an undated note Crump lamented that "it may be he is doing all he is capable to do—going around and making no impression. We are living in a different day."[50]

Soon after Kefauver's announcement, Edward J. Meeman, the editor of the local afternoon newspaper, the *Memphis Press-Scimitar*, was startled to learn that J. Charles Poe, an executive with the Nickey Bros. Lumber Company, was planning to vote for Kefauver.[51] To Meeman and others it was inconceivable that a respected business leader would openly break with Crump. Emboldened by Poe's decision, Meeman contacted the Kefauver campaign and invited the Chattanooga congressman to visit Memphis. Arriving in early June, Kefauver gauged his political chances in a meeting with Meeman, Poe, liberal attorney Lucius Burch, Jr., and businessman Edmund Orgill. After the meeting, Kefauver startled the local press by announcing his plans to "make a strong appeal for votes in Shelby County."[52]

Born in Indiana, Meeman became editor of the *Memphis Press-Scimitar* in 1931 and within a short time came to believe that he was operating "a free press under a totalitarian dictatorship . . ."[53] A fair-minded journalist, Meeman praised Crump for establishing honest and efficient government that improved the city's infrastructure while condemning Memphis's lack of political dissent. "What does it profit Memphis to have all these splendid physical accomplishments and have not freedom of mind and freedom of spirit?" Meeman rhetorically asked.[54] While Meeman struggled to remain objective, Crump, however, had no such qualms. "Your nature is so steeped in suspicion, disappointment, vanity, hate, envy and lust for power, you are a deadly enemy to fair play, charity and truth," Crump wrote to Meeman in 1943 in words that could just as easily have described the Memphis leader.[55] But this was not enough for Crump. Around the same time as this diatribe, an operative, acting ostensibly on Crump's orders, began to collect false affidavits from convicts at the state penitentiary who claimed Meeman was a homosexual. A lifelong bachelor, Meeman was theoretically susceptible to this charge, though there apparently was no truth to it.[56] The truth really didn't matter, so during a meeting of the city commission Mayor Pleasants read a statement which charged that Meeman had a "perverted and degenerate mind" and was known by many to be "one of those things," a crude euphemism for homosexuality.[57] The charges were then printed and mailed out to local voters. Despite the slanderous nature of the mayor's comments, Meeman wisely ignored them, which prevented the introduction of the false affidavits.[58] But the damage had been done. So Meeman had plenty of reason to oppose Crump in 1948.

Like the *Press-Scimitar* editor, Lucius E. Burch, Jr., was appalled by E. H. Crump's brand of politics. Born in Nashville, Burch established a law practice in Memphis after his graduation from Vanderbilt University Law School in 1936. Specializing in corporate law, Burch represented the Illinois Central Railroad and the Standard Oil Company of Louisiana.[59] However, Burch also defended the civil liberties of ordinary citizens. In 1940, for example, Burch challenged the organization when he represented a gambler who had been personally ordered to leave Memphis by Crump. As part of his defense Burch argued that, despite his political influence, the Memphis leader lacked any constitutional authority to order a citizen about. This defiance was not forgotten by Crump, and for his part Burch never wavered in his opposition to the Memphis leader's extralegal activities.[60]

Edmund Orgill, on the other hand, had never involved himself in politics before. As president of the Orgill Brothers hardware company, Orgill had concentrated on business affairs and civic organizations. Maintaining a cordial relationship with Crump, Orgill never felt the need to challenge Crump's political supremacy. The reason he attended the June meeting with Meeman and Burch, and later played a prominent role in Kefauver's campaign, had to do with events in Europe rather than Memphis.

In the summer of 1946 Burch sent Orgill a copy of Clarence Streit's book *Union Now*. Written in 1940 by an international reporter for the *New York Times*, *Union Now* argued that the democracies of the North Atlantic should unite in a "world federation" to preserve fundamental liberties and provide collective security.[61] The idea of a "federal union" to combat totalitarian governments sparked the imagination of Edmund Orgill, who worked tirelessly to promote Streit's ideas to his fellow Memphians. When Orgill learned that Kefauver supported the creation of a federal union, he joined with Burch and Meeman in forming an election committee on Kefauver's behalf. Adopting the slogan "The election of a U. S. Senator should be above local politics," the three principals were joined by other prominent white Memphians, including W. M. Barr, O. D. Bratton, Edwin Dalstrom, Henry Gotten, and Charles Poe. Anti-Crump sentiment coalesced around Kefauver and former governor Gordon Browning, who challenged incumbent Jim McCord. Browning had served as governor from 1936 to 1938 but was denied reelection when he tried, and failed, to destroy the Shelby County organization.[62] Although Browning was a potential threat, Crump focused most of his attention on defeating Kefauver.

With elements of the white middle classes groping for a political alternative to Crump-style government, the question became which faction African American voters would support. Given Crump's opposition to civil rights, the decision appeared to be an easy one. But it wasn't. For three decades those black voters who could had traded political support for access to city services which led to improved schools and parks for African American citizens. But at the same time their limited role strengthened segregation rather than weakening it. One concession they had been unable to wring from the white power structure was the opportunity for African Americans to serve on the police force. From 1867 to 1895 blacks served with distinction in the Memphis police department, most notably during the 1878 yellow fever epidemic.[63] In April 1919 African Americans George Isles, Matthew Thornton, Sr., and Will "Sweetie" Williams were appointed detectives by Mayor Frank Monteverde, but their tenure was brief. Three months after their appointment the men were dismissed after Williams shot and wounded a white saloon operator.[64] Adding black officers to the police department roster remained a goal of the Memphis African American community. In 1927 Crump and his mayoral candidate, Watkins Overton, agreed to consider the idea but reneged when their opponent, incumbent mayor Rowlett Paine, charged them with being a threat to white supremacy for considering the idea.[65] The desire to put blacks on the force was enhanced as police brutality against African Americans increased in the 1940s. One case in particular galvanized the black community.

On the evening of May 14 Ell Blaine, an employee of the Firestone Tire and Rubber Company, was in his apartment at 203 South Lauderdale when he heard a disturbance next door. Walking to the adjacent apartment, he attempted to console a crying woman when police officers L. E. Bryan and C. W. Brewer arrived at the scene.[66] The officers began a physical search of Blaine and the other occupants. During the course of the search one of the officers examined Blaine's wallet. Warning the occupants to keep the noise down, the police left. Blaine checked his wallet and discovered he had ten dollars missing, which left him with five dollars. Not sure what to do, he phoned his white manager at Firestone, Sam Holt. The manager asked Blaine to come to work where he "made me turn my pockets out then he ran his hand in my shirt pocket."

When Holt did not find the missing cash, he called the police and informed them of Blaine's accusation. Ordered to report to police headquarters, Blaine repeated his charge to an inspector and the accused officers. As Blaine accused the officers, one of them struck him in the face, breaking his eyeglasses and forcing him into a nearby wall. The blow was struck with such force that broken glass became embedded in Blaine's right eye. Exercising poor judgment, the inspector ordered Bryan and Brewer to take Blaine to the hospital. As Blaine was being transported to the medical facility in the back of a squad car, he fearfully asked the two officers if they were going to kill him. "You won't talk no more," one of the officers ominously replied. At some point in the journey the officers began to beat Blaine severely around the head and face with blackjacks. Finally arriving at the hospital, Blaine was examined by physicians who treated his wounds but were unable to save his right eye.[67]

After being informed of the incident, Fire and Police Commissioner Joseph Boyle visited Blaine in the hospital and was shaken by what he saw. Shortly after his examination, Boyle dismissed Brewer and Bryan from the force and had them arrested. Describing the attack as "outrageous and contemptible," Shelby County attorney general Will Gerber charged the two former officers with assault to murder.[68] The trial was held in July, and, despite the best efforts of Gerber, the jury handed down a very light sentence. Bryan was found guilty but only assessed a fifty-one-dollar fine, while Brewer was found not guilty.[69]

Understandably, Memphis blacks were outraged by such a light sentence. The *Memphis World* editorialized: "Something is fundamentally wrong when justice takes this sort of course."[70] Hoping to tap into public anger, the *World* stepped up its campaign for African American police officers. In a letter to Mayor Pleasants, editor Louis O. Swingler pointed out that Tennessee's other large municipalities, Chattanooga, Knoxville, and Nashville, had recently hired black officers, which benefited their localities in the "form of better race relationship, and reduction of crime."[71]

As the date of the primary neared, Crump and his lieutenants were deeply concerned that African American voters might support Kefauver. Hoping to outflank the black leadership, Pleasants called several of them together to coordinate political activities. To the mayor's surprise, the attendees thought the conference was called to discuss police brutality rather than politics. When the attendees demanded the hiring of black officers, the mayor refused to commit. In turn, the attendees refused to sign a resolution of support for the organization's candidates.[72] In a public statement issued the following day, Pleasants feigned surprise that African Americans wanted to exchange votes for black police officers. "We have made no promises and right here in the face of the election, we would not think of making one," the mayor exclaimed.[73] It was a curious statement given that the county organization had been trading services for votes for nearly forty years.

The refusal to hire African American police was a turning point in the campaign. Angry at having their wishes so callously dismissed, the Colored Democrats Club, which had been the African American wing of the Crump organization, endorsed Kefauver.[74] Crump attempted to paint Kefauver as anti-South and anti-American. In a full-page newspaper advertisement, Crump charged that the Chattanooga congressman had "Red tendencies" and refused to vote against "legislation which tended to abuse and humiliate the South . . ."[75] In late July, Mitchell echoed Crump when he traveled to Memphis and spoke to two thousand people in the ballroom of the Peabody Hotel. Mitchell reminded the audience that no one "has yet questioned my Americanism," and declared that the "government must not be allowed to encroach on States' Rights."[76]

When Memphis Democrats went to the polls, the issues of states' rights and anti-Communism did resonate with many of them as evidenced by the results on election day. Mitchell polled 37,792 votes while 27,855 ballots were cast for Kefauver. Although Mitchell outpolled his opponent by 10,000 votes in Shelby County, the large number of ballots cast for Kefauver prevented Mitchell from winning the statewide primary. When the votes came in from the rest of the state, Kefauver had won the nomination. The large number of votes for Kefauver in Shelby County sealed his victory over Mitchell, while Browning wrested the gubernatorial nomination from McCord. In light of these developments reporters kept a close watch on Crump's home and offices but he refused to comment. However, a persistent reporter from *Time* stationed outside Crump's home spied the Memphis leader through a bedroom window and began to question him. "Would he attempt a comeback?" the journalist asked. "Comeback? I haven't gone anywhere . . . Why should I come back? Any man who hasn't got enough to take a defeat is a poor man," Crump yelled from his window.[77]

Memphis blacks were naturally jubilant at the part they played in securing the Democratic nomination for Estes Kefauver. The *Memphis World* boldly declared: "'Boss' Ed Crump's Power Broken" and the *Washington Afro-American* stated in a headline that "Minority Vote Helped Ruin 'Crump Machine.'"[78] The jubilation did not last long, however.

On the evening of August 20, James Mosby, a World War II veteran and city garbage worker, began arguing with his wife. The police were called, and Corporal J. F. Nolan and Patrolman J. C. Coats were dispatched to the scene. The officers began to question Mosby, but he refused to answer. One of the officers struck Mosby, who then attacked Corporal Nolan. During the scuffle Mosby apparently bit Nolan in the arm, and the officer in turn shot him twice in the stomach. Mosby died shortly thereafter.[79] Mosby's death reenergized the campaign to hire black police officers in Memphis. Four days after the killing the residents of the Binghamton neighborhood held a mass meeting urging the city to act.[80] At the same time the Colored Methodist Episcopal Church Pastors Alliance and the East Memphis Citizens

Club sent petitions to the mayor's office calling for the hiring of African American officers.[81] The local branch of the NAACP supported the petition drive, while the two white daily newspapers, the *Memphis Press-Scimitar* and the *Memphis Commercial Appeal*, publicly supported the hiring of African American police.[82]

The results of the recent election combined with increased public pressure convinced the administration they had to act. After meeting with Mayor Pleasants, Fire and Police Commissioner Joseph Boyle announced to the press on September 9 that applications would be taken from African Americans who wished to join the police force. In his prepared statement Boyle took pains to ensure that the decision would not be viewed as an endorsement of black civil rights: "Negro police won't settle the negro problem by any means, when three candidates for the presidency of the Unites States are advocating FEPC and the elimination of the Jim Crow Law. In fact, they are advocating complete social equality, which will not happen in Memphis . . ."[83] On November 5 a segregated roll call was held for nine African American police officers. A month later thirteen African Americans began training to become patrolmen.[84]

With the decision made as to black police officers, another question faced organization leaders: whom would they support in the statewide races as well as the presidential election? The Republicans, hoping to exploit the split within the Democratic ranks, nominated well-known country music performer Roy Acuff for governor and former East Tennessee congressman B. Carroll Reese for the Senate. Despite Crump's earlier opposition, the Democratic nominees hoped the organization would join them in a united front against the GOP. Democratic organizers requested that representatives from the county organization serve on a statewide campaign committee, but Crump refused to appoint anyone.[85] Locally, the Memphis leader offered to support the statewide ticket as long as the Kefauver forces did not oppose the organization's candidates for the Tennessee General Assembly.[86] An agreement was apparently reached, but then Kefauver wrote a scathing article for *Collier's* magazine entitled "How Boss Crump Was Licked," which angered the Memphis leader and further split the Democratic Party.[87] Reneging on their agreement, Mayor Pleasants simply announced on October 31 that the organization would not endorse anyone for governor and senator.[88]

It will be remembered that Crump lobbied unsuccessfully to deny President Truman the Democratic nomination. When that failed, he flirted with the Dixiecrats but refused to endorse their ticket for fear of alienating black voters. With the primary campaign over, it appeared that the way was clear for him to endorse Strom Thurmond and the States' Rights Party. Soon after the ticket was formed, a local committee of political unknowns was established, which held rallies and distributed political circulars.[89] Ironically a rally was held on the same day the city announced it was hiring black police officers. Speaking at Bellevue Park, Mississippi senator James O. Eastland warned fifteen hundred white Memphians that a vote for Truman meant "the destruction of your family and our way of life." As Eastland droned on, fifty African American citizens stood on the edge of the park bearing silent witness to the southern way of life.[90] In addition to rallies, the committee also circulated advertisements that claimed that Truman's civil rights program would "provide for the discharge of 40% of all white employees to make room for the negroes [sic] to be employed under the act."[91]

Despite this flurry of political activity, Crump and his lieutenants remained publicly silent on whom they supported for the presidency throughout the month of September. When Eastland spoke in Memphis, several organization stalwarts, including county registrar Francis Andrews and mayoral secretary Marvin Pope, attended the rally in an unofficial capacity.[92] It was not until early October, however, that Crump announced his position. "We have decided to go for the States' Rights ticket for president," he declared to reporters.[93] Crump surely knew that the Dixiecrats had no hope of winning the presidency and that his disaffection would have little impact on the national election. It is likely he calculated that the majority of white voters would vote for Thurmond and that in order to maintain organization strength in Memphis he had to at least publicly support the Dixicrats. However, the election results in Shelby County suggested that Crump miscalculated. Thurmond did receive 26,246 votes in Shelby County, but 23,854 ballots were cast for President Truman, who did not even campaign in Shelby County, which suggested that Crump's electoral strength had again been severely weakened.[94] In the previous two presidential elections the results had been far different. The voters of Shelby County had strongly supported Franklin Roosevelt's third and fourth term reelection bids by casting 57,610 ballots for him in 1940 and 39,172 in 1944.[95] As in the August primary it was African Americans who voted heavily for the president and again handed the county organization an electoral defeat.[96]

The Dixiecrats were far more of a reactionary protest movement than a formal political party, but nevertheless they dominated the Democratic Party machinery in Alabama, Mississippi, Louisiana, and South Carolina.

As a result, Thurmond rather than Truman was listed on the ballot as the Democratic nominee in those states. This political sleight-of-hand undoubtedly contributed to the Dixiecrats winning a majority of votes in those four states. In addition to winning in Alabama, Mississippi, Louisiana, and South Carolina, Thurmond and Wright carried twelve counties in Georgia, three counties each in Arkansas and Florida, and Shelby and Fayette counties in Tennessee. However, they received only one-fifth of the popular vote, which was not enough to throw the election into the House of Representatives. Consequently Truman defeated Thurmond in the rest of the South and easily won the presidential election.[97] Dewey and Wallace fared little better. In Shelby County the Republican nominee received 13,668 votes, coming in third, and a paltry 223 ballots were cast for Henry Wallace.[98]

On the day after the election, Crump was walking down Second Street in downtown Memphis when a reporter asked him his reaction to the election results. "The vote that I cast for Thurmond and Wright was one of the best I've ever put in," he proudly replied.[99] As his statement suggests, Crump interpreted Thurmond's success in Shelby County as a victory for his organization, hollow though it was.[100] The events of 1948 did not fundamentally alter the political and social conditions in Memphis, but they did plant seeds that, if tended properly, had the power to establish a two-party political system and choke the foul weed of segregation. Whether or not these seeds of change would bear fruit was far from clear, but they were now securely set in the ground.

2

"My Family Ties in the South"

Mayor Pleasants was a tired man. Suffering from poor health and ashamed of his participation in the smear campaign against Meeman, Pleasants informed Crump in September 1948 that he wished to retire.[1] Concerned that Pleasants's resignation might affect the election, and wanting to choose a successor before the decision was announced, Crump asked the mayor to wait. The overriding consideration for the Memphis leader was to find an able administrator who could stem the perception that the county Democratic organization was tottering. As we have seen, the results of the 1948 Democratic primary and general election were perceived to be a defeat for the Crump machine despite their candidates outpolling the opposition in Shelby County.

The best administrator in Memphis was arguably former mayor Watkins Overton, who had been a close associate of Crump's until their relationship deteriorated in the late 1930s. In 1937 the Memphis leader criticized the mayor's handling of refugees fleeing from the Ohio-Mississippi Valley Flood, and a year later their relationship ended when the two squabbled over the city purchasing private electric and gas companies.[2] When the split became public, Overton vowed never to work with Crump again: "I will never bow my knee to any tyrant."[3]

But as time passed, his anger subsided. Overton refused to further criticize Crump, responding to periodic media questions by simply saying: "It was a difference of opinion. Mr. Crump has done a wonderful job for Memphis."[4] This mollified Crump, and in 1947 he asked Overton to serve as president of the Shelby County Board of Education, where he again demonstrated his considerable leadership skills.[5] Crump expressed his support for the school board president by attending local football games with him, so there was little surprise when it was announced that Overton would be Pleasants's successor.[6]

At 11:10 AM on January 15, 1949, over a thousand people crowded into city hall to watch as Watkins Overton again took the oath of office as mayor of Memphis. It must have been a moment of triumph for the new mayor, but he did have to pay a price. In his inaugural address Overton declared, "I don't return to office after nine years with any bitterness in my heart. I am proud to feel that I will have the friendship and counsel and guidance of the man who has done more than any other man for Memphis—to speak specifically, I refer to the Honorable E. H. Crump."[7] Despite feeling compelled to pay homage to Crump, Overton no doubt hoped his new administration would be more pleasant than in 1938–1939.

As Overton settled into the mayor's office, Lucius Burch and Edmund Orgill watched the revolving door at city hall with disgust. Their experience with the Kefauver campaign had convinced them that reform could come to Memphis if enough citizens agitated for it. Burch had emerged as the most vocal critic of the Crump organization, sparring with Mayor Pleasants over the low wages paid local police officers and constantly pointing out the weaknesses of the commission form of government. In particular Burch objected to the small size of the commission—only five men to govern a city of 292,000—and its easy dominance by an ambitious politician such as Crump.

In order to expand the wedge driven into local politics by Kefauver's victory, Orgill, Burch, and forty-eight other professionals formed the Civic Research Committee to "promote research, study and interest in our local government and to do it on a non-partisan, non-political basis."[8] Although officially nonpartisan, the committee clearly hoped to weaken the power of the local Democratic Party, as evidenced by Burch's comment that the end of "one-man" rule in Memphis was near its end.[9]

The committee adopted several long-term goals for the city, including civil service protection for government employees, permanent voter registration, the replacing of paper ballots with voting machines, and the adoption of a city manager form of government.[10] Although the others were important, the overriding goal for the Civic Research Committee was replacing the mayor and city commission with a city manager hired by a part-time city council. If adopted, this would fundamentally alter the structure of local government, which Crump and Overton knew full well.

In November the committee held a public forum where Lucius Burch outlined the steps needed to hire a city manager for Memphis. Because of his public role in the meeting, Burch emerged as the most eloquent spokesman for changing the government. He also earned more enmity, if that was possible, from the county organization. In a letter that was quickly made public, Overton lashed out at Burch: "What you are trying to do is to destroy Memphis' present efficient city government so you can take over."[11]

Burch had no intention of "taking over," but that mattered little to Crump.

The organization saw a threat and it moved quickly to check it. In addition to attacking Burch, Overton called for a referendum to "quit all the talk" and let the citizens decide if they wanted a new form of government.[12] Shaken by the mayor's outburst, Edmund Orgill replied that "we are only trying to obtain the best form of government for Memphis over a period of many years."[13] True enough, but there was a trace of elitism in the committee's rhetoric that prevented the building of a coalition that could alter Memphis's political landscape. With Orgill's statement the city manager debate abruptly ended, but as we shall see the committee remained a viable forum for municipal reform throughout the 1950s.

As the debate over the city manager faded from view, the relationship between Mayor Overton and the city commission began to crumble. In September 1951 Overton attempted to raise the salary of city research director Guy Bates, who was acting as the mayor's administrative assistant, but the move was blocked by Commissioner Joe Boyle, Crump's chief lieutenant.[14] Overton promoted Bates in January 1951, declaring he would not let Boyle "dictate" mayoral decisions to him.[15] Not long after Boyle's rejection of Bates's pay increase, public works commissioner O. P. Williams prevented the sale of the city asphalt plant to Sears, Roebuck and Company for forty thousand dollars which had been approved by the mayor.[16]

The split between Overton and the other commissioners grew wider in February when Overton opened his morning newspaper and learned that the Memphis Police Department was being reorganized. Angry at being left out of this decision, Overton lashed out at Commissioner Claude Armour, who professed shock that Overton was unaware of the reorganization.[17] Up to this point Memphians were not aware of the depths of the animosity that existed between the commissioners. It became clear when Boyle declared that it had been a mistake to dig "Watkins Overton out of the cemetery" because he "only likes those who will boot-lick him." Boyle then made public the details of the aborted sale of the asphalt plant to Sears. Describing the agreement as a "messed up deal," Boyle claimed the asphalt plant was worth $140,000 rather than $40,000.[18]

Once the details of the asphalt deal became public, it was nearly impossible for Crump to stay out of the conflict. In a brief statement to the press, Crump supported Williams's opposition to the asphalt plant sale, but he carefully avoided attacking the mayor.[19] Overton, however, was not in such a generous mood. Claiming he was being charged with "some sinister and dishonest motive," the mayor explained in detail the negotiations that led to the asphalt plant agreement. Although strident in his defense, Overton also took pains to avoid a feud with Crump.[20] But then the mayor miscalculated. In an interview with a reporter from the *Memphis Press-Scimitar*, Overton proposed several amendments to the city charter, which included granting the mayor full power to block commission decisions.[21] This was too much for Crump. Lambasting the mayor, the Memphis leader declared that Overton wanted to seize total control over the machinery of city government and exercise a "Russian veto" to block any measure he didn't like.[22] "I can never be a puppet," the mayor responded.[23]

A short time after this acrimonious exchange, Overton invited the organization leader to attend a city tax meeting where they had, in Crump's words, a "very pleasant talk." Although this ended the feud between the mayor and the other commissioners, Overton was far from mollified. When asked by *Commercial Appeal* reporter Bob Marks if the meeting meant he was "trying to be friends with Mr. Crump," Overton replied, "I am not giving any interpretation to it."[24] The uneasy truce struck between Overton and Crump allowed them to focus attention on the upcoming municipal election. In June the mayor visited Crump where the two chose candidates to fill the various government posts.[25]

It was agreed that Overton would seek another term, but the mayor had a condition. He wanted two of the commission candidates to come from outside the Crump inner circle.[26] This naturally required two sitting commissioners to withdraw from the election. Boyle and Commissioner Robert Fredericks retired from the commission, and city comptroller Frank Tobey and attorney John "Buddy" Dwyer were named their successors. The replacement of Boyle and the naming of Tobey and Dwyer were certainly victories for the mayor and suggested he had won the feud. But did he? When the mayor announced the compromise ticket on July 12, 1951, he stated that Crump had "given more of his time, thought and ability to the development of Memphis than any one person in the history of the city."[27] Hardly a cry of victory, but Overton was apparently satisfied with the arrangement. In addition to the city commission, the organization also slated candidates for tax assessor, city judge, and three school board positions.

Only one Memphian rose to challenge the Crump-sponsored ticket. Dr. J. E. Walker, a prominent African American business leader and former chairman of the Colored Democrats Club, stunned organization leaders and white citizens alike when he announced his candidacy for the Memphis school board in August. Under the chairmanship of black Republican leader

George W. Lee, a committee was formed to increase the number of registered voters.[28] One hundred fifty agents from Walker's Universal Life Insurance Company canvassed black neighborhoods, urging citizens to register.[29] At the same time, Ethyl Venson formed a committee of prominent African American women who also worked to increase the number of black registered voters.[30] When the registration period ended, twenty-five thousand African Americans were qualified to vote in Shelby County.[31] Walker chose twenty-six-year-old attorney Benjamin L. Hooks and undertaker Taylor Hayes as cocampaign managers who scheduled ward rallies throughout the city and radio addresses over several local stations.[32]

Meanwhile the county organization adopted a ten-point platform that attempted to draw support away from Walker by promising to establish "an adequate hospital for negroes [sic]."[33] Except for the promise of a black hospital, Crump and Overton ignored the issue of race for most of the campaign. However, on the eve of the election, the mayor openly criticized Walker and African American voters for attempting to "inject the racial issue into our school system." Arguing that Walker was trying to "destroy" public education, Overton urged citizens to express their "approval of the fine school system" by voting.[34] Although mild in tone, the mayor's message clearly played on white Memphians' deep-seated fear of black social equality. Even whites who were sympathetic to black aspirations could not shake their dread of integration. Edmund Orgill endorsed Walker, making the argument that his election would allow African Americans a greater sense of participation in educational matters and would prevent them from seeking "to have their children attend the same schools as white children."[35] Hoping to exploit the consternation felt by white Memphians, the organization printed circulars that included photos of all the candidates and check marks to indicate the recommended name. Walker's photo was included, but it had no check mark and was "so dark that there could be no doubt that he was a negro [sic]." These circulars were distributed in white neighborhoods, while another version without photographs was distributed to African American enclaves.[36]

To counter this, the Walker campaign printed a sample ballot with a check mark only by his name in the hope that black voters would ignore all of the other candidates and vote only for Walker. This "single-shot" voting technique was thought to be the best way to insure a victory.[37] Organization leaders understood this as well, so on election day they blocked Walker campaign workers from distributing their literature at polling places.[38] As might be expected, Overton and the rest of the organization slate won easily, including those running for the school board. Walker did receive 7,433 votes, but over 21,000 ballots were cast for his opponents.[39] Gracious in defeat, Walker proclaimed: "We lost the election but we feel our gain in self respect and better morale for all the people of Memphis will pay off in handsome dividends."[40]

Crump turned seventy-eight years old in 1952, and his health was beginning to deteriorate. In February of that year he had an elevator constructed at his home on Peabody Avenue so he and his wife would no longer have to climb the stairs to their bedroom. Newspaper reporter Null Adams phoned Crump when he learned of the addition. Crump caustically replied that he was "laboring under infirmities, heart very bad, all bent, couldn't walk, needed an elevator."[41]

Despite his infirmities, he could not bring himself to completely retire from politics. Shortly after the 1951 election, a Dickson attorney and former chief counsel for the politically influential Tennessee Railroad and Public Utilities Commission, Frank Clement, traveled to Memphis to discuss the upcoming 1952 gubernatorial race. Seeking the nomination, Clement wanted to sound out the Memphis leader about a possible endorsement.[42] Ill and unable to meet with Clement, Crump did speak with him over the phone and promised that they "would talk it over."[43] Weary of statewide politics, the Memphis leader had refused to become involved in the 1950 governor's race, and it appeared likely he would do the same in 1952. Crump's wariness was also influenced by the fact that two other Democrats, Clifford Allen, a Nashville restaurant owner, and Memphis attorney Clifford Pierce, were also running for governor.

However, when Governor Browning announced his intention to run for a third term, Crump decided to endorse Clement.[44] On March 6 Shelby County attorney general John Heiskell formed a "Clement for governor" campaign committee made up of businessmen, local politicians, and labor and civic leaders. When Heiskell announced the committee to the press, a newspaper reporter asked how Crump and organization leaders viewed his action. "We think it will be agreeable with them," replied the attorney general.[45] And of course they did. When the press conference ended, *Commercial Appeal* reporter Harry Woodbury quickly phoned Crump to confirm his support for Clement. "John has the right thought on the matter . . . [Clement] looks like a winner."[46]

Browning was furious. Traveling to Memphis in late March, Browning declared that Crump's "little stooge [Clement] will not be governor of Tennessee." The governor then charged that when Crump was mayor he received campaign funds from "bawdy houses, saloons and vice of all kinds."[47] "I have never accepted one cent of graft in my entire life [,]" the Memphis leader forcefully replied.[48] Speaking in his hometown of Huntington on May 24, Browning opened his campaign by repeating the charge that Clement was a "stooge candidate" and then described Crump as a megalomaniac. "I honestly think that the main reason E. H. Crump doesn't go to church any more than he does, he says to himself, 'why should I go to church and worship God when I can stay home and worship myself.'"[49] In the audience listening to the governor's speech were four operatives from the Memphis organization who transcribed the talk and took note of those in attendance. They carefully recorded the license plate numbers of all automobiles from Shelby County and then reported to the Memphis leader who the owners of the vehicles were.[50]

Browning's speech in Huntington contained the major theme of his re-election campaign: namely that Crump was a power-mad boss bent on recapturing the governor's mansion through the use of a puppet candidate. This was reinforced by posters with the bold headline "My Boy" above a photograph of Crump and Clement shaking hands. At a rally in East Tennessee, Clement noticed a young boy holding one of these posters, and he incorporated that into his speech. After declaring that he was not ashamed to be seen shaking the hand of any citizen, Clement roared: "You won't see a picture of me handing over a million dollars to my friends."[51] Clement was referring to the governor's approval of a controversial lease-purchase of an apartment complex for use as a state office building. It was alleged that the owners of the apartments were political supporters of the governor, and Clement made the most of these allegations. [52] The charge and counter-charge of bossism and corruption dominated the rhetoric of the campaign and overshadowed more substantive issues.

As in 1948 the election turned, at least in part, on the African American vote. George W. Lee, J. E. Walker and the Non-partisan Voters League organized a registration drive as they had in 1951 which increased to forty-two thousand the number of African Americans eligible to vote in Shelby County.[53] Recalling the 1951 school board race, Browning hoped to tap into black discontent by naming J. E. Walker a campaign manager and opening an office on Beale Street.[54] During one of several rallies held in Memphis, Reverend E. M. Johnson, pastor of a local African Methodist Episcopal church, declared that the "time has come for the Negro population in Memphis to go to the polls and destroy bossism."[55] As governor, Browning had courted the black vote by proposing improvements to Fuller State Park for Negroes, securing university status for Tennessee State College, and by hiring African Americans to work in a state employment office in Memphis.[56]

The opposition also reached out to the black community. The Clement campaign committee reached out to black voters by establishing a "Negro division" to coordinate activities in the African American wards. This included gaining permission from local religious broadcasters to air pro-Clement speeches on their radio programs and organizing several mass meetings. The largest took place at the Lincoln drive-in theater where five thousand African Americans expressed their enthusiasm for Clement's candidacy.[57]

During the election season Browning unwisely left the state several times to campaign for Estes Kefauver, who was attempting to secure the Democratic presidential nomination. Compounding the error, the governor attended the Democratic National Convention in Chicago on behalf of Tennessee's junior senator. During the convention, party regulars attempted to wring a loyalty pledge from southern Democrats to prevent them from bolting the party as they had in 1948. When the Virginia delegation refused to sign, the convention attempted to remove them from the gathering. Kefauver urged the Tennessee delegation to vote for the unseating of Virginia, and Browning reluctantly agreed. As a result, Tennessee became the only southern state to vote against its neighbor.[58] As might be expected, this deeply angered many white Tennesseans and strengthened the opposition. To make matters worse, Browning was further discredited when the convention rejected Kefauver, instead nominating Illinois governor Adlai Stevenson, President Truman's hand-picked successor.[59]

As we have seen, Crump endorsed Clement, but for the most part he stayed out of the gubernatorial race. Instead, he relied on Shelby County attorney general John Heiskell to oversee the operation of Clement's effort. Of greater importance to Crump was the reelection campaign of his old ally U.S. senator Kenneth D. McKellar. The two men had known each other for nearly fifty years, and despite an occasional misunderstanding, they remained steadfastly loyal to one another. For example, in March 1945 President Franklin Roosevelt mysteriously summoned Crump to the White House where he pleaded with the Memphis leader to withdraw political support from McKellar in order to keep the senior senator from running for reelection in 1946. Vowing that McKellar would be reelected, Crump refused to submit to the president's request.[60]

Always sensitive to political trends, Crump noticed in early 1951 that

Albert Gore, a fourteen-year veteran of the U.S. House of Representatives from the Middle Tennessee town of Carthage, appeared to be running for the Senate.[61] In order for McKellar to outmaneuver the Carthage congressman, Crump advised him to announce his reelection bid right away.[62] On June 15, 1951, McKellar called a press conference in Washington and announced his decision to run for a seventh term in the United States Senate. "I understand others are contemplating making the race on the theory that I will not be a candidate . . . ," McKellar explained.[63]

Gore publicly ignored the senior senator's announcement, but he continued to travel throughout the state and ostensibly campaign for the nomination. In early January 1952 Gore traveled to Memphis where he met with Mayor Overton and had his picture taken with him.[64] The Middle Tennessee congressman also desperately wanted to meet with Crump, but his phone calls and letters went unanswered.[65] Despite this rebuff, Memphis was central to Gore's senatorial campaign—so much so that he traveled to the Bluff City in early February 1952 to formally announce his candidacy. "I have no political machine supporting me," Gore declared. "The plan of my campaign will be simple, go to the people."[66]

Around the same time that Gore traveled to Memphis, McKellar forces began to organize his campaign. Overton, E. W. Hale, and Commissioner Francis Andrews joined Nashville mayor Ben West and other East and Middle Tennessee representatives in the state capital to plan strategy and choose campaign managers.[67] Eighty-three years old and suffering from rheumatism, McKellar did not have the physical stamina to endure a long campaign. Instead he relied on Crump's political instincts and the hard work of his campaign managers, James Gentry and Herbert Walters.

But it did not take long for the rheumatism in the senior senator's body to spread to his campaign. Crump canvassed the political situation and urged Gentry to establish an organization in each county, but by mid-May only forty-five out of the ninety-five counties in Tennessee had been organized.[68] Gentry and Walters informed Crump of this fact, and of McKellar's illness, in a meeting in Memphis on May 7.[69] On May 11 Walters traveled to Washington, where he told the senior senator that his chances for reelection were beginning to fade. The next morning Walters called Crump, and they apparently decided that McKellar should withdraw from the race. When he got off the phone with Walters, Crump called the senior senator and urged him to drop out. But he refused. In an anguished letter, McKellar wrote the Memphis leader that there "would be nothing dishonorable about it if I were defeated."[70]

Although now convinced that McKellar could not win, Crump decided to make the best of it. When Gore made McKellar's old age an issue, Crump issued a public statement comparing the senior senator to Winston Churchill, who had "also been attacked because of his age but despite his tremendous burdens and responsibilities he handles his huge tasks with speed and precision."[71] Along similar lines, the county organization published a large advertisement in Memphis newspapers with the headline "There Is No Substitute for Experience."[72] While the McKellar forces emphasized his credentials, Gore energetically crisscrossed the state, speaking in small, often ignored communities.[73]

One hundred thousand Shelby County citizens cast ballots on August 7, which had a profound effect on both the gubernatorial and senatorial races. Frank Clement received 50,863 votes in Memphis to Browning's 30,396, which helped him to defeat the incumbent governor by a 50,000-vote margin in the statewide balloting.[74]

In the Senate contest, McKellar won Shelby County by 5,000 votes, but this margin of victory in Memphis did not overcome Gore's strength in the rest of the state. Across Tennessee 303,346 ballots were cast for Gore, while McKellar received 223,083 votes.[75] The defeat of McKellar, although expected, was a bitter blow for Crump. What little political influence he had suddenly vanished and not even Clement's victory could restore his former glory. Writing to McKellar seven days after the primary, the Memphis leader regretted the outcome of the primary but was assured that "history will record you as the greatest senator Tennessee ever had."[76]

In the spring of 1952 Robert Church, Jr., the exiled head of the Shelby County Republican Party, returned to Memphis in hopes of reclaiming his lost political power. Church had been the most influential African American Republican in the United States, serving as a delegate to national conventions and advising the administrations of Warren Harding and Calvin Coolidge on federal patronage in the South during the 1920s.[77]

The ascendancy of Democrat Franklin Roosevelt to the White House stripped Church of his patronage influence, and in 1939 harassment by the Crump organization forced him to relocate to Chicago.[78] Although exiled from his home base and politically weakened, Church remained active in national Republican affairs. Like many Republicans, Church sensed that Democratic Party scandals and dissatisfaction over the Korean conflict boded well for the GOP's chances in the 1952 presidential contest. This feeling was strengthened when retired General of the Army Dwight Eisenhower announced his candidacy for the Republican presidential nomination. In addition to Eisenhower's widespread appeal, Church felt that civil rights legislation would be supported by the retired general.[79]

Shortly after arriving in Memphis, Church approached his former protégé George W. Lee, who was one of four Shelby County members of the Tennessee Republican Executive Committee. The two men had once been close friends, but Church felt betrayed that Lee continued to cooperate with the forces that had hounded him out of Memphis. Nevertheless, Church hoped the two could again work together on behalf of Eisenhower. To the dismay of Lee, his former mentor criticized him for being too conservative and then asked him to resign his executive committee seat in order for Church to take his place. Lee informed Church that he supported the conservative Ohio senator Robert Taft for the presidency and would not relinquish his committee membership. Angered by Lee's stand, Church vowed to defeat him in the August party election.[80]

Church vigorously campaigned for himself and Eisenhower, but the strain quickly took its toll on the sixty-five-year-old black-and-tan leader. While speaking to a supporter over the telephone, Church suddenly collapsed, gasping for breath. Rushed to a local hospital, the noted Republican was pronounced dead of a massive heart attack.[81] Concerned that Church's death might strengthen Taft's support in Shelby County, Eisenhower forces moved quickly to find another suitable candidate for the state executive committee. Recognizing the importance of the Church family name, local Republicans and Eisenhower's southern campaign manager, Pennsylvania congressman Hugh Scott, approached Church's daughter Roberta to run for the state executive committee in her father's place.[82]

Roberta Church enthusiastically agreed to run, joining white candidates Hugh Bosworth, Robert Redd, and Sallie McClure on an "Eisenhower Republican" slate.[83] Opposing them were the Old Guard Republicans George W. Lee, Lester Brenner, Mrs. C. Arthur Bruce, and Mrs. David Hanover.[84] Church and the other Eisenhower candidates held several rallies throughout the city, while Lee traveled to Chicago as a delegate to the Republican National Convention. During the convention the Taft campaign asked Lee to second his nomination. As television cameras broadcast the scene throughout the United States, Lee rose and gave a rousing speech on behalf of the Ohio senator.

> It is a matter of record that Senator Taft has supported every civil rights bill that has been before Congress . . . I have heard malicious charges to the effect

that the senator was against minority races. But, as a member of one of the denied races, I will never hang my political harp on a weeping willow. I shall sing his name in praise until the density of the air is thick with the echoes of my voice.[85]

In spite of Lee's eloquence, the convention rejected the conservative Taft for the more moderate Eisenhower. Lee then wasted little time in pledging his loyalty to the nominee. Meeting with the general in his hotel room, he promised to support the nominee "with everything I've got." Eisenhower was so pleased with Lee's pledge that he called his wife over and said, "This is the man who made the brilliant speech for Taft." Mrs. Eisenhower complimented him on the speech, to which Lee replied, "Madam, having paid my obligation to Senator Taft, I shall not hang my voice on a weeping willow, but shall use it in every section of the country in the crusade with General Eisenhower to gain a Republican victory." Vice presidential nominee Richard Nixon overheard Lee's remarks and replied, "That's a remarkable spirit."[86]

With the convention concluded, Lee returned to Memphis to continue his campaign for the state executive committee. Roberta Church's faction had already positioned themselves as the "official" Eisenhower ticket, and they refused to concede that Lee had now pledged loyalty to the party's nominee. Countering this, Lee contacted Eisenhower, who responded by praising his "untiring efforts on behalf of the Republican Party and the nation."[87] Eisenhower believed, although his advisors did not, that the South was fertile ground for his brand of moderate Republicanism, so he decided to campaign in the region in hopes of capturing some white Democratic votes while expanding the small African American base within the party.[88] Eisenhower was not the first Republican nominee to adopt a southern-based electoral strategy. In 1928 Herbert Hoover courted lily-white and black-and-tan factions in hopes of building a far-reaching GOP coalition in the South that would enfeeble the Democratic Party.[89]

On the eve of the election, Roberta Church and her fellow white candidates appeared on WMCT television where she urged her "father's friends" to vote for her the next day.[90] Many of them did. Miss Church had a stunning personal victory over the Old Guard, winning a place on the committee by sixteen hundred ballots. However, her popularity could not overcome the strength of the Lee faction, for the rest of the so-called "Eisenhower" group failed to poll enough votes and were defeated. Two thousand votes were cast for Lee, who returned to the state executive committee by a comfortable margin.[91] Although the Old Guard had won the majority of committee seats, they were also committed to Eisenhower, so the results had little impact on the ongoing presidential contest.

Hoping to capitalize on her victory, Church traveled to Denver, Colorado, to discuss strategy with the Republican nominee and several of his advisors. As she conferred with Eisenhower on political conditions in Tennessee, a photograph was taken which was flashed to newspapers across the country.[92] From Denver, Roberta Church flew to Washington, D.C., where she met with key Republicans regarding the presidential campaign. Eisenhower's willingness to meet with Church and have his photograph taken with her again reveals how important the South was to his electoral strategy.

African Americans were not the only southerners embracing the GOP's nominee. Many former Democrats, including some who voted for Strom Thurmond in 1948, grudgingly decided to vote for Eisenhower. For example, Roane Waring, one of the leaders of the Shelby County States' Rights Party, explained why he was supporting the Republican ticket: "It is my honest conviction that the Democratic party of my father's no longer exists . . . every precept of democracy is belittled, scoffed at and sneered at, and repudiated by the Trumanite socialist horde . . ."[93] In keeping with Waring's sentiments, the Tennessee States' Rights Democratic Committee endorsed Eisenhower in mid-October.[94] Eisenhower was very aware of white southerners' disaffection with the Democratic Party. In Houston and New Orleans he declared his belief in the preservation of states' rights because "otherwise an all-powerful Washington bureaucracy will rob us one by one of the whole bundle of our liberties."[95] In campaign literature produced by the Citizens for Eisenhower-Nixon Club of Memphis it was stressed that "Eisenhower is the only man who can rid us of the evils of the Democratic Party."[96]

Ultimately, Eisenhower's southern strategy created a temporary, and uneasy, alliance between African American Republicans and angry white Democrats throughout Dixie. Hoping to strengthen this tenuous coalition, the Republican nominee traveled to Memphis on October 15. Thirty-five hundred Memphians gathered at municipal airport to welcome Eisenhower to the Bluff City. Disembarking from the plane, the general was met by his Tennessee election coordinator, Millsaps Fitzhugh, a leading member of the black-and-tan coalition. Waiting with Fitzhugh was an integrated reception committee that included black attorney Benjamin L. Hooks. After the introductions and handshaking, Eisenhower climbed into a black Cadillac and was driven to the foot of the Mississippi River where he was introduced to a large, enthusiastic crowd. "I come here today with the feelings of kinship for the South—a feeling which goes back to my family ties in the South..." Eisenhower then made an important policy pronouncement: "Certainly there would be no disposition on my part to impair the effective working out of TVA."[97] Created in 1933, the Tennessee Valley Authority built, among other things, hydroelectric dams which provided inexpensive electricity to thousands of Tennesseans, including the citizens of Memphis. In effect, Eisenhower was signaling that if elected, his administration would not dismantle Franklin Roosevelt's New Deal reforms. After his speech, Eisenhower was driven down Beale Street where he happened to see George W. Lee standing outside his office. The general ordered the driver to stop, and he motioned Lee over to the car where the two leaders talked for at least five minutes.[98]

By the fall of 1952 the Crump organization was so enfeebled that it played only a minor role in Adlai Stevenson's presidential campaign. Crump attempted to advise the Democratic nominee on political strategy, but for the most part Stevenson ignored the Memphis leader. He didn't even visit the Bluff City during the election, opting to speak in Nashville instead.[99] Crump and his lieutenants did campaign for the Democratic nominee, but they were overshadowed by a rival Stevenson headquarters established by Albert Gore.[100]

On election day, Republicans were stunned to learn that despite all of the enthusiasm for General Eisenhower, he failed to carry Shelby County. Stevenson eked out a slim margin of victory, 71,194 to 64,832, but Eisenhower received the majority of votes in Tennessee, making him the first Republican to carry the Volunteer State since Herbert Hoover in 1928.[101] Despite the efforts of Roberta Church and George W. Lee, the majority of Eisenhower ballots came not from African Americans, but rather from white voters in affluent East Memphis.[102] This did not bode well for those who hoped the Republicans would become the party of civil rights. When asked why Eisenhower was so successful in Tennessee, Crump replied, "There was just too much Truman."[103]

To some Memphians there was also too much Crump. As 1953 began, the Civic Research Committee stepped up its campaign to reform city government, while younger politicians laid plans for the inevitable coming of the postmachine era. Even the mayor dreamed of slipping from E. H. Crump's orbit.

3

"All the Cooperation We Can Muster"

By February 1953 Mayor Watkins Overton had had enough. For several months the four other members of the city commission, Claude Armour, John T. "Buddy" Dwyer, Frank Tobey, and O. P. Williams, had voted against the mayor's proposal to construct a downtown parking garage and ignored his opposition to pensions for the widows of firefighters and police officers.[1] The rift grew wider in early February when the four commissioners requested a meeting with Overton to discuss concerns they had with the performance of city personnel director Stanley Dilliard. Appointed by Overton in 1949, Dilliard supervised the conducting of civil service tests to screen out unqualified candidates as well as maintaining a list of applicants for other city agencies to hire from. Commissioner Frank Tobey declared as the meeting began that he and his colleagues felt that an investigation of the personnel department was needed because of allegedly questionable practices.[2]

Claude Armour, commissioner of fire and police, reported that Dilliard ordered personnel department employees not to fail anyone taking an oral examination and frequently placed unqualified candidates on the civil service list.[3] Commissioner Tobey further alleged that Dilliard had listed an applicant who in a previous job had been responsible for a substantial money shortage. A vote was then called to decide Dilliard's fate. Unsurprisingly, Armour, Dwyer, Tobey, and Williams voted to dismiss Dilliard, while the mayor voted to retain his services. Storming out of the meeting, the mayor was asked by a reporter if he would resign. "Possibly," Overton replied.[4]

Brooding overnight, Overton announced to the press the following evening that "a hostile city commission" made it "impossible" for him to continue to serve as mayor. Consequently Overton announced his resignation effective March 1.[5] E. H. Crump, vacationing at the Arlington Hotel in Hot Springs, Arkansas, was informed of the mayor's resignation, but when a newspaper reporter pressed him about possible successors, the Memphis leader refused comment.[6] Despite the urgency of the city hall situation, Crump continued his vacation, but he did confer regularly over the telephone with Frank Tobey.[7]

This led many to believe that Tobey would be chosen to succeed Mayor Overton. Reinforcing this view were the endorsements Tobey received from several local organizations, including two African American religious groups, the Baptist Pastors' Alliance, and the Baptist Ministers' Conference.[8] On February 19, Tobey met with his commission colleagues and former commissioner Joseph Boyle in his office to discuss the succession. When the meeting ended, they announced to the press that Tobey had been appointed mayor and Boyle was taking his place as commissioner of finances. An enterprising reporter phoned Overton for his reaction: "I am not surprised . . . If I may, as a humble citizen, quote the immortal Shakespeare, I would say, 'Et tu, Brute.'" When asked if he was referring to Tobey, he replied, "If the shoe fits, let him wear it."[9] As previously discussed, Overton had been responsible for Tobey being slated on the 1951 organization ticket, so naturally he was bitter at this turn of events.

An avuncular man blessed with a beautiful singing voice, Tobey was a trained engineer who had served as chief clerk of Memphis's engineering department and as city comptroller before being elected commissioner of finances and institutions in 1951.[10] Although not a member of Crump's inner circle, the Memphis leader relied heavily on him during the Overton crisis and had great confidence in his abilities.[11] It certainly was true that Tobey was a recognized expert in municipal finances, but it was unclear whether he could heal the deep fracture that existed in city government.

It will be remembered that in 1949 the Civic Research Committee had unsuccessfully advocated changing Memphis's government to authorize a city manager to oversee municipal affairs. Their proposal had been swiftly condemned by the county organization, but as we have just discussed much had changed since 1949. Lucius Burch and Edmund Orgill, hoping to capitalize on public apprehension over the state of local government, organized a public forum to discuss "the three principal forms of municipal government." A representative from the CRC planned to talk on the city manager plan and Overton was invited to discuss his "strong mayor" proposal.[12] Mayor Tobey was also invited to defend the commission form of government, but he declined, citing a heavy workload.[13]

When Orgill and the CRC made plans to hold the forum anyway, Tobey changed his mind. Twenty-five hundred Memphians, including a small contingent of African Americans, packed the gymnasium of Memphis State College to hear Lucius Burch, Watkins Overton, and Mayor Tobey debate governmental structure. Scattered in the audience were many organization loyalists carefully placed there to insure that the mayor received ample applause.[14]

Avoiding any condemnation of Crump, both Burch and Overton argued effectively that their plan would bring more efficient government to Memphis. But it was Tobey who made perhaps the most salient point of the evening: "Experience has long demonstrated that the continued existence of any plan of municipal government depends not on what the political theorist and organizations think of it, but what it does." Each speaker was warmly applauded as he spoke, but when, in answer to a question, Tobey replied, "There is no American city as free from politics as your own city government[,]" he was roundly booed by some of the citizens in the audience.[15] When the forum ended, nothing had changed in Memphis. Despite this, the arguments made by Burch, Overton, and Tobey would subtly influence the city when it eventually modified its form of government in the 1960s.

While Tobey was formulating his defense of the commission form of government, racial tension erupted on a street in South Memphis. In early 1953 several white homeowners living on East Olive Street began placing their homes on the real estate market. To the dismay of some of their neighbors, they sold their homes to African Americans. The first African Americans to move to East Olive Street were Ms. Willie May Banks and her seventy-year-old mother. Shortly after moving, the two women began receiving threatening phone calls, which frightened them into abandoning their new house. This pattern was repeated when Mrs. Idel Winbush moved onto the street later that year.[16] White residents were not ignored either. One evening in May a mob of whites roamed the neighborhood tearing "for sale" signs from yards and threatening to tar and feather anyone who sold their home to an African American. When one white resident reported the incident to the mayor, she declared, "You do not pay attention to a racial thing until it is dumped in your lap."[17]

In June, Wren Williams, an African American employee of Memphis Light, Gas and Water, and his sister Annie Eggleston bought a two-story frame house on East Olive Street. Soon after they moved in they, too, received threats from some of their white neighbors, but unlike Banks and Winbush, they refused to be intimidated. When it became clear to white extremists that intimidation would not work on Williams, they decided to take more drastic measures.

At 1:30 AM on June 28, a stick of dynamite was tossed onto the front porch of Williams's home, shattering seven windows and blowing a hole in the concrete walk.[18] In defiance Williams vowed to never retreat. Mayor Tobey, in an interview with the editor of one of Memphis's black weekly newspapers, also defied the terrorists when he quickly reassured the black community that violence would "not be tolerated." Detectives were assigned by Commissioner Armour to investigate the bombing, and round-the-clock police patrols of the neighborhood were ordered in hopes of preventing further violence.[19]

But it didn't work. On a warm summer day in August, Mrs. Teresa Guard, a white real estate agent, visited East Olive Street with Mrs. Leslie Stewart, an African American looking to purchase a new home. As they inspected a house located at 481 East Olive, the two women were surrounded by a mob of twenty white residents screaming insults at them. When Mrs. Guard attempted to break free of the crowd and reach her automobile, Mrs. J. M. Beard sprayed her with a garden hose.[20] Mrs. Beard and three other East Olive residents were arrested and charged with disorderly conduct. Despite the fact that this was the second time violence had erupted in South Memphis, the judge hearing the case merely fined Beard and Norman Banks eleven dollars and dismissed the charges against the other two.[21]

Mayor Tobey was far more concerned about this incident than the judge was. "I'll see that the law is upheld if it takes all the police we have," he vowed. The mayor then called for a sixty-day moratorium on the selling of homes on East Olive Street.[22] Although he had no authority to prevent anyone from buying or selling a home, Tobey's cooling-off period was grudgingly accepted. Peace returned to East Olive Street, but racial tension in Memphis was far from over.

Just before President Truman left office, he submitted to Congress a proposed budget for fiscal year 1954. Included in Truman's proposal was $30 million for a TVA steam-generating plant thirty miles north of Memphis at Fulton, Tennessee.[23] The new facility was needed because it was estimated that by 1957 TVA would not be able to meet the electrical needs of Memphis, and consequently the city's publicly owned power company, Memphis Light, Gas and Water Division, was anxious to see the plant constructed. Eisenhower was not. The president let slip to newspaper reporters that he believe that TVA was nothing more than "creeping socialism," and, not long after making this statement, he mused to his cabinet: "By God, if we could ever do it, before we leave here, I'd like to see us sell the whole thing . . ."[24] In order to weaken TVA, the Bureau of the Budget trimmed $61 million from the proposed budget, which effectively canceled the Fulton steam plant.[25] The president's comments and the proposed reduction in TVA funds shocked government leaders in Tennessee, who became convinced that Eisenhower planned to destroy the Tennessee Valley Authority.

When Congress began debating the proposed budget cuts in May, Mayor Tobey joined Governor Clement and other state leaders in condemning the action before a committee of the House of Representatives. Failure to construct the Fulton plant would, in Tobey's words, "hamper and perhaps stop the industrial development and growth in Memphis and West Tennessee..."[26] Discounting the electrical needs of the Midsouth, Republican majorities in both the House and Senate voted for the reduced appropriation, killing the Fulton steam plant.[27]

However, the need for additional electrical power in Memphis was real and Eisenhower knew it. In order to provide that electricity, and at the same time weaken TVA "socialism," the president supported the construction of an electric-generating plant in West Memphis, Arkansas, just across the river from the Bluff City. The plant was to be built by the Mississippi Valley Generating Company, which was owned by Edgar Dixon and Eugene Yates. Eisenhower hoped that Memphis would purchase electricity from the privately owned Dixon-Yates plant and thus rob the Tennessee Valley Authority of its largest customer.[28]

Stunned by Eisenhower's proposal, Tobey and the city commission vowed never to purchase electricity from the West Memphis plant. But that decision created something of a quandary for the city of Memphis. Given that within a few years TVA would not be able to meet the city's electrical needs, the options were quite limited. The president of the Memphis Light, Gas and Water Division, Thomas H. Allen, informed the mayor that the only real alternative to Dixon-Yates was for the city to construct its own electric-generating facility. Either the Bluff City caved in and agreed to buy power from Dixon-Yates or they should begin to take steps to construct an electric-generating plant for Memphis. Tobey recognized this, but hoped that allies in the House and Senate would reject the Dixon-Yates contract.[29] If not, the mayor declared in December 1954, "there is really no other alternative than to construct our own plant."[30]

Time, however, began to run out for Memphis in the spring of 1955. As already discussed, TVA did not have enough electric-generating capability to continue to supply the Bluff City indefinitely, and Memphis's contract with TVA was scheduled to end in 1958. To make matters worse, pro-TVA forces in Congress failed to defeat the contract, leaving Memphis with little choice. Allen and the MLG&W board voted in late June to construct the steam plant, and the city commission concurred.[31] Speaking over WMCT television, Tobey assured Memphians that "we aren't going to permit you to run out of power."[32] There was concern, however, that the city was cutting it a bit thin. Fortunately TVA agreed to continue supplying Memphis until the plant was built.[33]

Memphis's decision had a profound effect upon the future of the Dixon-Yates contract. The Senate Appropriations Committee, emboldened by Memphis's action, voted to withhold funds for the proposed facility.[34] Realizing that Memphis was offering him an escape from a growing political controversy, Eisenhower declared in a press conference that he was "delighted" that Memphis planned to build its own electric facility.[35] But the president wasn't willing to capitulate just yet. He did, however, ask Tobey and Allen to come to Washington to discuss the matter. In a meeting at the White House, Eisenhower agreed to cancel the Dixon-Yates contract in exchange for a promise that Memphis would not seek federal funds to pay for the municipal plant. Tobey readily assented but wanted further assurances that TVA would continue to supply electricity until construction was finished. When Eisenhower promised that TVA would not cut off power, the fate of Dixon-Yates was sealed.

The two men spoke to waiting reporters, and the president announced that "immediate steps" would be taken to cancel the West Memphis project. Mayor Tobey put his arm around the president, and both smiled widely as camera flashbulbs popped. Although both men were undoubtedly relieved to have this controversy behind them, Tobey had far more of a reason to smile than the president. His decision to construct an electric-generating facility not only insured the public ownership of utilities for Memphis; it also preserved the Tennessee Valley Authority. Although Memphis did temporarily pull out of the TVA system, it continued to play a significant role in securing its future. In 1959 Clifford Davis introduced legislation granting TVA the authority to issue revenue bonds to pay for facility construction and equipment upgrades. Reluctantly signed by Eisenhower, Davis's TVA Self-Financing Bill insured that neither the president nor Congress could arbitrarily eliminate the publicly operated utility by slashing its budget.[36] In 1963 the city rejoined TVA when it leased its newly constructed steam plant to the utility for $6.9 million annually for twenty years which saved Memphis electricity customers about $300 million.[37]

Meanwhile the issue of civil rights remained an explosive one, especially when, in May 1954, the United States Supreme Court declared that segregated schools were unconstitutional. In a unanimous decision, the court concluded that "in the field of education the doctrine of 'separate but equal' has no place. Separate educational facilities are inherently unequal. Therefore we hold that the plaintiffs . . . are, by reason of the segregation complained of, deprived of the equal protection of the laws guaranteed by the Fourteenth Amendment."[38] White Memphians were subdued in their reaction to the decision. Mayor Tobey merely stated he was "sure the . . . Memphis City Schools will approach this new condition with the public interest uppermost in their minds." County commission chairman E. W. Hale also passed the buck, replying only that it was "a matter for the school board."[39]

Governor Clement declared that the "problems presented by the Supreme Court's decision must be solved only after careful study, deliberation and judicious appraisal," and Senator Gore called for "cool thinking." Other white southern leaders were not so temperate. Mississippi senator James Eastland defiantly vowed that his state would "take whatever steps are necessary to retain segregation in the Public Schools."[40] On the other hand, African Americans were delighted by the ruling. The Colored Methodist Episcopal Church, for example, praised the Court for making a "heroic and just decision." No one was quite sure how, or when, the Court's ruling would be enforced. The justices themselves did not have an answer either. One year later the justices ordered federal district courts to monitor the creation of desegregation plans created by local school districts in order for African Americans to be admitted "to public schools on a racially nondiscriminatory basis with all deliberate speed."[41] This year-long delay, as we shall see, gave opponents of the decision time to mount a counterattack to preserve segregated schools in the South.

As Memphians digested the Supreme Court's decision, E. H. Crump announced a slate of forty candidates, including Mayor Tobey, for the August city and county elections. The long-time Memphis leader personally selected the organization ticket just as he had been doing for forty years. Most of them were unopposed, save Tobey, who was challenged by J. O'Neill Bomar, a disbarred attorney who had moved to Memphis in hopes of "cleaning out the Crump machine." But he didn't get the chance. Bomar received a mere 3,669 votes to Tobey's 30,286.[42] The *Nashville Banner* argued that the "influence of 'Mister' Crump in his home county appears greater than ever."[43] Although the outcome was predictable, the 1954 election was significant for two reasons. For the first time in local history, voting machines were used in Shelby County,[44] and Memphians cast their final ballots for candidates handpicked by Edward Hull Crump.

As the summer wore down, Crump increasingly felt tired and was unable to work a full day in his office. A few weeks after the election he was admitted to Baptist Hospital for a thorough examination where doctors discovered he was suffering from heart disease. As the summer turned to autumn, Crump was unable to leave his home and could only move about with the aid of a wheelchair. Five days after his eightieth birthday his condition worsened and doctors placed him in an oxygen tent. As word spread of Crump's health, many Memphians reacted emotionally to the news. For example, Mrs. Barbara Mashburn's second-grade students at Berclair Elementary School sent cards of encouragement.[45] One student, James Richard Howles, wrote, "I know you feel bad. I hope you get well soon."[46] In mid-October he slipped into a coma, and at 4:53 PM on October 16, 1954, Crump died.[47]

The day after Crump's burial, the city commission held their regularly scheduled public meeting, where, in addition to opening bids for a construction project and condemning substandard properties, they sought divine guidance. "This being our first meeting after the passing of our great leader, we thought it would be appropriate to open with a prayer," Tobey intoned.[48] The leadership of the organization fell to Tobey, Shelby County Commission chairman E. W. Hale and Attorney General John Heiskell.[49] Many feared that political chaos would erupt after Crump's death just as it had when he was removed from the mayor's office for not enforcing Tennessee's prohibition law in 1915–1916. Fortunately for Memphis, Tobey was an able administrator who was committed to building consensus, especially with those whom Crump had alienated. This was particularly true of the Civic Research Committee. Tobey shared their view that Memphis needed an improved zoning plan and, acting on the CRC's recommendation, hired the noted urban planner Harland Bartholomew to update the city's existing program.[50] Despite this cooperation, Tobey disagreed with the Civic Research Committee's position on the city manager form of government.

On the same day that Tobey and the city commission prayed for heavenly assistance, several members of the Civic Research Committee formed a separate organization to further promote the city manager plan for Memphis.[51] Headed by business leader R. A. "Dick" Trippeer, the committee organized a televised public debate for early November in hopes of further educating the public on the need to reform local government. Tobey agreed to participate but soon realized that to discuss changing the city charter so soon after Crump's death might create a sense of political panic in the Bluff City. The mayor believed that commission government "has served the people of this community well and . . . we should be reluctant to give up a plan that has proven to be successful."[52] Trippeer disagreed with Tobey's assessment, but did consent to cancel the debate for fear it "might give some people the idea that the Memphis Committee for Council-Manager government . . . is in the same way opposed to Mayor Tobey and his associates in the city government."[53]

In January 1955 entertainer Danny Thomas, the star of the popular television comedy *Make Room for Daddy*, began making plans to construct a hospital for underprivileged children in Memphis. Believing that faith and prayer had led to his show business success, Thomas wanted his hospital to serve as a permanent monument to the patron saint of lost causes, St. Jude. The entertainer chose Memphis because one of his principal advisors, Archbishop of Chicago Samuel Cardinal Stritch, had started his pastoral career in the Bluff City and considered it his "hometown."[54] In order to gauge Memphis's interest in such a project, Thomas sent Sol Rubin, a close friend and board member of a Los Angeles hospital, to Memphis to meet with attorneys John Ford Canale and Edward F. Barry.[55] Rubin also met with Tobey, who enthusiastically supported the construction of a children's hospital in Memphis. No doubt Tobey saw the economic advantages in such a medical facility being headquartered in the Bluff City, but he also had a more personal reason. In 1915, his wife, Lucille Adams, had suffered a miscarriage, which instilled in him a deep interest in hospitals and children's health issues.[56]

Tobey was so excited about the project he promised the city would purchase a suitable tract of land and give it to the hospital free of charge.[57] Impressed with Tobey's offer, Thomas invited him to Hollywood to further discuss the project. "We want to follow through on this with all the co-operation we can muster," promised the mayor as he prepared for his trip.[58] Joining him were Edward F. Barry, banker W. W. "Bill" Scott, and Paul Molloy of the *Commercial Appeal*. Wanting to make a good impression, Thomas toured the group around 20th Century Fox studios where they watched two movies being filmed, had lunch with actors Walter Brennan and Jane Russell, and met famed gossip columnist Louella Parsons. While the Memphians were lunching with the movie stars, a singing group serenaded them with a rendition of "Dixie."[59] In between the entertainment, the principals agreed that St. Jude Hospital would be a one-hundred-bed, $2 million facility for underprivileged children. Thomas agreed to raise $1.5 million while the Memphians promised to collect $500,000 from the contributions of midsoutherners. "The City of Memphis pledges itself in wholehearted support of the St. Jude project," said Mayor Tobey when he arrived back in Memphis.[60]

A few days after returning from Hollywood, Tobey met with prominent physicians and hospital administrators, where he outlined the project and requested their support. Those attending gave the proposed hospital their "enthusiastic support."[61] Other Memphians also embraced the project. The Memphis Junior Chamber of Commerce passed a resolution urging "all citizens and civic organizations of Memphis to pledge their support to Mr. Thomas . . ."[62] As Tobey began to build support for the project in Memphis, Thomas and his advisors selected Paul R. Williams, a noted African American architect, to design the hospital facility. Like everyone else involved, Williams refused to accept compensation for his work.[63]

In May, Thomas made his first trip to Memphis, where he described the hospital to local business and civic organizations and began to collect donations.[64] For example, the Knights of Columbus presented him with a check for thirty-five hundred dollars, and the Memphis Lebanese community contributed eighteen hundred dollars.[65] Thomas briefly left Memphis to appear on Bert Parks's popular television game show *Break the Bank*. Introduced as "Mr. Buford Williams" of Memphis, Thomas delighted the audience by speaking in an imitation southern accent. "Y'all evah been down to Memphis? I been working down there for Mayor Tobey—sweeping out the city hall." As the crowd roared in laughter, Thomas dropped the fake accent and asked everyone watching to send a dollar "to help a sick child."[66] Within three days of Thomas's appearance, thirty-five thousand dollars was sent to Memphis for St. Jude.[67]

On May 27 Thomas held a fundraising concert at Crump Stadium with Dinah Shore and his young costar of *Make Room for Daddy* Rusty Hamer. Fifteen thousand Memphians contributed a hundred thousand dollars[68] to watch an energetic performance highlighted by Thomas singing a new composition that contained the lyrics "give us back our Beale Street and take back your Avenue." Thomas was referring to the fact that in 1905 Memphis changed the name of world-famous Beale Street to Beale Avenue to conform to a city ordinance that designated all roads running east to west "avenues." Nearly everyone in Memphis ignored the ordinance, including W. C. Handy, who penned the "Beale Street Blues" in 1917. Sitting in the audience was Mayor Tobey and the city commission. At an impromptu meeting, the leaders quickly decided to rename the street. Tobey rushed to the stage to inform Thomas and the audience, who roared their approval. Thomas embraced the mayor, who clapped the entertainer on the back and laughed heartily.[69]

Tobey's willingness to commit governmental resources to the construction of St. Jude was perhaps the most significant political decision made by a Memphis mayor in the second half of the twentieth century. Opened on February 4, 1962, St. Jude Children's Research Hospital quickly became one of the city's leading industries and established Memphis as one of the nation's top medical communities. Within forty years of its opening, the hospital had 3,461 employees and a budget of $409 million.[70] More important, St. Jude saved the lives of thousands of children. In 2005, for example, the hospital treated 4,200 patients.[71] Because of its emphasis on research, a treatment for acute lymphoblastic leukemia was developed by the St. Jude staff and currently has a cure rate of 85 percent.[72]

Around the same time Danny Thomas was laying plans for St. Jude, Watkins Overton stunned political observers with the announcement that he planned to seek the mayor's office in the upcoming municipal election.[73] As we have seen, Overton was a fierce critic of the commission form of government and an advocate of the "strong mayor" plan. Ostensibly the former mayor remained a popular figure, and his criticism of the commission struck a cord with some Memphians. Consequently, the former mayor's announcement caused Tobey and his fellow commissioners a great deal of consternation. This was particularly true of Tobey, who was making plans for his own reelection campaign. A week before Overton's pronouncement the mayor met with several business executives to outline the administration's ticket. To the surprise of the assembled group, Tobey announced that he, Claude Armour, and John T. Dwyer would seek reelection, but Joseph Boyle and O. P. Williams would not. In their stead two unnamed candidates would be slated to run on the administration ticket.[74]

Caught off guard by Overton's declaration, Tobey huddled with his fellow commissioners to assess the new situation. Concerned that the shake-up would lend credence to Overton's anticommission platform, it was decided that Boyle and Williams would abandon their decision to retire. The five commission members then affixed their signatures to a document which pledged each man's loyalty to the ticket.[75] The day after Overton's announcement, Tobey made one of his own. "I have faith in the commission form of government," the mayor proclaimed when he shared the formation of the administration ticket with reporters.[76]

Despite the appearance of unity, Overton continued plans to establish a citizens' committee to support both his candidacy and the "council-mayor" form of government. Meanwhile the *Press-Scimitar* newspaper reported in March that park commission member Henry Loeb III was considering a run for the commission as an independent.[77] Born into a prominent Memphis Jewish family in 1920, Loeb attended Phillips Academy and Brown University before serving as a PT boat commander during World War II. After the war he returned to Memphis to work in his family's laundry business. Active in civic organizations, Loeb was appointed to the park commission in 1949. He was well regarded for championing park improvements, but was little known outside of business circles. The front page *Press-Scimitar* article no doubt enhanced his visibility, but more publicity was needed if he was to challenge the prominent Tobey and Overton factions. Fortunately for Loeb an opportunity for increased notoriety presented itself not long after the newspaper story appeared.

In the spring Loeb heard rumors that commission chairman John B. Vesey was using park employees, equipment, and supplies to improve his home at 316 North Avalon. Investigating the matter, Loeb sent a questionnaire to several employees asking if they had ever worked at Vesey's residence. All replied in writing that they had. Truck driver Joe Williams stated that he had worked at the chairman's home on twelve separate occasions when he took "paper off Mr. Vesey's walls, worked on floors, general cleaning of house and other odd jobs." Half the time Williams was paid by Vesey and the other half by the park commission, according to the truck driver's written statement.[78] Along similar lines, subforeman R. M. Child reported that he was ordered to take twenty-five boxwood trees from the park commission's nursery and plant them in Vesey's yard. "I never drew a dime for this private job . . . ," Child declared.[79] However, in his statement, foreman L. E. Cox related that "our men and trucks have done work on Mr. Vesey's property on their time off and were paid by Mr. Vesey."[80]

Alarmed by these findings, Loeb reported the information to fellow commissioner Sam Nickey, and the two requested a meeting with Chairman Vesey. He refused. The commissioners then sent the evidence to the mayor and city commission.[81] Tobey turned the matter over to city attorney Frank Gianotti, Jr., who investigated the matter and advised the commission to bring charges against Vesey and hold a hearing to determine his guilt or innocence. "We do not see how under the circumstances these charges can be ignored," Gianotti reported to the mayor.[82] No doubt this was the last thing Tobey wanted to deal with in the midst of a political campaign, but he had little choice. On July 7 the mayor filed nine charges of official misconduct against Vesey and suspended him from the park commission chairmanship.[83]

Just before charges against Vesey were filed, Loeb's term on the park commission came to an end. Wanting to remain on the board, Loeb wrote the mayor requesting reappointment.[84] Tobey, however, had other ideas. Two days before announcing Vesey's suspension, the mayor informed the press that the city commission had decided not to reappoint Loeb. "It is our opinion that Mr. Loeb is contemplating running and in fact he is actually campaigning right now for a place on the city commission[,]" Tobey explained.[85] That may have been a factor, but the embarrassment caused by Loeb's revelations of Vesey's activities no doubt played an even larger role in their decision.

The hearing began on July 27 with Gianotti introducing several witnesses who confirmed the allegations Loeb had collected in May. Vesey's defense counsel argued that the park commission had been reimbursed for all work done and employees had been paid by the chairman for their labor.[86] On the fourth day of testimony Commissioner Armour ignored the mounting evidence against Vesey and introduced a motion to drop all charges, reprimand the chairman, and reinstate him. Stupefied, Giannoti requested more time to introduce further evidence. Instead, Tobey recessed the proceedings.[87] To the surprise of no one, Vesey was acquitted the following day.[88] The shabby way in which the Vesey affair ended angered many Memphians and tarnished Mayor Tobey's image. In a letter to the mayor, "a disgusted law abiding citizen" described the hearing as a "farce," and went on to write: "It is time for counsel [sic] city management to replace this unhealthy condition."[89] Vesey's acquittal also affected Henry Loeb as well. Although certainly pleased over the publicity he garnered during the investigation and hearing, Loeb could not have been comforted by the end result. A fiscal conservative who abhorred corruption, Loeb was no doubt appalled at the commission's decision.

On September 7 Tobey met with members of the commission to discuss plans for an expressway system to relieve Memphis's chronic traffic problems. As the meeting dragged on, Commissioner Boyle noticed that the mayor looked as though he was sick to his stomach. Confirming that he didn't feel well, Tobey rested on his couch until he felt better. That evening he joined his wife, son, and daughter-in-law for dinner but around 11 PM became ill again. A physician was called and by early the next morning it was clear that Tobey had suffered a severe heart attack. Placed in an oxygen tent, Tobey remained in critical condition until his death on September 11 at 10:35 AM.[90] Many were deeply saddened to learn of Tobey's passing, none more so than Danny Thomas. Devastated by the news, the founder of St.

Jude declared from his Beverly Hills home that "America has lost one of its finest sons. Always shall I cherish the memory of his beautiful cherubic face and kind heart, I have suffered the loss of a great friend."[91]

The untimely death of Frank T. Tobey had a profound effect on the history of Memphis. As we have seen, he successfully held the Shelby County organization together while ably governing the city. Shortly after Tobey's burial the political vacuum that failed to materialize after Crump's death took form. Rudderless, the Shelby County organization began to splinter while new leaders emerged who offered Memphians an alternative to the machine politics of the past. Which faction would prevail was far from clear as Memphis prepared for its first election without the formidable presence of Edward Hull Crump.

4

"Why Didn't Someone Tell Us This Before?"

Henry Loeb was ready. On September 16 he formally announced what nearly everyone already knew, that he was a candidate for a seat on the city commission. Distancing himself from the administration and Overton tickets, Loeb declared that "I offer myself without political ties or obligations. I will be free, if elected, to represent all the people without fear of favor."[1] Loeb's independent stance distinguished him from the other politicians who were running as part of a slate of candidates.

Shortly before Loeb's announcement, Overton revealed his running mates for the commission and his platform. Chosen were former city personnel director Stanley Dilliard, Malcolm R. Futhey, president of the American Federation of Labor's Building Trades Council, and railroad superintendent Henry K. Buck.[2] Comprising seventeen points, Overton's platform included a provision to appoint a citizens' committee to "draw up for Memphis the finest, most modern city government they can plan."[3] Overton received a key endorsement from Will Gerber, former Shelby County attorney general and confidant of Crump. Although no longer holding public office, Gerber remained an organization stalwart, and his endorsement of Overton was a significant victory for the former mayor.[4]

Meanwhile the administration was thrown into turmoil because of Tobey's unexpected death. Two decisions faced the remaining commission members. First, the city charter required them to appoint an interim mayor to serve until the end of the year, and second, they needed an acceptable candidate to replace Tobey. Ideally that would be the same person, but when the commission met on September 17 they were only able to accomplish the first of these tasks. Former mayor Walter Chandler agreed to serve as interim executive but refused to run for a four-year term.[5]

While the administration sought a suitable mayoral candidate, the Council-Manager Committee, who had earlier endorsed Tobey for reelection, was carefully considering the new political reality. Dissatisfied with the Overton and administration tickets, many members of the committee wanted a more liberal candidate to run for mayor. Perhaps the most recognizable reformer in 1950s Memphis was Edmund Orgill, a leader in the 1948 Kefauver campaign, former president of the Civic Research Committee, and an outspoken supporter of the council-manager form of government.

Heeding the call of the Council-Manager Committee, Orgill entered the race in late September. During an enthusiastic campaign meeting on September 27 Orgill was praised by African American educator J. Ashton Hayes and received the endorsement of former mayor Rowlett Paine.[6] With Orgill in the race, the question became who the third mayoral candidate would be. Chandler announced that they were interviewing local businessmen but were unable to find anyone willing to serve. In desperation they asked former Shelby County attorney general John Heiskell to run, but he, too, declined. Resigned to the situation, Chandler, Armour, Boyle, Dwyer, and Williams announced they were running as the "good government ticket" without a mayoral candidate.[7] "We don't need any head to our ticket; let the two mayor candidates fight it out for themselves . . . ," Chandler declared at a campaign meeting in Overton Park.[8] Despite this boast, the "good government" candidates did not garner much enthusiasm. Even the campaign rally in Overton Park was attended mostly by city employees who were ordered to appear.[9]

In early October two hundred African American church leaders met at the Church of God in Christ's Pentecostal Temple to organize for the upcoming election. Christening themselves the Ministers and Citizens League, they held a series of rallies in area churches to encourage blacks to register to vote.[10] Joining the church officials on the executive committee were George W. Lee and J. E. Walker. Although the two leaders cooperated on the registration effort, they differed on who should be mayor. Walker strongly endorsed Orgill while Lee halfheartedly supported Overton. A firm believer in organization, Walker established the Citizens League for Edmund Orgill, which also endorsed Henry Loeb, John T. Dwyer, and Stanley Dilliard for the commission.[11] The two organizations also supported the school board candidacy of Roy Love, pastor of Mt. Nebo Baptist Church and the only African American in the race.[12] Despite the division over the mayoral race, the voter registration drive was an astounding success with 38,847 African Americans registering to vote in Memphis.[13]

The Walker organization held parties in black neighborhoods to build support for Orgill's candidacy. Ward leaders were appointed who organized rallies and distributed campaign literature in a door-to-door canvass of African American neighborhoods.[14] Recognizing the importance of the black vote, Orgill attended Coca-Cola parties while his campaign staff worked closely with Walker's Citizens League.[15] Overton, on the other hand, had little support in the African American community save the endorsement of George W. Lee and a handful of ministers.[16] Although his campaign was not terribly organized in the black community, Overton continued to pick up key endorsements from members of the old Crump machine. Shelby County Commission chairman E. W. Hale endorsed the former mayor,[17] as did former county attorney general John Heiskell, his successor Phil Canale, and county court clerk Hickman Ewing.[18]

Television was an important tool exploited by both mayoral candidates. Speaking over one local station, Orgill declared that a major reason for his candidacy was "to prevent the creation of a selfish political machine." Overton countered over the Memphis airwaves that he was not attempting to "build some kind of a sinister political organization."[19] The charge that Overton wanted to re-create the Crump machine in his own image became the favorite rhetorical flourish of the Orgill camp, while the former mayor argued that his opponent wanted to establish an undemocratic government that would hire an outsider to direct the affairs of Memphis. "I don't want anybody running our city who doesn't know where Main and Madison is," Overton quipped.[20] As election day drew near, Orgill seemed to have the advantage. He received endorsements from local business leaders including contractor W.L. Sharpe, who had been a close friend to the late Mayor Tobey.[21] Political observers speculated that Orgill would win if there was a large turnout of voters "without past political ties."[22]

And they were right. Eighty-six thousand Memphians, the largest turnout in municipal history up to that time, went to the polls on November 10. Orgill led the way with 51,789 votes, while Overton received only 33,154. Administration candidates Armour and Dwyer reclaimed their seats on the city commission, but their colleagues Boyle and Williams were defeated by Henry Loeb and Stanley Dilliard.[23] Nineteen thousand six hundred and one ballots were cast for Roy Love, the only African American in the race, which were not enough for election but were 12,000 more votes than J. E. Walker had received in 1951.[24] The black vote was far more decisive in the mayor's race. In many black-populated wards Orgill received a majority of votes cast. For example, in ward 14, which was located near LeMoyne College, Orgill received 515 votes while only 65 ballots were cast for Overton.[25]

The same week of the election the Southern Historical Association met in Memphis at the Peabody Hotel for its annual conference. Wanting to address in a meaningful way the Supreme Court's 1954 *Brown vs. Board of Education* decision, which, as we have already seen, declared school segregation unconstitutional, the president, Bell I. Wiley, and the program committee chair, James W. Silver, scheduled a conference session to discuss the decision and its impact on the future of the American South. Silver, a history professor at the University of Mississippi, asked his neighbor, the Nobel laureate William Faulkner, to speak at the session. The renowned novelist agreed, joining conservative Nashville attorney Cecil Sims and Morehouse College president Benjamin Mays on the panel. In order for Mays to appear at the conference, Silver and Wiley had to convince management to do the unthinkable—to allow an integrated gathering in "the South's grandest hotel."[26]

Entitled "The Segregation Decisions," the session convened on the evening of November 10 at the association's Phi Alpha Theta banquet in the Peabody's continental ballroom. After introductions, Cecil Sims discussed the historic background of the *Brown* decision and then argued that the court only outlawed compulsory separation, not segregation itself. When Sims finished his legal brief, Benjamin Mays rose and spoke passionately about the injustice of legalized separation. "The chief sin of segregation is the distortion of human personality . . . It gives the segregated a feeling of inferiority which is not based on facts and it gives the segregator a feeling of superiority which is not based on facts." Faulkner, who had been sitting quietly, puffing on his pipe, came last. Speaking in low tones, the noted writer charted a more moderate course. "I am not convinced that the Negro wants integration in the sense that some of us claim to fear he does . . . I think what he wants is . . . equal right and opportunity to make the best one can of one's life . . . without fear of injustice or oppression or threat of violence. If we had given him this equal right to opportunity 90 or 50 or even 10 years ago, there would have been no Supreme Court decision about how we run our schools."[27]

A month after the proceedings Silver asked Faulkner to expand his thoughts for publication. In the version that was published by the Southern Regional Council, the celebrated novelist offered a trenchant observation: "We speak now against the day when our Southern people who will resist to the last these inevitable changes in social relations, will, when they have been forced to accept what they at one time might have accepted with dignity and goodwill, say, 'Why didn't someone tell us this before? Tell us this in time?'"[28] Unfortunately for Memphis and the rest of the South, few were listening.

○ ○ ○

Not long after his inauguration, Mayor Orgill found himself in a very isolated position. The four commissioners, Armour, Dilliard, Dwyer, and Loeb, had all been elected independently of the mayor and consequently owed him no loyalty. This became clear in January when Orgill suggested to the commission that J. E. Walker be appointed to the board of the city-owned John Gaston Hospital. Uneasy about appointing an African American, the commission rejected the proposal. The mayor however, refused to give up. During an appearance on WMCT's *Know Your Government* program, Orgill was asked if the city had ever considered appointing an African American to the board. The mayor confirmed that the commission had considered the matter and if adopted it "would give the Negroes a feeling of belonging . . ."[29]

Many white Memphians did not want their African American neighbors to have a sense of belonging. Angry whites reacted to the mayor's proposal by reporting to the fire and police departments that nonexistent violent disturbances and fires were taking place at Orgill's residence. The suggestion was no more welcome to the city commission. At the next scheduled meeting each commissioner publicly condemned the mayor's proposal. Caving to the pressure, Orgill abandoned his plan to appoint an African American to the hospital board.[30] The John Gaston incident not only set back race relations at a time when, as William Faulkner pointed out, cooperation was sorely needed, but it also created a split in local politics which would have profound consequences for the Bluff City. One month after the mayor's hasty retreat, the surviving members of the old Crump machine attempted to exploit Orgill's weakness, and recapture their former glory, by forming a new political organization called the Citizens for Progress.

One hundred sixty-four political leaders, including commissioners Armour and Dwyer, U.S. Representative Clifford Davis, and former mayor Walter Chandler, met in the Empire Room of the Hotel Claridge to select candidates for the upcoming legislative election who were committed to segregation and the commission form of government. "We should have a delegation go to Nashville pledged to . . . vote to have Tennessee interpose with other states against the Supreme Court decisions on segregation[,]" declared former judge Samuel O. Bates to the assembled crowd.[31] The CFP later adopted the slogan "Keep Memphis and Shelby County Down in Dixie." The formation of the Citizens for Progress was part of a wider movement by whites across the South to block implementation of the Supreme Court's school desegregation orders. Commonly referred to as "massive resistance," it was perhaps best expressed by the Southern Declaration of Constitutional

Principles (also known as the Southern Manifesto), which was introduced in Congress in March 1956, one month after the formation of the Citizens for Progress.

The declaration, signed by nineteen senators and seventy-seven representatives (including Clifford Davis), stridently argued that the "Supreme Court of the United States, with no legal basis for such action, undertook to exercise their naked judicial power and substituted their personal political and social ideas for the established law of the land." The leaders also promised to use "all lawful means" to overturn the Court's barring of school segregation.[32] The Southern Manifesto not only comforted the segregationist members of the Citizens for Progress but also emboldened their campaign to elect an anti-integrationist bloc to the Tennessee General Assembly. Meanwhile the increasingly isolated Mayor Orgill took notice of his enemy's actions and began to build his own coalition.

On May 26 a picnic to celebrate the mayor's first five months in office was held in the Shelby County community of Bartlett at a farm owned by Thomas L. Robinson. Thirty-five hundred Memphians sampled barbeque, cole slaw, ice cream, and watermelon while a guitar player performed popular songs of the day. According to *Commercial Appeal* reporter James Gunter the crowd gave Orgill "Elvis Presley–type applause" when he thanked them for their support. Commissioner Loeb attended the event while Armour, Dilliard, and Dwyer were noticeably absent.[33] The mayor must have been gratified by the enthusiasm of the attendees, and it certainly influenced his decision to create his own political organization shortly after the picnic ended. Organized by the mayor's old ally Lucius Burch, a luncheon was held at the Hotel Chisca for nonaligned Democrats and Republicans to gauge interest in forming a new coalition. Sixty people attended the event and enthusiastically supported the creation of an Orgill organization.[34] As a result the mayor announced the formation of the Good Local Government League to not only expand municipal reforms but also endorse candidates and campaign for their election.[35]

When the league held its first full meeting on June 26, George Grider, Orgill's campaign manager, was elected president and a platform was adopted that included calling for the passage of legislation to regulate the activities of political parties, including a prohibition on government workers participating in election campaigns, and granting home rule status for Memphis. Unlike their opponents, they did not deem defending segregation worthy of mention.[36] However, as the segregationists seemed to gain ground, Grider pointed out that the GLGL did not endorse any integrationist candidates.[37]

A few weeks later, the issue of government workers engaging in political activities became a major issue when Peggy Irvin, an employee of the Memphis Light, Gas and Water's personnel office, reported to Henry Loeb that all of her assigned tasks for the past month had been of a "partisan political nature." Irvin also reported that she was about to be terminated because she had "expressed admiration" for Loeb and Mayor Orgill.[38]

Deciding to see for himself, Loeb invited a *Commercial Appeal* reporter and photographer to accompany him to the personnel department. When they arrived they witnessed a Memphis firefighter hand a MLGW employee a list of names. "Doing a little ward work . . . ?" Loeb asked personnel director George Sneed. "You stepped right in the middle of it," Sneed replied. In answer to several questions the personnel director admitted that he was a member of the Citizens for Progress and that at least one employee was engaged in political work during office hours.[39] Loeb's grandstanding infuriated the leaders of the CFP, most notably Claude Armour. In addition to charging that the public works commissioner was a "publicity seeker," Armour declared to the press that Loeb "has a habit of exposing every confidential matter discussed at commission executive sessions and you cannot deal with him on a confidential basis." As we shall see, Loeb's maverick streak and his inability to cooperate with his fellow municipal leaders had profound consequences for the city of Memphis.

During Loeb's "raid" on MLGW, reporters learned of a scheduled ward meeting two days hence at Barksdale Police Station. On the appointed day, two *Commercial Appeal* reporters and a photographer entered the police station, startling twelve city and county employees who quickly fled. The organizer of the meeting, deputy county tax assessor Alton B. McHenry, scooped up a large stack of papers and headed for the door. A reporter followed him outside the building, where McHenry hastily admitted he had been conducting a ward meeting just as he entered his automobile and drove off.[40] Hoping to exploit the issue, the GLGL requested that the city commission adopt a resolution forbidding all city employees from working at the polls on election day. Unsurprisingly Armour, Dilliard, and Dwyer rejected the proposal.[41] Despite this, Orgill continued to hammer away at the issue. "I think one of the most important issues is the question of a little Hatch Act for Memphis patterned after the federal Hatch Act which prevents federal employees from participating actively in politics," the mayor declared to the press.

As the Citizens for Progress defended segregation and the Good Local Government League promoted political reform, Memphis blacks continued their struggle to achieve equality through voting. When the GLGL was organized, African Americans were invited to participate, which led to forty black leaders joining the group, including Reverend S. A. Owen, who was named head of a committee charged with interviewing perspective Republican candidates. Dr. J. E. Walker also joined the group, and he, too, was appointed to a committee.[42] As we have seen, throughout the 1950s African American Memphians hoped to elect black candidates as a first step in dismantling segregation. Twice before, in 1951 and 1955, they had failed to elect a candidate to the local school board. In 1956, they set their sights much higher. Not long after the formation of the GLGL, the black-led Democratic Voters League was formed to support the candidacy of African American labor leader James Thomas Walker for the Tennessee House of Representatives. Secretary of the Coopers' Union Local 99, vice president-at-large of the Tennessee Federation of Labor, and president of the North Memphis Civic Club, Walker garnered a great deal of support in the black community, largely because J. E. Walker agreed to serve as his campaign manager.[43] George W. Lee and the Republicans nominated three African Americans, William C. Weathers, Benjamin L. Hooks, and T. L. Spencer, to run for seats in the state house and senate, but Walker's candidacy received the most attention.[44]

In the final days before the primary, the rhetoric on both sides became more strident. Claude Armour, speaking during a rally at the Northgate Shopping Center, charged that the opposition candidates were men of low station "with criminal records for bootlegging, forgery and strong-armed robbery." Calling attention to the fact that the Good Local Government League was an interracial organization, Armour referred to them as the "Meeman-Orgill-Dr. Walker ticket" and distributed photographs of blacks and whites attending meetings together. The police commissioner also lambasted Henry Loeb as having "the mind of a child and the body of a man." On the same day supporters of the GLGL, including Lucius Burch and Henry Gotten, spoke on WHBQ-TV to encourage citizens to participate in local government. Arguing that the CFP was nothing more than a reenergized Crump organization, Dr. Gotten declared that "[t]here's no such thing as a benevolent dictatorship."[45] Not long after, Dr. Walker reminded black voters: "If you don't vote against the CP [Citizens for Progress] ticket you'll wake up and find yourself like the Negro in Mississippi, unable to vote."[46] And so it went until the voters went to the polls on August 2.

Turnout was light, but the Citizens for Progress received the majority of votes, electing not only delegates to the Tennessee General Assembly but also attorney general, sheriff, tax assessor, and county trustee.[47] The leaders of the CFP, especially Claude Armour, walked away from the August 1956 election believing they had created a political apparatus that rivaled the old Crump organization. For African Americans, the results were more sobering. Few blacks chose to vote for James Walker. For example, in the rural Shelby County hamlet of Stewartville, African American voters were in the majority but only eleven votes were cast for James Walker. The rest went to the segregationist ticket.[48] The defeat of the Good Local Government League did more than embolden segregationist sentiment in Memphis; it also further strained the mayor's relationship with his fellow commissioners. Orgill sometimes came across as an irritable schoolteacher lecturing his students, and this tendency became more pronounced as his term continued. During a commission meeting in 1957 Orgill shouted at Henry Loeb, "Now wait a minute; I'm running this hearing. Be quiet." In a letter to the mayor, Loeb chastised him, declaring, "I resent this type of peremptory treatment and do not expect it to happen again—ever."[49] Nonetheless he was able to accomplish several important things for Memphis, including the construction of expressways, expansion of the city through the annexation of the Frayser community, and the adoption of an urban renewal program for the inner city.[50] But his dream of altering the city's form of government remained lost on a sea of acrimony.

On Sunday, July 29, 1956, a new post office opened in Memphis. Located in a prominent African American neighborhood, the post office was named for George W. Lee, and a black federal worker, A. L. Moreland, was appointed postmaster.[51] An elaborate ceremony, including a band concert and parade, was held to mark the occasion. Carroll Reece, Republican U. S. representative from East Tennessee, spoke at the event, as did an assistant postmaster general of the United States.[52] With the naming of a federal building in his honor, George W. Lee emerged as Memphis's most influential national political figure in the early post-Crump years. Lee's chief Republican rival, Roberta Church, no longer lived in Memphis, owing to her appointment as the Department of Labor's consultant for minority groups by President Eisenhower in 1953.[53]

The ceremony also marked the beginning of the 1956 presidential campaign in Memphis. As the post office suggests, the Eisenhower campaign looked to Memphis to increase the president's electoral strength in the South. Later that summer, Lee, along with Dr. R. Q. Venson, traveled to San Francisco to attend the Republican National Convention as delegates. After Eisenhower's nomination, Lee returned home to plan the campaign. White attorneys Armistead Clay and Walker Wellford, along with black insurance executive O. T. Westbrook, were appointed cochairs of the president's reelection effort in Shelby County, but Lee oversaw the details of the campaign. For decades Lee had employed grassroots electoral techniques, and he used all of his considerable political talents during the 1956 presidential campaign. Workers fanned out across the city and county, ringing doorbells and distributing eighty-nine thousand pieces of campaign literature. Large rallies were held in the African American wards, while Lee negotiated with ministers to use their influence to get out the vote on election day. The negotiations worked. The Friday before the election over one hundred black religious leaders issued a statement requesting their parishioners to vote for the president.[54]

Tireless in his efforts, Lee was out front during the campaign, giving speeches and writing editorials on behalf of the president.[55] In one particular address Lee passionately argued that it was the responsibility of African Americans "to go to the polls and give . . . full strength to re-elect Dwight Eisenhower who has done more to extend equality of opportunity to American Negroes than any other president since Lincoln."[56] In spite of the fact that Eisenhower had only tepidly endorsed the Supreme Court's school integration decision, Lee's argument swayed many black voters who for two decades had cast ballots for a succession of Democratic candidates. A rival, lily-white organization, the Citizens for Eisenhower-Nixon, was formed by several prominent businessmen and champion golfer Dr. Cary Middlecoff. The organization crudely attempted to appeal to segregationists by prominently displaying the Confederate battle flag on their campaign literature.[57] Their efforts amounted to little, however. As the Eisenhower campaign knew full well, the black-and-tan coalition was the key to a Republican victory in Shelby County in 1956.

Despite the efforts of the Citizens for Eisenhower-Nixon, most Tennessee segregationists remained, albeit uneasily, within the Democratic fold. Shortly before the party's convention in Chicago, Governor Clement traveled to Atlanta for a strategy meeting with other southern leaders. Southern Democrats decided at the Atlanta conference to use their 336 delegate votes to insure that the convention adopt a vague platform that did not endorse school integration. Most conferees expressed their support for front-runner Adlai Stevenson, but they were determined to block the nomination of a pro–civil rights northerner for vice president.[58] Clement, scheduled to give the convention's keynote address, hoped that the southern caucus would look favorably upon him as the party's vice presidential choice. He wasn't the only one. Tennessee senators Estes Kefauver and Albert Gore both expressed an interest in the second spot, as did Massachusetts senator John F. Kennedy.

When Clement arrived in Chicago, he dined with former president Harry Truman, who had declared previously that the Tennessee governor would "make a very good vice president."[59] The former president was a conspicuous figure at the convention, where he unsuccessfully attempted to deny Stevenson the nomination and, as he had in 1948, argued before the platform committee that a moderate civil rights plank favored by southern leaders was necessary to achieve "harmony" within Democratic ranks.[60] Emboldened by Truman's stand, southern delegates pressured Stevenson to accept the moderate plank by refusing to pledge their votes until a platform was adopted. A group of northern representatives tried to adopt a plank that endorsed the Supreme Court action, but after a personal appeal from Truman, the convention consented to a platform that recognized the school integration decision but did not pledge to enforce the law.[61] With the platform fight behind them, the Democrats nominated Adlai Stevenson for president and, in an unusual move, he announced that the delegates would make the vice presidential choice rather than the nominee.[62]

For Estes Kefauver, who had been campaigning steadfastly for both himself and Stevenson, the nominee's decision came as something of a disappointment. Stevenson forces had hinted they might throw open the selection in order to outflank the die-hard southerners who never forgave Kefauver for not signing the Southern Manifesto, but a firm commitment was never given. Consequently, the Tennessee senator feared this was a move to humiliate him. Only after meeting with Stevenson did Kefauver agree to continue his campaign.[63] The Tennessee delegation was bitterly opposed to Kefauver, especially those from Memphis. Claude Armour explained their position: "I felt the primary reason my people sent me to Chicago was to keep Kefauver off the ticket." As a result, they pledged their votes to Clement, who began to campaign in earnest.[64] When the governor's candidacy stalled for lack of delegate support, they switched to Senator Gore, who also failed to garner widespread support. While the Tennessee delegation remained intransigent, John F. Kennedy began to pick up votes. As the night wore on, it became clear that either Kefauver or Kennedy was going to win the vice presidential nomination. The Tennessee delegation, unwilling to vote for a northern liberal, reluctantly switched to Kefauver. The convention hall erupted in cheers as Kennedy conceded defeat, making the Tennessee senator's nomination unanimous.[65]

Enthusiasm for the Stevenson-Kefauver ticket was hard for southern Democrats to muster, but they tried their best. Governor Clement, along with political leaders from the former Confederate states, joined the nominees in Knoxville to pledge their loyalty and support.[66] In Memphis, former mayor Walter Chandler called for harmony, declaring that he planned to "support the Democratic ticket from top to bottom."[67] Not everyone agreed. The cochairmen of the Citizens for Progress, Sam O. Bates and W. Percy McDonald, refused to campaign for the Democratic ticket, while Shelby County Democratic Executive Committee chairman John Heiskell failed to organize an effective local campaign for Stevenson.[68] As the Democrats floundered, George W. Lee and his black-and-tan coalition continued to work on behalf of President Eisenhower. In the end, the unnerved Democrats could not overcome the superior organizational skill of the African American community.

For the first time in its history, a Republican presidential candidate received a majority of votes in Shelby County. The president received 65,999 votes, while 62,037 ballots were cast for Stevenson. Most of Eisenhower's support came from African American wards and suburban white neighborhoods which continued the longstanding political alliance between black and white middle-class voters in Memphis.[69] The only difference was that it was for a Republican ticket rather than a Democratic one. Although not readily apparent in November 1956, the election weakened further the Democrats' steely grip on the South. As one Memphis Republican put it, "It's the beginning of a two-party system in Shelby County."[70]

Meanwhile, the issue of segregation remained the most divisive issue in the South. In early 1956 federal judge Robert L. Taylor ordered the school district of Clinton, Tennessee, to integrate, making it the first community in the Volunteer State instructed to do so.[71] To the relief of many, on August 27 twelve African American children enrolled in the local high school without incident.[72] But the peace did not last. On the third day of integration, violence erupted as segregationist demonstrators, led by John Kasper, the charismatic executive secretary of the Seaboard White Citizens' Council, attacked one of the black students. Judge Taylor, alarmed by the violence, issued a restraining order against Kasper and five others.[73] The situation further deteriorated when Kasper was arrested, quickly tried, and sentenced to a year in prison for inciting a riot. Seething with anger, fifteen hundred white segregationists massed in front of the Anderson County courthouse to listen to North Alabama Citizens' Council leader Asa Carter harangue the

Supreme Court. When a rumor spread that Carter was about to be arrested by federal marshals, the crowd went berserk, stopping traffic and beating several African American tourists passing through East Tennessee.[74] Violence continued sporadically over the next two days, which forced Clinton mayor W. E. Lewallen to request state assistance. Governor Clement, faced with an escalating riot, ordered the highway patrol and National Guard to restore order.[75] Although primarily designed to crush resistance, the governor's action in effect applied the power of Tennessee state government to enforce integration.

On January 7, 1957, the new general assembly convened in Nashville amid lingering consternation over the violence in Clinton. When the session opened, the speakers of the house and senate, James L. Bomar and Jered Maddux, introduced a resolution condemning the U.S. Supreme Court and pledged to "resist all illegal encroachments upon the powers reserved for the State of Tennessee . . ."[76] Christened the "Tennessee Manifesto," it was enthusiastically endorsed by the Shelby County delegation to the general assembly. Two days later, speaking to a joint session of the legislature, the governor introduced a legislative package to promote "peaceful and harmonious relations between the races and for the preservation and efficiency of our public school systems." The legislature wasted little time in enacting the governor's program. A mere twelve days after the governor made his proposal, the major points became law.

Local school officials were given the power to assign and transfer students within their districts, maintain segregated schools if parents elected to do so, and amend the school bus transportation law to eliminate any mention of race. All of Clement's proposals were clearly designed to circumvent the Court's ruling and preserve the separation of black and white schoolchildren. Along similar lines, the Shelby delegation introduced several bills designed to crush the NAACP in Tennessee.[77] The actions of the 1957 general assembly appeared on the surface to strengthen the segregationist cause in the Volunteer State, but they did little to discourage African Americans from chipping away at the second-class fortress white southerners had placed them in.

On April 26, 1956, O. Z. Evers, a black postal clerk, stood at the corner of Bellevue and Lamar waiting for a bus to take him downtown. A native of Arkansas, Evers had lived in Chicago until he went to work for the post office in Memphis. When the bus arrived, Evers entered the conveyance, paid his fare, and sat down just behind the driver. Unaccustomed to segregated transportation, Evers did not realize he had broken a state law. The driver, horrified that a black man dared to sit in a seat reserved for whites, informed Evers that he could not sit there. "Why?" Evers asked. The driver replied that state law required "that the negroes sit in the back." The driver stopped at a nearby fire station and called the police when Evers refused to move. Officers soon arrived and ordered Evers to "get in the back of the bus, get off, or be arrested." Not wanting to go to jail, the postal clerk sheepishly left the bus.[78] But he did not remain docile for long. A longtime member of the NAACP, Evers contacted the local branch, which referred him to its president, civil rights attorney H. T. Lockard.

Quickly realizing that Evers's complaint held the potential to weaken segregation in the Bluff City, Lockard eagerly agreed to represent him and informed the national office, which dispatched famed attorneys Robert Carter and Thurgood Marshall to assist in the lawsuit.[79] As filed, the suit argued that Tennessee's segregated streetcar law was unconstitutional, and as a result African Americans had "suffered great injury, inconvenience and humiliation" when forced to ride in the back of the bus.[80] Four months after the suit was filed, on November 13, 1956, the U. S. Supreme Court upheld a lower court ruling that Alabama's law requiring segregated seating on public transportation was unconstitutional. The decision was the culmination of a year-long boycott, led by Dr. Martin Luther King, Jr., of the buses operated in Montgomery, Alabama. Lockard and Evers were understandably emboldened by the Supreme Court's action, and when a three-judge panel finally convened to hear the case in January 1958 they were confident that the Montgomery precedent would cover Memphis. This view seemed to be borne out when Judge John D. Martin, the presiding member of the tribunal, informed defense counsel that if it was found that the Montgomery decision applied to the Evers case then they would have to follow its tenets.[81]

Three hundred Memphians, most of them African Americans, sat nervously in the courtroom as the trial began. In his opening statement defense attorney Walter Chandler shocked the audience by declaring that the case was merely a crude attempt to increase NAACP membership. Chandler then went on to further chastise the NAACP by advising them to abandon the goal of equality and instead focus on improving the physical, mental, and moral conditions of African Americans.[82] The most important witness was Evers himself, and Lockard wasted little time in calling him to the stand. In his initial testimony Evers explained in detail what happened on April 26, 1956, while Lockard, through his line of questioning, emphasized that his client was removed solely because he was black. Cross-examining Evers, city attorney Frank Gianotti tried, and failed, to make the plaintiff admit that the NAACP instigated the bus ride and the subsequent lawsuit. For example, Ginanotti asked at one point, "And you deny, then, that you got on this bus on this particular day for laying the foundation for this suit?" Evers defiantly replied, "I do deny it." Despite his emphatic denials, cross-examination uncovered two points that, on the surface at least, cast doubt on Evers's testimony. First, he admitted that before April 26, 1956, he had never ridden a bus in Memphis and had not since the date in question and that he owned an automobile. If the Montgomery decision was to be the tribunal's guide, then none of this should have mattered, but it did.

Six months after the trial, the panel handed down its verdict. Strongly influenced by the defense, the judges declared that Evers had boarded the bus in 1956 "for the purpose of instituting this litigation." According to the judges this fact meant that the case was not "an actual controversy" and Evers was not deserving of redress because "his own testimony shows that he has not been injured at all."[83] "Lord, have mercy on American justice...," Evers exclaimed when he heard of the verdict.[84] The United States Supreme Court seemed to agree when, in a unanimous decision, they overturned the lower court decision and ordered a new trial.[85] The same tribunal heard the case a second time and in August 1960 they abstained from issuing an order but instead instructed the plaintiffs to bring suit in the courts of Tennessee since they were being asked to rule on the constitutionality of a state law.[86] A few weeks after the judgment of the court, the matter finally came to an end when the Memphis Street Railway formally ended segregated seating on local buses.[87] It had taken four years of litigation, but O. Z. Evers, H. T. Lockard, and the NAACP had secured the first true victory over segregation in the Bluff City. But the struggle was far from over.

On June 17, 1957, the cashier of the Tri-State Bank, Jesse H. Turner, walked into the main branch of the Memphis Public Library at Peabody and McLean and requested a library card. Normally this was a routine matter, but Turner's visit was far from ordinary because he was black. Caught off guard, library staff called the director, Jesse Cunningham, who curtly refused to issue Turner a card.[88] This was not the first time Turner had challenged America's racial status quo. Born in Longview, Mississippi, Turner graduated from LeMoyne College in 1941 with a degree in mathematics. Two months after his graduation Turner was inducted into the United States Army where he earned high scores on the military's aptitude tests. Despite this, Turner was assigned to Fort Knox, Kentucky, to train as a cook because the army only assigned African Americans to menial roles. Any college graduate would be offended by this decision and Turner especially so. Refusing to submit to the army's decision, Turner decided he would rather be placed in military prison than become a cook. Recalling his feelings decades later, Turner stated, "My ultimate decision was guardhouse or equal opportunity."[89]

The army removed Turner from Fort Knox and assigned him to a noncommissioned officers' school to become a first sergeant. Not long after becoming a sergeant, Turner was accepted into Officer Candidates School where he continued to agitate for equality. When he discovered that African Americans could not use a swimming pool on the army post, he protested to the base commander, who ordered the facility open to all officer candidates. Assigned to the 758th Light Tank Battalion after his commission as a second lieutenant, Turner eventually attained the rank of captain. Participating in the invasion of Italy, Captain Turner was awarded the Bronze Star for "bold combat leadership" in April 1945. After the war Turner earned a master's degree in business administration from the University of Chicago and became a certified public accountant when he returned to Memphis.[90] Disturbed that he could not use the main public library, Turner decided to challenge discrimination as he had in the army.

When director Cunningham refused him a library card, Turner contacted H. T. Lockard, who drafted an appeal to Wassell Randolph, the chairman of the library board, requesting permission for Turner to use the main library. Lockard pointed out to Randolph in his letter that Tennessee law did not prohibit African Americans from using public libraries, but did not expressly mention legal action if the board did not grant Turner access.[91] Three months passed before the library board met in special session to discuss Turner's appeal. Lockard had expressed to a newspaper reporter that he did not expect Turner's request to be rejected, but it must have come as no surprise when library officials did exactly that. The board reminded Lockard and Turner in their reply that all books in the library system were available to African Americans on request at the Vance Avenue Negro Branch. "Thus, the circulating library facilities are available equally to all citizens, but . . . to avoid regrettable incidents . . . the Directors have designated the Vance Avenue Library as the headquarters for the distribution of books to Negro citizens."[92] Of course, the board completely missed Turner's point. Access to books was not his primary motivation; it was equal treatment and the elimination of segregated public facilities.

The board's decision seemed to settle the matter until the following summer when a petition circulated among the white faculty of Southwestern at

Memphis College, Memphis State University, and the University of Tennessee Medical College, calling upon the board to allow all citizens equal access to public libraries. Southwestern professor Rowland M. Hill presented several petitions containing 180 signatures to the library board on June 20, 1958.[93] Library officials met in special session three days after the petition was received to discuss the situation. The pressure exerted by local college faculty apparently convinced the board to slightly modify its original position. They promised that when renovations to the downtown Cossitt Library, which housed an extensive research collection, were completed then African Americans would be allowed to use the facility.[94] The white petitioners also had an effect on Jesse Turner. It had been over a year since he had first requested equal use of library properties, but in all that time he had refrained from filing suit to adjudicate the matter. Apparently emboldened by the action of his white neighbors, Turner and Lockard sued the library board in federal court. In addition to arguing that no law prevented Turner, or any other black citizen, from using library facilities designated for whites only, the suit also directly challenged the board's assumption that racial incidents were bound to occur if all libraries were opened to African Americans. "Equal use of the library facilities in Memphis certainly would not result in creation of racial tensions or animosities," Lockard declared.[95] The suit dragged on for several years and, as we shall see, played an important role in the destruction of segregation in the Bluff City.

In 1958 Frank Clement was prevented by law from seeking a third term as governor of Tennessee. He hoped that his widespread popularity would secure the Democratic nomination, and the governorship, for his former campaign manager and protégé Buford Ellington. However, Estes Kefauver had other ideas. Still smarting from his vice presidential defeat in 1956, Tennessee's senior senator hoped to elect a friendly governor in order to secure his Tennessee base for a possible run for the presidency in 1960. The deeply conservative Ellington, as well as the archsegregationist Judge Andrew "Tip" Taylor, who was also seeking the nomination, would not do, so Kefauver turned to his old friend Edmund Orgill.[96] The Memphis mayor, besieged and isolated at home, decided Kefauver's idea had merit and announced his candidacy in the spring of 1958.[97] Another faction that was interested in the governor's race was the Citizens for Progress. Encouraged by their sweeping victory in the 1956 elections, the CFP leadership believed they could influence the state's choice for governor as the Crump organization had done in years past.[98]

Around the time Orgill announced his candidacy, Claude Armour visited Nashville to attend a meeting of the Tennessee Municipal League. While there, the commissioner was approached by representatives of the Ellington campaign with an enticing offer. In exchange for the endorsement of the Citizens for Progress, they promised Armour he would be Ellington's official liaison on matters related to Memphis and Shelby County.[99] Due in large part to Armour, the organization's executive committee voted to endorse Ellington in July.[100] Not every member agreed, however. Several believed that Taylor, whose segregationist rhetoric was more palatable than Ellington's, was the better choice. Despite this, a thin veneer of unity covered the Citizens for Progress throughout the campaign.[101]

Naturally African Americans were equally interested in the governor's race. Faith in the power of voter registration, though battered by recent defeats, remained steadfast in the black community. In keeping with this belief, volunteers from the Citizens Non-Partisan Registration Campaign fanned out across African American neighborhoods, knocking on doors and urging blacks to register. At the same time, the black-oriented radio station WDIA broadcast urgent appeals throughout the registration period. These tactics influenced many who took the time to become voters. One such person was Sam May, a sixty-three-year-old retired sawmill worker who "was home lying on my bed and heard them announce . . . that it was the last day to register so I got up, caught the bus, and came on down here and registered."[102] Despite the enthusiasm of May and the dedication of volunteers, the group only succeeded in registering 56,576 African Americans, which was a far cry from the white total of 146,038.[103]

Meanwhile, segregation, as might be expected, was the most important campaign issue to white Tennesseans, and the candidates were quick to defend it. Ten thousand white Memphians enthusiastically cheered when Taylor, speaking at the fairgrounds, declared, "I was the first candidate to say that he is opposed to mixing the races in our schools . . . I am the only candidate with a plan to prevent it."[104] Even Orgill, who enjoyed widespread black support, felt compelled to describe himself as a segregationist.[105] Even so, the *Tri-State Defender* endorsed his candidacy.[106] Not all African Americans paid attention to their weekly newspaper, however. Shortly before election day the Citizens for Progress organized a political gathering in the rural Shelby County hamlet of Millington. Included in the audience were 450 African Americans who listened intently to what was being said. Blair T. Hunt, principal of Booker T. Washington High School and former ally of E. H. Crump, bluntly told the audience to vote for the CFP candidates because "[w]e must work with those who have the jailhouse keys, sit on the judges' seats, and occupy positions at the police stations."[107] On the day of the election, the Citizens for Progress resorted to even more unsavory tactics.

The week before the election, the *Tri-State Defender* published a sample ballot to guide black voters in making their choices. The CFP, in order to exploit white fears of black political domination, reprinted the ballot and passed it out at polling places throughout the county. As they did so, they reminded white voters that "this is the way the Negroes are voting." At several polling places white CFP workers attempted to intimidate African American voters. In one case, Orgill worker Doris Johnson was told she was "nothing but a damn nigger" when she objected to a CFP supporter referring to her as a "girl."[108] Of course, this did little to intimidate determined black voters, but determination alone could not make Edmund Orgill the Democratic nominee. The Memphis mayor came in second, polling 40,809 votes, which was far more than was expected but not enough to win the nomination. Taylor received 43,996 votes, while only 18,570 ballots were cast for Ellington. Statewide, Ellington barely received a majority to become the nominee, but Memphis played no part in that victory.[109] Ultimately, the results of the 1958 Democratic primary humiliated the Citizens for Progress and ended their dreams of statewide power.

In many places across the South, African Americans were moving beyond political and legal strategies to confront segregation. Boycotts and other forms of protest were staged in Birmingham, Nashville, Miami, and Washington, D.C., as the 1950s drew to a close.[110] Some African American Memphians were increasingly dissatisfied with the lack of success political participation had brought. The *Tri-State Defender*, for example, lamented in an editorial that "[v]irtually no mention is made of getting Memphis Negroes more days to visit the zoo, or use the facilities at the fairgrounds. There is no appreciable comment about public school desegregation."[111] The situation remained the same until frustration over a municipal election channeled the issue of civil rights into a new direction, away from the strategy of using the ballot box and the courts to achieve equality and towards employing civil disobedience on the streets of Memphis.

5

"To Compel the White Race"

Russell Sugarmon had a plan. In early 1959 he became convinced that conditions were ripe for him to become the first African American in the twentieth century to achieve electoral office in Memphis. The Tennessee General Assembly had recently passed a law requiring political candidates in municipal elections to run for a specific school board or city commission post rather than the past practice of assigning seats to those who received the highest number of votes.[1] The law was specifically designed to limit the impact of African American voting on local elections. As previously mentioned, since 1951 black voters had been employing the technique of "single-shot" voting—that is, casting their ballots for a black candidate while ignoring all other races in the hope of electing African Americans to political office.

The strategy had not led to black officeholding, but in 1955 Roy Love had nearly been elected to the school board, and S. A. Wilbun almost won a seat in the state legislature in 1958. Memphis segregationists, alarmed that blacks might actually win an election, were determined to curb their political aspirations and their answer was the anti–single shot voting law. While those in the white power structure were smug in their belief that they had checkmated black voters, Sugarmon sensed an opportunity. He quickly realized that the new law did not hamper black electoral opportunities but rather strengthened them if the white vote was split between two or more candidates. On May 22, as Sugarmon was making his calculations, public works commissioner Henry Loeb announced his decision to run for mayor against Edmund Orgill, who had announced his reelection bid two days before.[2]

Just as Sugarmon had hoped, several whites immediately announced their candidacy for Loeb's commission seat, including city personnel director William W. Farris, John Ford Canale, county commission administrative assistant, and city engineer Will Fowler.[3] With so many white candidates in the race, Sugarmon believed that, given the anti–single shot voting law, he had a real chance of being elected public works commissioner himself. A graduate of Rutgers University and Harvard Law School, Sugarmon had practiced law in Memphis since 1956 and had managed S. A. Wilbun's unsuccessful race for the state legislature in 1958. Therefore he was quite aware of how difficult it was for a black candidate in a white-dominated political campaign, but nevertheless he announced his candidacy in early June.

Sugarmon's candidacy electrified the black community and spurred other African Americans to seek public office. Elihue Stanback, a leader in the Binghampton Civic League, announced his candidacy for tax assessor, while O. Z. Evers declared his intention to run for the city commission.[4] Around the same time, former army chaplain and pastor of Mount Olive Christian Methodist Episcopal Cathedral Henry Bunton and Roy Love of Mt. Nebo Baptist Church ran for seats on the school board. The two black religious leaders joined with Sugarmon to form a unified black political campaign, which they called the Volunteer Ticket. In order to round out the slate and gain the support of George W. Lee and the GOP, Sugarmon and his campaign manager, A. W. Willis, Jr., induced Republican Benjamin L. Hooks to join the ticket as candidate for juvenile court judge.[5] Archie Walter Willis, Jr., was born in Birmingham but relocated to Memphis where he graduated from Booker T. Washington High School. A graduate of the University of Wisconsin Law School, Willis opened the first integrated legal firm in Memphis with his friend Russell Sugarmon.[6]

Describing their campaign as a "Crusade for Freedom," the Volunteer Ticket organized a voter registration drive which resulted in 57,109 African Americans becoming voters.[7] Secretaries from Universal Life Insurance Company culled the African American names from the registration rolls to compile a master list of black voters, but the list was stolen from the ticket's Beale Street headquarters.[8] Despite this setback, 1,200 African Americans served as campaign workers for the Volunteer Ticket.[9] While workers distributed campaign literature, Sugarmon attended rallies, spoke at countless church and civic organizations, and appeared on WMCT's "meet your candidates" television program alongside his white opponents.[10] Meanwhile, the ticket's finance committee organized a mass rally at the Church of God in Christ's Mason Temple to raise needed campaign funds and encourage the electorate to vote. The committee invited Dr. Martin Luther King, Jr., the leader of the Montgomery bus boycott and head of the Southern Christian Leadership Conference, and famed gospel singer Mahalia Jackson, which no doubt guaranteed a large crowd.[11]

Arriving at the Memphis airport on a hot July afternoon, Dr. King was met by a large crowd of young people who chanted, "Two, four, six, eight, who do we appreciate? King! King! King!" as the hero of Montgomery exited the terminal.[12] The five thousand people who crammed into Mason Temple shared their enthusiasm. Among the speakers that night was George W. Lee, who promised to "fight till hell freezes over and then skate across the ice." As the crowd laughed and applauded, Dr. King came to the podium. "I am delighted beyond power of word to see such magnificent unity," the civil rights leader exclaimed to the audience. King then called upon the crowd to elect Bunton, Hooks, Love, and Sugarmon "because this election will give impetus for our whole civil rights struggle to every Negro in the United States." As the applause became deafening, King lifted his voice and reminded black voters to "start out early, walk to the polls. Walk together, children, for we just want to be free."[13] In addition to the mass rally, which raised thousands of dollars for the campaign, the finance committee also held a fund-raising dinner with keynote speaker Daisy Bates, the president of the Little Rock, Arkansas, NAACP, who had played a prominent role in the integration of that city's Central High School.[14]

As the Volunteer Ticket basked in the glow of Dr. King's visit, most white Memphians were paying little attention. Rather, they were watching closely the mayoral race between Loeb and Orgill. When he announced his candidacy Loeb declared that he was an ardent segregationist. "As far as social change goes, I am not for it . . . I would fight any integration order all the way. Separate but equal, but I mean equal in all fairness. I have tried to do that in my department."[15] That, of course, depended on your point of view. As public works commissioner, Loeb expanded the rate of street repairs throughout the city but refused to replace worn-out equipment, which worsened the working conditions of the department's African American labor force. Obsessed with balancing his department's budget, Loeb also kept wages low, which did nothing to improve his standing with black voters.[16]

The commissioner's pledge to defend segregation was met with approval from the majority of white voters and placed Mayor Orgill in an untenable position. It will be remembered that the mayor had received enthusiastic support from many black citizens in the previous city election. But that was before white resistance against integration began to harden in Memphis and throughout the South. Loeb's vow to defy the federal courts made matters worse for those white Memphians, including the mayor, who wanted to chart a more moderate course. Consequently, Orgill felt compelled to state that he was in favor of continuing segregated facilities because "Memphis has enjoyed the best race relations of any Southern city." However, he did take pains to say that he would not oppose a decision of the federal courts. Despite this qualification, Orgill was roundly criticized in the local African American press. The *Tri-State Defender* ridiculed the mayor's position, saying that "if the chief executive of our city honestly believes that the unlawful, unconstitutional, unChristian policy of denying rights to the 175,000 Negroes in Memphis builds 'the best race relations,' he should closet himself in his study and pore over some law volumes, the Constitution of the United States and the Holy Bible."[17]

Loeb, along with many other white Memphians, viewed the Volunteer Ticket, especially Sugarmon's candidacy, with a great deal of discomfort. He asked city attorney Frank Gianotti to investigate the possibility of Memphis enacting a runoff law which would require a candidate to receive a plurality of votes cast rather than a simple majority. In practical terms this would decrease Sugarmon's chances of winning the election, a fact Loeb well understood. "My interest in bringing this matter up is to try and see that an office holder in Memphis is elected by the Majority and not by any single-shooting. I am sick and tired of politicians the country over currying favor of minority groups," Loeb explained to reporters.[18] In order for Loeb's proposal to become law before the election, a special session of the state legislature would have to be called. Governor Ellington was approached by Loeb, but he refused to call a special session.[19]

Increasingly obsessed with Sugarmon's candidacy, Loeb anonymously floated the idea of holding a citywide poll to choose two candidates who would then remain on the ballot while the other candidates withdrew from the race.[20] Presumably this straw poll would include only white Memphians which, if held, would prevent Sugarmon from appearing on the ballot. The legality of Loeb's scheme was questioned by the city attorney and was quickly dropped,[21] but he continued to search for a way to derail Sugarmon's candidacy. Loeb even went so far as to reach out to his political nemesis Claude Armour.

The two rivals met with four of the five white candidates, John Ford Canale, William Farris, Will Fowler, and Sam Chambers (the fifth white candidate, Samuel A. Hawkins, was not invited presumably because he was an unknown) in hopes of convincing at least two of them to withdraw.[22] The reaction to Armour and Loeb's proposal ranged from lack of interest to outright hostility. "I'm not going to be pressured out by professional politicians . . . ," Chambers angrily replied.[23] When the meeting ended, none of the candidates agreed to withdraw, at least not right then. Weighing the situation, Fowler bowed out of the race, explaining to the press that he had "deep affection and respect for the good old Southern Negro and I do not wish to see the harmonious relation disturbed."[24]

Of course, as we have repeatedly seen, a "harmonious" relationship hardly existed between the races, but many white Memphians longed for it to be true. African Americans knew better. As fears grew in white neighborhoods that a black man might actually become an elected official, some turned to more unsavory tactics to prevent that from becoming a reality. Death threats and obscene phone calls were delivered to all of the African American candidates, while false alarms were reported to the police and fire departments at their homes. More ominously, someone fired a weapon at Hooks, Sugarmon, and Willis while they drove the streets of Memphis.[25] Nevertheless, the Volunteer Ticket refused to abandon their commitment to integrate local government. "Negroes represent a third of the city's population. They should be represented in the government," Hooks declared during a rally at Mt. Olive CME Cathedral.[26]

Meanwhile, Mayor Orgill was campaigning hard against Henry Loeb. On July 3 the mayor shook the hands of voters for three hours during a tour of the city. Toward the end of the tour Orgill's right arm lost all sensation, and he was unable to grip anything with his hand. A blocked carotid artery was discovered in the left side of the mayor's neck during a routine examination by Orgill's physician, Dr. Henry Gotten. Alarmed by the news, Orgill decided to withdraw from the mayoral race.[27] The mayor's supporters were shocked by his decision, especially after he successfully survived bypass surgery two days after his withdrawal.[28] Annexation of outlying communities, the abolition of city employees engaging in political work, investigating changing the Bluff City's governmental structure, and the consolidation of Memphis and Shelby County were included in Orgill's campaign platform, and when he resigned there was great consternation among his supporters that these goals would never be achieved.

Consequently the mayor's campaign organization formed the Dedicated Citizens Committee to further Orgill's proposed reforms and to bring together the various political factions.[29] Each candidate was asked several questions, including whether they were willing to appoint a committee to investigate amending the city charter. From those answers the committee then decided which candidates to endorse. Henry Loeb, as well as Claude Armour, John T. Dwyer, William W. Farris, and James W. Moore for the city commission received the nod from the Dedicated Citizens Committee. Styling their endorsements the Unity Ticket, the DCC tried in vain to convince the chosen candidates to campaign together, but most agreed with Loeb, who refused to associate himself with the group.[30] The Unity Ticket never lived up to its name, but it did offer a clear choice for those voters who yearned to maintain white supremacy.

With Orgill out of the race, several political unknowns entered the mayoral contest, the most notable being local furniture retailer and former champion wrestler Partee Fleming.[31] None, however, had much of a chance against the politically astute Loeb. In spite of this dearth of credible opposition, Loeb left little to chance. Crisscrossing the city, he appeared at various rallies and civic functions. On one typical day he shook hands with workers at several industrial plants in Northeast Memphis from noon to 5 PM, then attended a steak dinner sponsored by the Masonry Contractors Association. Afterwards he visited a rally sponsored by the Glenview Civic Club, attended a meeting of the American Legion, and finished up the day at a Coca-Cola party.[32] The other white candidate who campaigned as effectively as Loeb was William Farris, who was running against Sugarmon for public works commissioner. Farris organized a group of dedicated campaign workers, dubbed the "blitz committee," who concentrated their efforts on visiting upper-middle-class white neighborhoods to expand Farris's base of support.[33]

As Loeb's attempt at derailing Sugarmon's candidacy suggests, no leading white citizen endorsed the Volunteer Ticket, which disappointed and angered many black organizers. "It goes to show you that even though the white man is divided on many issues which affect our local scene, he is together on one issue—the Negro[,]" explained George W. Lee, who had expected organized labor and the Dedicated Citizens Committee to support at least some African American candidates.[34] Much of this anger was directed at Loeb. The *Tri-State Defender* pleaded with African Americans to "flock to the polls to vote AGAINST Loeb" by casting ballots for Partee Fleming, while Volunteer Ticket workers handed out sample ballots to voters in the predominantly black sections of the city.[35]

A total of 130,276 voters, reportedly the highest turnout in Memphis history, did flock to the polls on the day of the election, but it did not turn out the way the *Tri-State Defender*, or the Volunteer Ticket, hoped. The candidate who received the highest number of ballots was Henry Loeb, who garnered 85,282 votes, while Partee Fleming secured a mere 32,170. In the public works race 35,268 ballots were cast for Sugarmon, but he placed second to William Farris, who received 58,964.[36] The other Volunteer Ticket candidates fared no better. Neither Bunton, Hooks, nor Love were able to overcome their white opponents.[37] Disappointment certainly spread within the black community as the totals were announced, but, more important, Memphis was now a part of the region-wide struggle to end segregation as Dr. King's visit suggested. The Volunteer Ticket was similar in scope to the Southern Christian Leadership Conference's "Crusade for Citizenship," which was launched in 1957 by King and his lieutenants to sponsor voter registration drives "to arouse the masses of Negroes to realize that, in a democracy, their chances for improvement rest on their ability to vote."[38] Memphis was thus integrated into the larger, national movement that was battling on many fronts to crush segregation and secure full citizenship for black Americans. As Nat D. Williams wrote in a postelection article for the *Tri-State Defender*, "[T]he Memphis Negro's election effort gained him a respectable place among the Negro freedom fighters over the nation. At last Memphis was in the 'cause' . . . and the headlines."[39]

Despite their defeat, Sugarmon was determined to expand black political power in Memphis. In late 1959 he joined with A. W. Willis, A. Maceo Walker, H. A. Gilliam, and Jesse Turner to turn the formerly ad hoc Shelby County Democratic Club into a structured organization. An executive committee was created to oversee the operation of the club and establish precinct-level organizations in African American neighborhoods. A central committee was also formed to screen candidates and recommend who would receive the organization's endorsement. The precinct groups enlisted memberships and elected members to the organization's executive and central committees. A file was maintained of each member from which campaign volunteers were drawn and voters mobilized during the election season.[40]

Walker was chosen chairman of the executive committee, while Sugarmon was named executive secretary. Under Sugarmon and Walker's skilled leadership the organization grew quickly. Within a year of its creation the club included sixty-five precinct groups comprising hundreds of members.[41] In addition, the organization was successful in electing Jesse Turner to the Shelby County Democratic Party's executive committee, the first African American to achieve this distinction.[42] In practical terms Turner's election did little to change the segregationist tenor of the local Democratic Party, but it did insure that the votes of black Memphians would not be completely taken for granted in the 1960 presidential race.

As discussed previously, President Eisenhower won a majority of Shelby County votes in the 1956 election, the first Republican to ever do so. Largely because of the GOP's stunning success in Memphis, the state of Tennessee emerged as a key battleground state in the 1960 presidential race. Vice President Richard Nixon was recognized as the Republican Party's presumptive nominee, but for the Democrats the situation was not so clear-cut. Massachusetts senator John F. Kennedy had emerged as the frontrunner by winning several state primaries, but as the convention opened on July 10 in Los

Angeles he was still 409 votes shy of those needed to secure the nomination.[43] Kennedy's most serious challenger was Senate majority leader Lyndon B. Johnson of Texas, who was perceived to be more conservative than the Massachusetts senator on the issue of civil rights and thus was the favored candidate of southern delegates. This was particularly true of the Tennessee delegation, which was headed by Johnson's close friend, Governor Ellington.

Caucusing at the Green Hotel in Pasadena, Clifford Davis placed Senator Johnson's name before the delegates, who enthusiastically endorsed the majority leader. A handful of the delegates, most notably former governor Clement and Mayor Loeb, were leaning toward Kennedy, but they did not oppose the endorsement of Johnson.[44] The enthusiasm of Tennessee for Johnson could not, however, prevent Kennedy from picking up delegate votes from such key states as Pennsylvania and New York.[45] By the second day of the convention Kennedy seemed unstoppable, but Ellington and the other Tennesseans still hoped that Johnson could somehow stop his momentum. As the Massachusetts senator's candidacy gained ground, southern delegates kept a watchful eye on the drafting of the party's platform.

A twenty-man subcommittee was given the task of writing a platform which was introduced during a contentious meeting on July 11. A strongly worded, pro–civil rights document, the proposed platform went farther than any previous convention's declaration. The plank called not only for the elimination of segregation in public schools and housing, but also for the elimination of poll tax and literacy test requirements for voting. Former president Truman's proposal for a Fair Employment Practices Commission was also added to the platform.[46] The delegations from Alabama, Arkansas, Florida, Georgia, Louisiana, North Carolina, South Carolina, and Virginia filed a protest which vowed to "resist the kind of change that will turn us more and more into a super-state." Conspicuously absent from the minority report were the delegations from Tennessee and Texas, who did not want a platform fight to further diminish Johnson's chances for the nomination.[47]

Conservative southerners tried in vain to launch a stop-Kennedy movement, while Johnson attacked the Massachusetts senator for being a wealthy dilettante who owed his position to the support he received from corrupt political machines.[48] But it was all in vain. When the roll call of states began, Kennedy quickly received more than enough votes to secure the nomination. Florida governor LeRoy Collins, who was serving as chairman of the convention, made a motion for all delegations to approve Kennedy's nomination by acclamation. Southerners rushed to their microphones to denounce Collins's proposal. A delegate from South Carolina roared that the Palmetto State voted "unanimously not to be unanimous," but Collins refused to recognize any other delegations. "I didn't have a chance," Governor Ellington lamented as Kennedy's nomination was confirmed.[49]

A few hours after his nomination, Kennedy met with several key Democrats in his suite at the Biltmore Hotel. Closeted with the nominee was Chicago mayor Richard J. Daley, Carmine DeSapio, the head of the Tammany Hall political organization, Ohio governor Michael V. DiSalle, and Pennsylvania governor David L. Lawrence. The southerners' angry outburst unnerved the assembled group, who discussed ways to hold Dixie in line. Daley and the others suggested to Kennedy that the only way to prevent a southern walkout was to offer Johnson the vice presidential slot. Bowing to their judgment, Kennedy placed a phone call to the majority leader on the morning of July 14 asking for a meeting later in the day. Kennedy did not reveal the reason for the conference, but Johnson was too canny a politician not to understand what was happening. He sought the opinion of several southern leaders, including Georgia senator Richard B. Russell, Speaker of the House Sam Rayburn and Tennesseans Davis and Ellington, and then decided to accept the nomination if offered it by Kennedy. Kennedy arrived at Johnson's hotel room later that morning and offered him the second spot, which he quickly accepted. Johnson's nomination dismayed many liberals, but it mollified southern delegates, who abandoned any notion of splitting the party.[50]

As Democrats adjusted themselves to the Kennedy-Johnson ticket, Republicans traveled to Chicago for their convention. Included among the Tennessee delegates was George W. Lee, whose importance to the party's victory in 1956 had not been forgotten.[51] Most Republican delegates enthusiastically supported the nomination of Richard Nixon, but GOP conservatives, led by Arizona senator Barry Goldwater, briefly attempted to wrest the nomination from the vice president. However, as with their Democratic counterparts, the real struggle of the convention was over civil rights. Nixon wanted a strongly worded platform to strengthen the black-and-tan coalition, and he warned southern delegates that a fight would be waged on the convention floor if they pushed for a vaguely worded plank.

Nixon's defense of civil rights led some southern delegates to flirt with the conservative, lily-white wing. For example, the Louisiana delegation threatened to switch to Goldwater if Nixon's plank was adopted, but it quickly became an empty gesture when the Arizona senator withdrew his name from consideration.[52] Concerned that the conservatives could tear the party apart, Nixon visited with many of them and successfully convinced them of the need for unity. In the end his civil rights plank was adopted, and Nixon and his chosen running mate, United Nations ambassador Henry Cabot Lodge, were easily nominated.[53]

Because a majority of Tennesseans had voted the Republican ticket in 1956, Tennessee was perceived by both campaigns as an important battleground state. Consequently both candidates decided to campaign vigorously in the Bluff City. The Nixon campaign appointed the white chairman of the Shelby County Republican Party, Millsaps Fitzhugh, to serve as head of the overall local campaign, while George W. Lee again used his considerable organizational skills in marshalling black votes for the Republican ticket.[54] Meanwhile Senator Kennedy's younger brother Robert contacted Henry Loeb and asked him to coordinate campaign efforts in Memphis.[55] With organizations in place, each nominee laid plans to visit Memphis.

The first to visit was Senator Kennedy, who arrived in the Bluff City on a sunny afternoon in September after first speaking in Knoxville and Nashville earlier in the day. Joined by Governor Ellington, Senator Gore, and Mayor Loeb, Kennedy was greeted by forty thousand Memphians who lined the streets as his motorcade traveled from the municipal airport to downtown Memphis. Ten thousand citizens jammed the area between Riverside Drive and Court Avenue to hear the Democratic nominee.[56] Speaking cautiously, Kennedy criticized the Eisenhower administration for attempting to gut TVA with the aborted Dixon-Yates power plant but refused to address the South's most pressing problem, civil rights. "I want to see an America which is free for everyone which develops the constitutional rights of all Americans," the nominee lamely explained.[57] Kennedy's speech may not have been a memorable one, but he was the first Democratic presidential candidate to visit Memphis in the twentieth century. (In 1860 Stephen Douglas had campaigned in the Bluff City, and the Populist candidate William Jennings Bryan had spoken in Memphis in 1896.[58])

The weather was not as hospitable when Vice President Nixon and his wife, Pat, arrived in Memphis on September 27. A drizzling rain began to fall before Nixon's arrival, and it continued throughout most of his visit. Despite the rain, sixty thousand Memphians, twenty thousand more than cheered Kennedy, lined the route between the airport and downtown. Unlike the Democratic nominee, Nixon stopped his motorcade several times to shake hands and speak to citizens. At the corner of Lamar and Parkway he shook hands with two hospital patients and was mobbed by a large crowd of well-wishers. Later he stopped near Union and Cleveland to confer with an elderly African American woman, and on Beale Street Nixon and his wife visited W. C. Handy Park, where they placed a bouquet of flowers at the base of the blues composer's statue and shook hands with a large crowd of African Americans.[59]

As the vice president arrived downtown to give his address, a chill wind arose and heavy rain began to fall. Twenty-five thousand people shivered as Nixon praised Memphis as "the only city in America with more churches than service stations." Like his opponent the vice president avoided mentioning civil rights except to declare that "I support my program." After his speech Nixon shook hands with many in the crowd and had his photograph taken with Benjamin Hooks and George W. Lee. As they left, Mrs. Nixon said, "We enjoyed our visit very much, especially your southern hospitality."[60] Between the two candidates Nixon probably made the better impression on local voters. In contrast to Kennedy, who completely ignored the black community, Nixon, through handshaking and visiting the memorial to the father of the blues, at least made a personal effort to reach African Americans.

Lyndon Johnson visited Memphis two days later. Arriving at the airport, Johnson was met by Clifford Davis, Governor Ellington, Mayor Loeb, and a thousand supporters who listened to the Texan compare Kennedy to Franklin Roosevelt. As with the previous visitors, there was no mention of civil rights in Johnson's remarks.[61] However, when LBJ attempted to spend the night in a local hotel he experienced the humiliation of segregation firsthand. Traveling with the vice presidential nominee was an African American physician from Texas who attempted to register for a room at the Claridge Hotel along with the rest of the party. To Johnson's dismay the manager refused to allow the African American to stay at the hotel. Turning on his considerable charm, Johnson tried to convince the manager to change his mind, but he refused to budge. Consequently the black physician was forced to sleep in the black-owned Lorraine Motel.[62]

As the campaign neared its end, the Democrats hoped to peel off enough black votes from Nixon to secure the White House. In an editorial published in the *Tri-State Defender*, Jesse Turner argued that the Republicans had done little for black Memphians. They "named a segregated U.S. post office for a worthy Negro; and the Vice President stopped by and laid a wreath on the W.C. Handy monument. For these meager handouts, they have the nerve to ask us to give them our votes."[63] Advertising heavily in the *Tri-State Defender*, the Kennedy campaign received that paper's endorsement.[64] The Democrats also sent to Memphis several prominent African Americans, including the wife of baseball great Willie Mays, the daughter of singer Lena Horne, and boxing champion Henry Armstrong, to campaign on behalf of Kennedy.[65] This last-minute campaigning did bring some African Americans back to the Democratic fold, but it could not overcome the defection of white southerners to the GOP.

Nixon won Shelby County, but only by 916 votes; 87,181 ballots were cast for the vice president, while Kennedy received 86,265 votes. Although Kennedy failed to carry Shelby County, he did capture many African American votes. For example, in the predominately black precinct 11-2 Kennedy received 543 votes to Nixon's 201. The result was just the opposite in white neighborhoods. In ward 56, located in East Memphis, 1,390 ballots were cast for Nixon, while Kennedy received only 628 votes. Nationally, however, Kennedy barely won a plurality to become the thirty-fifth president of the United States. Memphis may not have played a decisive role in who became president, but the local election results hinted that a major political realignment was taking place in the American South.

It will be remembered that in August 1959 Henry Loeb was elected mayor of Memphis on a segregationist platform. As he prepared for his inauguration, the mayor-elect learned that the public library board was having second thoughts about their refusal to allow African Americans use of all library facilities. Therefore the board decided to open the reference department at the Cossitt branch to black Memphians. This decision was made not to bring about integration of library facilities but rather to strengthen the notion of separate but equal, because, unlike circulating books that could be requested at the black Vance branch, reference books could not be transferred and checked out. In addition, the restrooms remained segregated, with black customers having to use the janitors' bathroom located in the basement of the library. Loeb opposed even this tepid decision but agreed not to challenge the board's authority.[66] Meanwhile, the courts had yet to hear arguments on Jesse Turner's 1958 lawsuit. This delay, along with the defeat of the Volunteer Ticket, concerned many younger African Americans who began to lose faith in their elders' strategy of relying on politics and the courts to dismantle segregation. As some Memphis blacks groped for a more effective way to challenge discrimination, a handful of college students in North Carolina implemented a radical strategy that would bring Jim Crow to its knees.

On February 1, 1960, four North Carolina Agricultural and Technical College freshmen entered the Woolworth's department store in downtown

Greensboro and sat down at the whites-only lunch counter. Word of this brave act quickly spread, and it had a powerful impact on black students across the South.[67] Inspired by the Greensboro students, they organized sit-ins in many towns and cities throughout the region, including Memphis. On the afternoon of Friday, March 18, seven students from Owen Junior College entered the McLellan's Variety Store on Main Street, walked past the blacks-only lunch counter, and sat down at the white lunch counter located in the back of the store. The group ordered coffee, but the manager, J. D. Fields, refused to serve them and the store was closed.[68] Police were not called to the scene, but Commissioner Armour was quick to condemn the protest. "This department will not tolerate this type of unlawful demonstration. Our men have been instructed to be firm but fair and to enforce the law."[69] The warning, however, was not heeded.

The following day a group of LeMoyne College students, frustrated by the lack of progress in desegregating the libraries, laid plans to hold simultaneous demonstrations at the Cossitt and main branches.[70] Coordinated by NAACP youth council president David L. Moore, forty LeMoyne and Owen students divided into two groups and entered both libraries around 12:15 PM. Mrs. Jan Karpinski, assistant circulation librarian, was working the registration desk at the main library when the students arrived. According to Karpinski, the students walked through the children's department and "distributed themselves throughout the library, bunched up in the card catalog area, making it impossible for other library users to get into the card index area, and occupied a good many of the seats."[71] Police were called to both locations, and the demonstrators were arrested when they refused to leave. Gwendolyn Yvonne Townsend, a twenty-year-old LeMoyne sophomore, defiantly explained after her arrest that "I felt that since I was a citizen, I had the right to attend the library."[72] Loaded into a patrol wagon, the protesters were subjected to curses and threats by the officers but otherwise were unharmed.[73]

Taken to police headquarters, the demonstrators were charged with disorderly conduct, loitering, and threatened breach of peace, which, of the three, was the most serious. One of the protesters placed a phone call to Russell Sugarmon, who, in addition to his political work, was then serving as a member of the NAACP's Legal Redress Committee. Sugarmon and A. W. Willis eagerly agreed to defend the protests, and they were joined by Benjamin Hooks and the other seven African American lawyers in Memphis. As the protesters were being arraigned before Judge Beverly Boushe, the local NAACP held a mass meeting at Mt. Olive Cathedral to express support for the students. "We will go to jail and we are willing to suffer," one attendant declared. Around midnight at least a hundred supporters arrived at the criminal courts building, where they cheered and sang while eight police officers armed with nightsticks kept a watchful eye. The police did not interfere as the crowd burst into "Onward, Christian Soldiers" each time a defendant was released, but when the final protester left the courtroom at 1:30 AM Sunday morning, they ordered everyone to go home. "Okay, let's get off the streets before we lock you up for loitering," one officer exclaimed.[74]

During church services later that morning several African American ministers urged their congregations to stand with the students. Reverend W. Herbert Brewster, the pastor of Trigg Avenue Baptist Church and a noted gospel songwriter, explained to his parishioners that the young people "were merely applying Gandhi and Nehru's tactic of passive resistance to compel the white race to live up to its own political and religious philosophy."[75] Several hundred black Memphians heeded their pastor's appeal, arriving at the criminal courts building early Monday morning, but the police did not allow them to enter the courtroom. Standing on the sidewalk, they sang "The Star Spangled Banner" while a small group of young white men glared at them from a nearby parking lot. Fearful that violence might erupt outside the courthouse, Dr. Vasco A. Smith, Jr., and other NAACP leaders organized a mass meeting at Mt. Olive Cathedral which drew at least two thousand people and raised three thousand dollars. To many African Americans the sit-ins and the subsequent rallies were the beginning of a broad, grassroots movement that signaled the end of the segregated social order. The unity and determination exhibited during the Mt. Olive meeting overwhelmed many in the crowd who began crying. Surveying the crowd, Dr. Smith declared, "People are shedding tears, tears of joy . . . The day we have been waiting on for years has finally come. Thru all the persecution, we have said that a better day is coming. Things are going to be changed here in Memphis."[76]

Back at the courthouse, Benjamin L. Hooks argued that "the defendants were arrested because they are Negroes." "They were arrested because they violated a city ordinance," countered city prosecutor Arthur N. Shea. This verbal sparring continued for five hours before Judge Boushe reached his verdict. "There is no doubt in my mind that this was a concerted effort to use this court as a platform for your propaganda. This demonstration was an open invitation to violence and mob rule," the judge explained as he found all defendants guilty of disorderly conduct and levied a twenty-six-dollar fine.[77] Despite Boushe's harsh assessment of the demonstration, he did drop the loitering and threatened breach of peace charges. The white establishment hoped that the combination of Armour's threat, along with Boushe's admonishment and leniency, would deter further demonstrations.

It didn't. The day after the trial, demonstrators again targeted the Cossitt library, while others protested at the city-owned Brooks Memorial Art Gallery.[78] In order to maintain discipline and insure that the protest remained nonviolent, group captains were assigned to each demonstration.[79] When this disciplined cadre began to systematically target downtown lunch counters, city officials became more desperate to curb the demonstrations. Several protesters were charged with conspiring to interfere with trade and threatened with being charged with incitement to riot. Citing the city charter, which granted police the power to detain individuals when the municipality was in a "state of Tenseness," Boushe ordered the students held without bond.[80] Elements within the white community also took action to stop the protests. In several cases, white youths spit on the demonstrators while others poured hot coffee and itching powder on the students.[81] When two students entered the Woolworth's at 59 North Main Street, four young white men physically threw the protesters out of the store.[82] Several other demonstrators were also manhandled by a group of sailors and marines during a sit-in at the downtown Walgreen's.[83]

Seven months after the sit-ins had begun, in October 1960, local African Americans won their first major battle against Jim Crow when the commission desegregated all public libraries.[84] The victory was temporarily short-lived, however, when the library board refused to allow black patrons to use the restrooms at the main library. In July 1961 a federal judge ordered the library to open its restrooms to African Americans, which Loeb and the library board reluctantly agreed to do.[85] Meanwhile the sit-ins continued until November of 1961 when the majority of downtown restaurants and lunch counters agreed to integrate and hire some African American personnel.[86] From March 1960 to November 1961, 318 demonstrators were arrested, resulting in 163 convictions. The bravery exhibited by the students had severely crippled segregation, but the struggle continued.

As discussed previously, in 1957 the Tennessee General Assembly passed the pupil assignment law, which was designed to circumvent the Supreme Court's *Brown* decisions by allowing local school officials to assign and transfer students within their districts. The measure did create the possibility of a black student being transferred to a white school, but it was unlikely this would ever happen. When African American secretary Marjorie McFerren applied to have her son Gerald Young attend the all-white Vollentine

Elementary School in September 1958, the board denied her request even though it was much closer to their home than Hyde Park School, which Young had been attending.[87] In December 1959 the NAACP formally requested that the Memphis city schools implement a desegregation plan, but their entreaty was ignored.[88]

Because Memphis had stubbornly used the Pupil Assignment Law to prevent integration, the national office of the NAACP encouraged its local chapter to challenge the school board's policy in court. Claiming that Memphis was operating a "compulsory bi-racial school system" in violation of the Supreme Court's desegregation decisions, Sugarmon, Willis, and Hooks, along with national civil rights attorneys Thurgood Marshall and Constance Baker Motley, filed suit in federal court.[89] The school board countered that African Americans, including Mrs. McFerren, had never appealed school assignments despite having the right to do so.[90] Several months later, during a pretrial deposition, school board president Walter P. Armstrong, Jr., informed the court that Memphis city schools were no longer designating schools by race. Instead they would assign each student to the school they had attended the previous year, which in practical terms meant continuing a segregated system.[91]

The board's decision strongly influenced Judge Marion Boyd, who presided over the hearing convened to argue the matter. After three days of testimony, Boyd ruled in favor of the school board, stating that the Pupil Assignment Law was an adequate desegregation plan despite the fact that not a single black child had been admitted to an all-white school. "The court hopes very much . . . that we can go forward with the education of our children without discrimination." [92] Vague though it was, Boyd's ruling did at least suggest that some form of integration should take place in the near future. When registration for classes began in late August 1961, the parents of fifty-three African American students applied to attend all-white schools. The board, wanting to validate the appeals process, rejected all of the black students.[93] When forty-two students appealed the decision, the board turned the appeals over to a three-member panel of "hearing officers" to carefully review the applicants as prescribed by state law.

The students were interviewed by hearing officers Paul M. Bryan, Hunter Lane, Jr., and John Richardson and visited by social workers in order to be chosen for reassignment. After this careful scrutiny the hearing officers recommended to the board that thirteen African American students be transferred to the all-white schools of Bruce, Gordon, Rozelle, and Springdale. The board concurred and quickly informed Loeb and the city commission of the decision. Not wanting to give die-hard white supremacists time to organize and create havoc, board of education president William D. Galbreath delayed announcing the "good faith" integration plan until the night before the scheduled transfers. Ever the segregationists, Mayor Loeb and the commission took another swipe at the *Brown* decisions when they expressed support of the board's action: "Many people feel that the decision of the Supreme Court . . . was ill timed and ill advised. At the same time, all of the people of this city recognize that they must obey the law. Law abiding citizens do not resort to violence because they disapprove of a law."[94]

Claude Armour was more direct. All those, "regardless of race, creed, color, that crossed the police lines with anything in mind other than going to school were going to be arrested," the commissioner explained.[95] This was no mere rhetoric on Armour's part. As we have seen, the police commissioner was deeply committed to maintaining the segregated social order in Memphis, but he was equally committed to keeping the peace. As one Memphian remembered, Armour "said he was going to maintain law and order and he didn't care whose ass, black or white, he had to run out of town in order to do it."[96] Two hundred officers were hand-picked by the commissioner to carry out the operation. In each of the four schools, detectives with radios walked the hallways and reported conditions to a squad car patrolling the streets outside. Uniformed officers also ringed the schools, while others patrolled the routes the students would take to get to school. The news media was kept a block away from each school, and any spectators who arrived were escorted from the area.[97]

The night before the scheduled arrival, the parents of the thirteen students met with NAACP officials, who arranged transportation and escorts for the children.[98] Maxine Smith, the newly chosen executive secretary, escorted Deborah Ann Holt and Jacqueline Moore to Springdale, while A. W. Willis's wife, Annie, arrived at Bruce Elementary with her son Michael, Dwania Kyles, and Harry Williams. At the same time Joyce Ann Bell, E. C. Freeman, Leandrew Wiggins, and Clarence Williams arrived at Rozelle with Jesse Turner, and Russell Sugarmon transported Alvin Freeman, Pamela Mayes, and Shelia and Sharon Malone to Gordon Elementary.[99] Everything worked according to plan, with no incidents to mar the students' first day. The students were, for the most part, made welcome by their classmates, and most white parents accepted the integration without protest. Of the 1,580 white children enrolled in the four schools, only 95 were absent on that first day.[100] The peaceful conditions at the schools persisted and the police were eventually withdrawn.

Memphis was no less a raucous place than any other city in the South, but several factors made violence unlikely. First, city officials were quite aware of the damage that had been done to the economy of Little Rock in the wake of its disastrous handling of the integration of Central High School in 1957, and they were determined to avoid the mistakes made in Arkansas's capital. Second, the school board worked closely with both the police department and NAACP in developing a plan to ensure a smooth transition for the African American children. Perhaps the most significant ingredient was Claude Armour himself. Having risen from the ranks to head the police department, the commissioner was respected, and feared, by the majority of officers, and they obeyed when he ordered them to maintain the peace.

By all accounts the integration of Memphis's schools was a success, but it did not magically erase the stifling effects of segregation nor ease racial strife. For the brave six-year-olds, the transition was a difficult one. Dwania Kyles, the daughter of Samuel "Billy" Kyles, then an emerging leader in the civil rights movement, was informed by a white classmate that "black people were supposed to have tails" and asked to see hers. A. W. Willis's son Michael had an even more difficult time. Frequently harassed for being a "rich nigger" because he was driven to school in a Cadillac, he never fully adjusted to his circumstances. Looking back, Willis described first grade as being "a very difficult year. I feel like I was always on the defensive . . . I was just not on a solid foundation. It made me more reserved as a person, more defensive, and never sure if I was doing the right thing."[101]

By 1963 de jure segregation was fading from daily life in Memphis as it was in many places across the region. In addition to the public libraries, downtown restaurants, and schools, movie theaters were also integrated. The head of the Malco theater chain, Richard Lightman, worked closely with Vasco Smith, the NAACP, and the Congress of Racial Equality to implement a desegregation plan which integrated its movie houses in 1962.[102] As in Memphis, businesses throughout the South were negotiating with local civil rights organizations to desegregate peacefully to avoid further economic disruption. The zoo, Brooks Memorial Art Gallery, and three golf courses had been integrated, but the entire public parks system remained strictly segregated.[103] In response to an NAACP lawsuit, the Memphis Park Commission adopted a gradual desegregation plan that was scheduled to take ten years before full integration was achieved. The park commission argued that their plan met the Supreme Court's standard for achieving integration "with all deliberate speed." Judge Boyd and the U. S. Court of Appeals for the Sixth Circuit ruled in favor of the gradual plan, but Willis, Sugarmon, and the rest of the NAACP legal team appealed to the Supreme Court, hoping for a more favorable outcome.[104]

In a unanimous decision written by Justice Arthur Goldberg, the court ruled against the park commission's gradual plan in *Watson v. City of Memphis*. Chastising the city, Goldberg found that denying African Americans the use of local parks was "patently unconstitutional racial discrimination..." Not stopping there, the court also declared that "*Brown* never contemplated that the concept of 'deliberate speed' would countenance indefinite delay in elimination of racial barriers in schools, let alone other public facilities not involving the same physical problems or comparable conditions."[105] With the Supreme Court's decision, formal, legalized segregation came to an end in the Bluff City. Pockets of resistance remained, but the fate of Jim Crow had been settled in the streets, ballot boxes, and courtrooms of Memphis.

No white person was more frustrated by this than Mayor Loeb. The Memphis executive had effectively used segregation to win the 1959 mayoral race and hoped it would carry him even farther. In early 1962 Loeb explored the possibility of running for governor of Tennessee. Voter signatures were collected throughout the state in order for him to qualify as a candidate.[106] Wishing to make headlines across the state, the Memphis mayor attacked Governor Ellington for collecting campaign funds from state employees in what he described as a "political shakedown."[107] His campaign quickly fell apart, however, when he realized he would have to resign the mayoralty to run for governor. This would have resulted in Claude Armour becoming mayor, a fact he could not abide.[108] Consequently, Loeb requested that the chairman of the state Democratic executive committee remove his name from consideration in the upcoming primary.[109]

Loeb was equally frustrated by his relationship with the Kennedy administration. Earlier it was mentioned that Loeb had campaigned vigorously for his fellow PT boat commander in the 1960 presidential contest. Despite his important contributions the mayor was not invited to attend the inaugural festivities in January 1961 and he was furious.[110] After a discreet investigation, it was discovered that the state Democratic executive committee had failed to submit his name to the Kennedy inauguration committee.[111] The president's brother Robert Kennedy apologized profusely for the error, but the damage was done.[112] When the Justice Department began to hold Memphis up as a racially progressive city whose desegregation efforts should be emulated by other southern localities, the relationship deteriorated further. In a letter to the mayor, Attorney General Robert F. Kennedy wrote that he had "talked to the president about our conversation on the telephone and about the fine record your city made during the very difficult start of integration in your schools."[113]

Loeb didn't want to make a "fine record." In his reply, he reminded the attorney general that it "was my thinking that we could better handle our own problems. Even though the duty was extremely distasteful, I intend to continue to do my duty."[114] The mayor was even more adamant when Assistant Attorney General Burke Marshall sent a telegram of congratulations regarding the city's handling of the desegregation of downtown restaurants and lunch counters. "My advice has been and is 'keep your nose out of our affairs,'" Loeb wrote at the bottom of a typewritten copy of Marshall's telegram.[115] From Loeb's perspective, Memphis blacks, with the encouragement of the Kennedy administration, had robbed him of his greatest political issue.

Like many whites, the mayor of Memphis never forgave either the Democratic Party or African Americans for the revolutionary changes in the southern social order. The hostility that many white southerners harbored led many of them to make common cause with western Republicans to create a grassroots conservative movement. At the same time, blacks in Memphis, and across the South, swelled the ranks of the Democratic Party in hopes of capitalizing on the advances gained with the collapse of segregation.

6

"Please Don't Do That"

A. Maceo Walker was very pleased. In March 1961 he became the first African American in the twentieth century to serve on a permanent city board when he was appointed to the Traffic Advisory Commission. Walker was nominated by Commissioner William Farris, and his appointment was widely applauded by both the black and white communities.[1] The son of Dr. J. E. Walker, Antonio Maceo was born in Indianola, Mississippi, in 1909. Maceo and his family moved to Memphis in 1920 in order to expand the family's life insurance business and to avoid white harassment. We "were a sore spot in the eyes of the whites of that community. They began to pick on us, and there was nothing to do except move," Walker remembered.[2] In 1923 J. E. Walker and his son founded Universal Life Insurance Company, which quickly grew into the largest black-owned business in the Midsouth. Walker earned a baccalaureate degree from Fisk University in Nashville and then went on to receive a master's degree in business administration from New York University. By 1961 Walker was serving as president of both Universal Life and the Tri-State Bank, making him the leading African American businessman in Memphis.[3] Walker's appointment was accepted without comment from white supremacists, which was in stark contrast to the proposed appointment of his father to the John Gaston Hospital board in 1956. A few months later, however, a second black appointment resulted in a far different reaction.

In July former mayor Orgill resigned his seat on the Memphis Transit Authority board, which oversaw the city's public transportation system, in order to accept a similar position on the light, gas and water division's governing body. Several prominent African Americans, including Walker, Sugarmon, and Jesse Turner sent letters to the city commission requesting that they nominate A. W. Willis to the MTA board. Armour replied that he would vote for Willis, which no doubt strongly influenced the other commissioners.[4] Consequently at the next commission meeting William Farris nominated Willis, while Armour, John Dwyer, and James Moore approved the motion. However, to their surprise, Loeb voted against it.[5] Undoubtedly the reason for his nay vote was to bolster his credibility as a segregationist.

It worked. Within a few hours of the vote irate white citizens began phoning and writing the mayor's office complimenting Loeb on his vote and expressing dismay over Willis's appointment. "We certainly don't need an NAACP lawyer on any city board," one caller exclaimed.[6] For Richard T. Ely, president of the white Memphis and Shelby County Council of Civic Clubs, Willis's selection was an example of unscrupulous politicians "selling out their elective offices to minority groups . . . for a political advantage."[7]

Encouraged by this support, Loeb vowed to veto the appointment at the next commission meeting. The city charter did contain a vague provision requiring "the approval of the mayor before it shall take effect," but it had almost never been used by previous mayors.[8] Despite his bluster, Loeb at the same time hinted at a compromise. He was willing, he said, to appoint a "moderate" African American to the MTA board, but not an "extremist" like Willis. At first, the four commissioners stood by their decision, but as they got closer to the next meeting, they began to waver. Meanwhile, African American leaders issued statements of support for Willis in hopes of blocking Loeb's threatened veto. Leaders of several black organizations, including Walker, Russell Sugarmon, Jesse Turner, Benjamin L. Hooks, and George W. Lee, urged the commission to sustain Willis's appointment.[9] In response to a letter sent by the group, Armour promised that he would support Willis, and over the weekend he and the other three commissioners met privately in the mayor's office to discuss the situation. Farris and the other commissioners were adamant that an African American be appointed to the board, but their commitment to Willis had weakened considerably in the face of such vocal white opposition.

Loeb really didn't care if an African American was appointed to a city board, but he was determined not to reward an activist like Willis while at the same time bolstering his segregationist credentials. Consequently he suggested that in exchange for removing Willis, he would agree to vote for A. Maceo Walker to take his place. At first Farris and Dwyer refused to agree to Loeb's proposal, but when Armour and Moore agreed to compromise, they reluctantly abandoned Willis.[10] Walker agreed to the appointment, which was announced when the commission met at its regular Tuesday afternoon session.[11] Understandably Willis felt humiliated by the commission's action, and in a fit of hyperbole lashed out at the commission. "Out of the darkness came once four courageous men now reduced to boys, soaked in the soup of race hatred, prepared by the hands of Henry Loeb . . . We would rather be dead than kneel and humble ourselves to a racist dictator."[12] The controversy surrounding Willis's removal and Walker's appointment to the MTA board in Willis's place not only had an effect on the relationship between the two men; it also influenced the outcome of the 1962 state elections.

In March 1962 thirty-eight-year-old public works commissioner William Farris announced his plan to seek the Democratic nomination for the Tennessee governorship. Farris was virtually unknown outside of Memphis; his statewide political experience was limited to a brief term as director of the Tennessee Department of Old Age and Survivors Insurance in 1951. Before his election to the city commission Farris had served as executive assistant to mayors Tobey and Orgill, which no doubt taught him the inner workings of municipal government but did nothing to help him win a statewide contest. To make matters worse, his chief opponent was former governor Frank Clement, who longed to succeed his former protégé Buford Ellington, who was prevented from seeking a third consecutive term by the state's constitution. Also seeking the Democratic nomination was Chattanooga mayor P. R. Olgiati, but Clement was the presumptive frontrunner.[13] The campaign season began in earnest when the three major candidates spoke before the Tennessee Voters Council, a statewide black political group. A large delegation of Memphians was on hand to hear the candidates when the organization assembled at Fisk University in Nashville. During a raucous meeting the majority of delegates voted for Clement, but it was not unanimous. Two Olgiati supporters from Memphis, labor leader James T. Walker and his wife, Willa, resigned when Chattanooga civil rights leader C. T. Vivian called them traitors for refusing to support Clement.[14]

Meanwhile in Memphis the Shelby County Democratic Club began deliberations on whom to endorse in the Democratic primary. A screening committee, which included Walker, Sugarmon, Turner, H. T. Lockard, and Willis, was formed to make recommendations to the organization's Central Committee. The screening committee was evenly divided between Clement and Farris partisans, but when the names were presented to the Central Committee, Clement was overwhelmingly selected to receive the club's endorsement. In addition, Southwestern College political science professor Ross Pritchard, who was also Mayor Loeb's brother-in-law, was endorsed for the ninth district congressional seat held by Clifford Davis.[15] This put Maceo Walker in something of a quandary. Presumably he felt some sense of loyalty to Farris for his appointment to the transit authority board. On the other hand, in order to support him in the governor's race he would have to split the club's membership and, by extension, the black community. Despite whatever reservations he may have felt, Walker decided to leave the organization his father had helped found.

Not long after the Democratic Club's endorsement of the former governor, Walker resigned from the organization and formed the Citizens for Farris and Davis Committee to campaign for the white candidates in African American wards. Leaving no doubt of his feelings, Walker declared in an hour-long speech that the club had made a "serious mistake" in supporting Clement and Pritchard and that "some of these self-styled Negro leaders have done nothing in the area of civil rights . . . unless they have been motivated by personal recognition."[16] Walker's organization recruited two hundred volunteers to canvass black neighborhoods and held receptions in forty different wards across the city. At the same time rallies were held at several locations, including the Handy Theatre and Mitchell Road High School.[17] The Shelby County Democratic Club engaged in similar activities on behalf of their candidates. Pritchard paid particular attention to the club, even going so far as to address the membership during an evening meeting.[18] The Farris campaign organized several political gatherings around Shelby County, including a massive rally at the fairgrounds. Thousands of hot dogs and soft drinks were served to twenty thousand attendees who listened to the candidate along with former governor Browning and commissioners Armour and Moore. "Make your voice heard," Farris urged his fellow Memphians.[19]

On election eve Farris returned to the Bluff City, where he toured the downtown area shaking hands with citizens and appearing on WHBQ television. The other gubernatorial candidates also visited Memphis—Olgiati visited the Plough pharmaceutical facility and toured the downtown business district, while Clement greeted workers at the International Harvester plant, toured the Cotton Exchange, and visited with firefighters at the main fire station on Front Street.[20] The voters of Tennessee spoke the following day, but the sound was not what William Farris wanted to hear. Although the public works commissioner carried Shelby County by twelve thousand votes, he could not overcome the former governor's widespread popularity across Tennessee. In the end, Clement won the Democratic nomination and a third gubernatorial term because there was no Republican opposition in the fall general election. Unsurprisingly, Clifford Davis also secured the Democratic nomination for the ninth district congressional seat over Ross Pritchard.[21]

Unlike in previous elections, black voters were not a significant factor in the outcome of the 1962 Democratic primary. In the election precincts with African American majorities, no candidate received the bulk of the vote. For example, in precinct 11-1, Pritchard received 217 votes, while 76 ballots were cast for Davis. In precinct 11-1, 1,259 blacks were registered to vote, but fewer than 300 actually cast ballots. The reason, of course, was the split in the ranks of the Shelby County Democratic Club. According to George W. Lee, the African American electorate was "split into too many splinters."[22] While the Shelby County Democratic Club played an important role in Clement's and Davis's victories, it was by no means a complete one. The feud that erupted between them and Walker's faction severely weakened the leverage black voters employed in the election.

George W. Lee remained the most powerful, and popular, Republican leader in Memphis despite the fact that thousands of black Memphians were deserting the party. In early June 1962, thirty-five hundred people, including Commissioner Armour and Shelby County sheriff M. A. Hinds, attended an event honoring Lee's years of dedicated service to the Memphis community.[23] Lee was then in the midst of his reelection campaign for another term as a member of the state Republican executive committee, and the tribute no doubt assisted in that effort. In fact he needed all the help he could get. Since Nixon's defeat, the conservative, lily-white wing of the party, nominally led by Arizona senator Barry Goldwater, converted thousands of suburban whites in the South and West to their philosophy of states' rights, rigid anti-Communism, and fiscal restraint.[24] Memphis was no exception to this trend. Determined to purge the Shelby County GOP of its moderate, civil rights–oriented leadership, a group of white professionals formed the Republican Association with the express purpose of removing Lee from the state committee. The group also planned to challenge the Democrats for the ninth congressional seat, but its most fervent wish was to remove Lee and thus make the local Republican Party an all-white organization.[25]

The New Guard, as the Republican Association was nicknamed to distinguish it from Lee's Old Guard, stated publicly that it opposed Lee because he had created a "closed corporation" that excluded conservatives from the party's ranks. However, one does not have to look hard to discern their true purpose. In effect the New Guard was little more than the old lily-white faction which had been trying for decades to "reform" the southern wing of the GOP by purging African Americans from party leadership positions.[26] Lee certainly understood their real motivation. "Their chief indictment against me is that I do not resemble them in face and features," Lee wrote to the state committee chairman, Congressman Howard Baker, Sr.[27] Both factions fielded a full slate of candidates for the primary, but the two most important races were for the executive committee and the congressional seat. One of the staunchest conservatives in the Republican Association, Robert James, was chosen to run for the congressional seat, while Lee's Old Guard slated white attorney Raymond Briggs.

Born in Iowa, James moved to the Bluff City in 1936 to serve as a salesman in the Memphis office of the Firestone Company. Two years later he opened his own business, the Memphis Housecleaning Company, which employed five hundred people by the early 1960s. After service in the navy during World War II, James devoted much of his energy to combating Communism. He chaired the local American Legion's "Crusade on Communism" for which he received the Freedoms Foundation's George Washington Honor Medal.[28] In his campaign platform James declared that his "unchanging goal is ultimate victory over Communism."[29] For James, anti-Communism was no doubt a useful political tool, but it appears that his true goal was to crush Lee's influence within the Republican Party. The New Guard organized parties at the homes of prominent white citizens where James brought his conservative message to the fertile ground of suburban Memphis.[30] The chairman of the Republican National Committee, William Miller, shared James's political views and provided the New Guard with substantial assistance during the campaign.[31]

Meanwhile Lee received the endorsement of 150 black ministers who distributed pamphlets to their parishioners arguing that Lee was "fighting for Negro Democrats as well as Republicans" to improve job opportunities for African Americans.[32] Echoing this statement, Lee called on "progressive Republicans, Negro and white Democrats to vote for me..."[33] Many African Americans did rally behind Lee and his Old Guard slate, including the Lincoln League and the influential black disc jockey and newspaper columnist Nat D. Williams, but collectively they were not enough to convince black voters to return to the Republican fold.[34] Indeed, African American voters in Memphis had overwhelmingly cast ballots for the Democrats in the 1960 presidential election, and, as the campaign progressed, they did not appear to be inclined to go back to the GOP in 1962. Unfortunately for Lee and the Old Guard most African Americans voted in the Democratic primary rather than the Republican one. Lee received 5,228 votes, but he came in third behind two white candidates, which ended his tenure on the state Republican executive committee.[35]

James defeated Briggs by over four thousand votes in the congressional nominee race to become Clifford Davis's opponent in the fall general election. In a telegram to Briggs, James declared that he wished to "unify the Republican Party and to bring the two-party system to Memphis..."[36] Of course, the two-party system that James envisioned was a segregated one, with the

GOP being the party for white people while all African Americans would become Democrats. The local Republican organization may have emerged from the 1962 primary as a white-dominated apparatus, but it did not quite make them a majority party. To the surprise of the Democratic establishment, Davis narrowly defeated James in the November general election by a mere 479 votes. They had expected to defeat the Republican nominee handily, but James's aggressive campaigning was in stark contrast to Davis's rather lackadaisical electioneering. In the end, it was African American Democrats who sent Davis back to Washington for a twelfth congressional term.[37] The fact that a majority of Memphis blacks voted in the Democratic primary and beat back a Republican insurgency in the fall contest was not lost on the Kennedy administration. Hoping to make further inroads in the local black community, President Kennedy appointed Russell Sugarmon a special ambassador to represent him at ceremonies honoring the independence of Trinidad and Tobago.[38] In addition, Vice President Johnson corresponded with Lee regarding the Committee on Equal Employment Opportunity, which Johnson chaired.[39]

1962 was not a good year for Mayor Loeb. Not only had he seen his political future wane as segregation collapsed; he also watched impotently as William Farris emerged as a statewide political figure in the wake of his unsuccessful gubernatorial bid. As 1963 began, the mayor became increasingly cantankerous, feuding with public officials and newspaper reporters alike. Just before the new year, commissioners proposed their budgets totaling $42 million, which would increase the city's property tax rate by fourteen cents. Appalled by the increase, the mayor vetoed the budget and vowed to eliminate capital improvement projects and reduce the number of city employees.[40] However, when the mayor and commission met in regular session, it was apparent that the other members would override the veto. Faced with the commissioners' unwillingness to cut the budget, Loeb glumly withdrew his veto, and the tax increase remained intact.[41] The impasse between mayor and commission continued over the construction of expressways to relieve the city's growing traffic problems.

By 1963 Memphis had only 18.2 miles of expressways which connected the city with the federal interstate highway system.[42] However, much more was needed. Commissioner Farris proposed to issue $19.9 million in city bonds to accelerate construction of the rest of the expressway system.[43] The mayor, again concerned about the cost, voted against issuing the bonds but did not attempt to veto the proposal. Farris's plan was adopted, and by the end of 1964 construction began on the rest of the expressway system.[44] Loeb got along with the news media about as well as he did the commission. Angry over the coverage he received from the *Commercial Appeal* and *Press-Scimitar*, the mayor announced he would only answer written questions submitted by reporters in advance rather than submit to an unscripted interview. When the newspapers declined to accept this restriction, Loeb proposed to hold a daily televised press conference, but the three television stations refused to cover the event.[45] So, by mid-1963, as Memphis prepared for a municipal election, Loeb had alienated the city commissioners, the local press, and no doubt many voters.

Despite his frustrations, Loeb was not quite prepared to abandon his political career, nor was he ready to announce his reelection bid. Loeb remained silent as to his plans even when a group of his supporters strongly urged him to announce his candidacy.[46] With Loeb wavering, several others announced their intention to run for mayor. The first to do so was traffic court judge William B. Ingram, who had been engaged in an ongoing dispute with police commissioner Armour regarding his department's enforcement of city traffic laws.[47] When he announced his candidacy, Ingram issued a ten-point campaign platform which promised, among other things, to "stop the constant confusion, indecision and bickering at city hall."[48] Joining him in the race was Sheriff M. A. Hinds, former police department chief of detectives, who had become Shelby County's head law enforcement official in 1958.[49] Missing from this list was William Farris, who many, including Loeb, assumed would also seek the mayoralty.[50] Meanwhile Loeb continued to vacillate.

The mayor was not at all sanguine about the possibility of Farris, Hinds, or Ingram becoming his successor. He was particularly concerned with Hinds because of his past ties with the old Crump organization. But neither could he make up his mind to become a candidate himself. However, when the mayor learned that Shelby County Quarterly Court member Herbert B. Moriarty, Jr., was being touted as a possible candidate, he declared that he "would step aside for Moriarty. I think he is a smart young man."[51] However, Moriarty declined to run, so Loeb was right back where he started. For years Loeb had sponsored a monthly public affairs discussion series, called the Dutch Treat Luncheon, and it was there that Loeb finally announced his decision.

After explaining his inability to find a candidate "who stands for the same things I do," Loeb announced his reelection bid. "I don't intend to sit back and watch while a three-headed police state is resurrected from remnants of the old machine," the mayor informed a boisterous crowd of two hundred supporters.[52] Loeb was obliquely referring to the fact that Hinds, as well as commissioners Armour and Dwyer, had served in the police department during the Crump era. The specter of machine politics was no doubt a convenient excuse, but the real reason for Loeb's campaign was that none of the other candidates was as fiscally and socially conservative as he was. As expected, two days later Farris entered the race. Promising to send Loeb back to private life, Farris lambasted the mayor's polarizing leadership. "We should not be surprised that he [Loeb] is a reluctant candidate. He has been a reluctant mayor for four years. Reluctant to give Memphis anything that would contribute to its progress ... Memphis, I say, is tired of this 'no' government."[53]

Loeb's reelection campaign did not last long, however. In late September the veteran president and general manager of Loeb's Laundry, Frederic Thesmar, suffered a heart attack and died. According to Loeb, his mother and brother William pleaded with him to leave public office and return to the family business. Ostensibly Loeb decided his first duty was to his family, so he resigned the mayor's office and withdrew from the contest.[54] When the commission met to accept the mayor's resignation, Farris hoped to be named interim executive, but Loeb threatened to stay on if he, or any other candidate, was named to the post. Bowing to Loeb's wishes, Farris recommended Claude Armour be named acting mayor, and the rest of the commission agreed. It is difficult to determine exactly why Loeb made the decision to resign. The fact that he dithered for so long before announcing his candidacy, as well as his threat to remain in office if Farris was appointed mayor, suggests that family loyalty was not the motivating factor in his decision. Regardless of the reason, his resignation seemed to put an end to the politics of divisiveness that had dominated city government and that Loeb had come to represent. On his first day as a private citizen, Loeb arrived at the laundry plant and was met with a reminder of what he had just given up. On the first rack of clothes he came to were several campaign neckties for Farris, Hinds, and Ingram. The former mayor reportedly laughed at the sight, but it must have caused him a moment's discomfort to be reminded of the seeming end of his political career.[55]

On the same day that Farris entered the mayor's race, attorney Hunter Lane, Jr., challenged incumbent public services commissioner John T. Dwyer, whose reelection campaign was in disarray after it was revealed that two of his employees had engaged in questionable real estate deals. Pledging to "clean up the mess" in the public services department, Lane stressed the need for harmony in local government. "Our city officials must put aside their personal differences and subordinate their ambitions and emotions for the greater good of the city which they represent."[56] In addition to the public services position, the public works commission seat was also available owing to Farris's decision to run for mayor. Two candidates emerged for that position, Charles A. Oswald, president of the Industrial Maintenance Corporation, and insurance executive Pete Sisson. An attorney and former president of the Memphis Jaycees, Sisson was a well-known leader in civic affairs.[57] Another attorney, John Ford Canale, also entered the race, and like Sisson, pledged to work harmoniously with the other commissioners.[58] Meanwhile, as the various candidates jockeyed for position, African American leaders began organizing voters for the upcoming election.

Shortly after the 1962 elections, A. Maceo Walker and his faction established the Ninth Congressional District Democrats from the remnants of his Citizens for Farris and Davis Committee. Russell Sugarmon and the Shelby County Democratic Club, concerned about the growing rift in the black community, proposed to reactivate the Volunteer Citizens Committee to endorse candidates and coordinate the activities of both organizations. Walker agreed to this proposal, as did George W. Lee and O. Z. Evers.[59] By bringing together the ninth district Democrats, the Democratic Club, Lee's Republicans, and Evers's Binghamton neighborhood association, Sugarmon hoped to unify the black vote and influence the outcome of the election.[60]

An executive committee screened candidates and presented their recommendations to a mass meeting held at Metropolitan Baptist Church. White candidates Armour, Canale, Farris, and Lane received the organization's nod, as did Benjamin Hooks, who was running for a city judgeship. The Volunteer Citizens Committee also endorsed Dr. Vasco Smith, LeMoyne College president Hollis Price, and Olivet Baptist Church pastor E. W. Williamson, who were all running for school board seats.[61]

Opening its headquarters on Beale Street, the Volunteer Citizens Committee organized receptions at several people's homes and arranged campaign appearances at black churches and Universal Life Insurance Company offices.[62] The other two mayoral candidates did not ignore black voters despite the endorsement of Farris by the Volunteer Citizens Committee. In October, Farris, Hinds, and Ingram appeared at Reverend James Lawson's Centenary Methodist Church to outline their positions relative to the black community. Hinds pointed out that he had hired twenty-one African American deputies, while Farris touted the improved wages of sanitation workers, most of whom were black. Ingram, on the other hand, found himself in a shouting match when A. W. Willis accused him of threatening NAACP lawyers during a trial of sit-in demonstrators. Ingram denied the charge, and Willis countered by calling the judge a liar.[63] Campaign literature was distributed throughout the city with photographs of Farris, Hooks, Price, Smith, and Williams, emphasizing the fact that the ticket was an interracial one.[64]

Many hailed the Volunteer Citizens Ticket as a sign of racial progress, but others viewed it as a threat. A brochure circulated in white neighborhoods by "a small group of thinking citizens" pointed out that Farris had the support of "diehard NAACP integrationist leaders." The broadside also snidely mentioned that "Bill Farris and his wife attended Maceo Walker's daughter's wedding." [65] Farris proudly confirmed his attendance at the wedding and pointed out that he had welcomed African American Olympic gold medalist Wilma Rudolph to Memphis when Mayor Loeb had refused to attend the ceremony.[66] Despite being the victim of a smear campaign, Farris was not above employing negative tactics to further his political ends. In a widely distributed advertisement, Farris declared that "Ingram for mayor means dictatorship" and "Hinds for mayor means machine rule."[67] Receiving the endorsement of the *Tri-State Defender*, Farris appeared to have the lead as the campaign neared its conclusion.[68] This seemed to be confirmed when *Press-Scimitar* reporters interviewed eligible voters and discovered Farris far ahead of his opponents. However, among the African Americans questioned, Ingram actually outpolled Farris and Hinds.[69]

Ignoring this trend, Farris predicted he would win the election by 65,000 votes.[70] When the returns began to trickle in on election night, Farris was actually ahead by 8,000 votes, but the tide began to turn for Ingram as the night wore on. The former traffic judge received an unusual combination of African American and white working-class support, which secured victory over his opponents by 7,825 votes. In the city's largest African American precinct, for example, 625 ballots were cast for Ingram, while Hinds received 346 votes, and a mere 185 ballots were cast for Farris. At the same time Ingram carried every precinct in the white working-class community of Frayser, which meant in practical terms that an unwitting coalition of white segregationists and African Americans elected Ingram mayor of Memphis. In addition to Ingram, Hunter Lane, Jr., and Pete Sisson also secured seats on the city commission, defeating their opponents John T. Dwyer and John Ford Canale.[71] The new mayor promised, as he had in the campaign, to bring harmony to the commission. However, he struck an ominous tone when asked how he would get along with the reelected Claude Armour. "I am the mayor . . . I see no problem in getting along with Commissioner Armour as long as he abides by the law and respects my office."[72]

The reason for Farris's defeat is rather murky, but the scurrilous brochure distributed by the "small group of thinking citizens" clearly persuaded many whites to vote for Ingram, who did not have the support of an organized bloc of African Americans. Perhaps the biggest loser of the 1963 elections was not William Farris but rather the Volunteer Citizens Committee. The established black leadership was, for whatever reason, repudiated by a large number of African American voters. This was true not only in the mayor's race but also in the city judge and school board contests. Despite their aggressive campaigning, they were unable to elect either Benjamin Hooks as city judge or Hollis Price, Vasco Smith, and E. W. Williamson to the school board. In reality both the Shelby County Democratic Club and the Ninth District Democratic League were severely weakened by the elections of 1963.[73] As the year came to a close, no one was sure whether they could reorganize in time to influence the 1964 elections, which would elect not only the next president but also a U. S. representative and members of the Tennessee General Assembly.

President Kennedy, deeply disturbed by the escalating violence directed against African American demonstrators in the South and worried that the publicity surrounding these events was weakening America's position in its cold war with the Soviet Union, outlined a daring civil rights program in a televised address to the nation on June 11, 1963. "We face, therefore, a moral crisis as a country and as a people. It cannot be met by repressive police action. It cannot be left to increased demonstrations in the streets. It cannot be quieted by token moves or talk. It is time to act in the Congress, in your state and local legislative body and, above all, in all of our daily lives."[74] True to his word, the president sent a special message to Congress on June 19 which called for the adoption of civil rights legislation to ensure that "race has no place in American life and law." Kennedy's proposals included equal access to all public spaces including "hotels, restaurants, places of amusement and retail establishments," accelerated school integration, "fair and full employment" for African Americans, and the elimination of voting restrictions.[75]

The president attempted to build a broad-based coalition that would embrace an expansion of civil rights legislation, but Congress would have none of it. As his bill languished in committee throughout the summer and early fall, Kennedy became increasingly worried about his electoral prospects for 1964. He was determined to do all he could to hold on to the South, particularly Texas. Consequently Kennedy convinced his reluctant vice president to schedule a campaign visit to the Lone Star State to raise money and unify a fractious Democratic Party.[76] Two weeks after the November Memphis elections, President Kennedy traveled to Texas, where he was assassinated in Dallas on November 22. When the news reached the Bluff City, Memphians, like the rest of their fellow citizens, were shocked and bewildered by the event. *Commercial Appeal* reporter E. W. Kieckhefer surveyed reaction on Beale Street. Service station attendant Dempsey Chalmers shook his head emphatically and declared, "To think it could happen in this country." Continuing his tour, Kieckhefer visited George W. Lee's office. Kennedy's "death will not stop the march that Lincoln started more than a century ago. It will simply cause a wave of freedom to cover the country like water in the woodland," the Republican leader exclaimed.[77]

Although it was not immediately apparent, the new president was determined to bring true Lee's prediction. Not long after his unexpected inauguration, President Johnson made Kennedy's moribund civil rights package his own and worked assiduously to make it become law. Hearings on the bill began in January 1964, and the House passed the measure on February 10. But the bill stalled in the Senate as southern Democrats engaged in a filibuster which lasted seventy-five days.[78] The Senate finally passed the bill, and the president signed it into law on July 2.[79] Naturally African Americans were pleased with the passage of the Civil Rights Act of 1964, but too much had happened for them to believe the struggle was now over. As Russell Sugarmon explained, "I think it would be a mistake to assume this bill will cure all of our problems."[80] Nevertheless it was a historic piece of legislation that banished legal segregation from the American landscape. Johnson recognized that the law was a crowning achievement of his presidency, but it came at a political cost. Resting in his bedroom after the signing, the president glumly turned to his aide Bill Moyers and said, "I think we just delivered the South to the Republican Party for a long time to come."[81]

There were those in Memphis who hoped to make Johnson's prediction come true. The New Guard Republicans, emboldened by their victories in 1962, removed county chairman and black-and-tan leader Millsaps Fitzhugh from his post in May 1963. Calling his removal illegal, Fitzhugh appealed to the state executive committee for reinstatement. Instead they ordered a new election scheduled for October. After several Fitzhugh supporters walked out of the October caucus, Robert James was elected chairman of the Shelby County GOP.[82] Committed to an extreme form of conservatism, James and his followers were unwilling to compromise with either moderate Republicans or the African American wing of the party. Successful in seizing control of the local party's machinery, the New Guard then turned their attention to the 1964 presidential campaign.

In March of that year a party caucus was held to slate candidates, choose delegates to the national convention, and elect a new chairman. Representatives from several black precincts were challenged by Lee because they had not been chosen by his organization. Attempting to further marginalize Lee, James announced that debate on contested delegates would be limited. Lee, protesting this decision, harangued the group for ignoring the plight of African Americans. When James cautioned him to finish his speech, Lee walked out of the convention with his followers in tow. They did not travel far. Meeting in the foyer just outside the auditorium, Lee and his colleagues voted to form a rival ninth congressional district Republican organization and chose Lee and Benjamin Hooks as delegates to the national convention and David Marks and Anne Moody as alternates. As Lee's rump caucus ended, the regular Republicans chose James and Lewis Donelson as delegates, along with alternates Peggy Spurrier and Mrs. C. G. Richardson.[83]

Lee continued his struggle at the state Republican convention in Nashville. "My only desire is to make whatever contribution I can to keep the party from becoming an all-white party," he declared. But Lee's vision of the Republican Party as an inclusive, multiracial organization was rejected out of hand by the besotted followers of Goldwater. The convention then handed Lee the worst political defeat of his career by seating James and Donelson as the official Shelby delegates to the national convention in San Francisco.[84] With Lee callously disposed of, the convention then endorsed Goldwater and condemned the Civil Rights Act of 1964. As the convention ended, delegates paraded through the auditorium wearing Goldwater hats, waving banners and chanting for their presidential choice.[85] Despite all of this, Lee did not give up. He hoped that Nelson Rockefeller, leader of the moderate wing of the Republican Party and Goldwater's opponent, would secure the nomination and resurrect his political fortunes.[86]

As Lee made plans to challenge the New Guard in San Francisco, Goldwater emerged as the Republican frontrunner by winning several primaries, including California, where he defeated Rockefeller, who withdrew from the presidential contest.[87] With Rockefeller out of the race, moderates rallied around Pennsylvania governor William Scranton, who was determined to stop Goldwater at any cost because of his opposition to the Civil Rights Act.[88] The Pennsylvanian believed he could secure the nomination for himself if he could only convince a majority of delegates that Goldwater's anti–civil rights stand would cripple the party's chances in November. As Scranton surveyed delegations in Illinois, Oregon, and Utah, sources in the Goldwater campaign pledged that the Arizona senator would vigorously enforce the Civil Rights Act of 1964. Undaunted, Scranton's supporters fought to insert language in the Republican platform that endorsed the constitutionality of the Civil Rights Act and denounced "extremism."[89] At the same time, Scranton approached Lee and offered legal and financial support in the latter's struggle to wrest delegate seats from James and Donelson.[90] This two-pronged strategy was Scranton's last hope of wresting the nomination from Goldwater.

Lee quickly became the center of attention when he arrived in San Francisco as the convention was getting under way. George Bloom, Scranton's chief political strategist, and Henry Cabot Lodge issued statements supporting Lee's position, while Knoxville attorney R. C. Smith, Jr., made plans to defend the Memphian at the convention's credentials committee. The Scranton forces hoped to link their platform fight with Lee's credentials struggle to paint Goldwater as a racist demagogue and thus block his nomination. To put pressure on both the platform and credentials committees, Scranton supporters staged a rally in downtown San Francisco. Fifty thousand demonstrators carried placards with slogans such as "Vote for Goldwater—Stamp out Peace" and "I'd Rather Have the Scurvy than Barry-Barry." Henry Cabot Lodge reminded the boisterous crowd that "justice delayed is justice denied and justice has been delayed a long, long time," and Nelson Rockefeller condemned Goldwater's position on civil rights.[91]

The following day the credentials committee convened in the Italian Room of the St. Francis Hotel to hear arguments over the contested delegate seats. Inexplicably, R. C. Smith avoided the issue of race and instead argued that the "New Guard" had employed unfair tactics to remove Lee from his position of power. Smith pointed out that Lee had attended every national convention since 1940 and that Tennessee had sent African American delegates for the past fifty years, but refrained from saying that the Memphian had been removed because he was black.[92] Robert James, however, was not so restrained. "I believe the whole thing was at least partially inspired by those who wanted to inject the race issue at this convention to embarrass Senator Goldwater." After three hours of testimony, the credentials committee voted sixty-six to nineteen to seat James and Donelson as the recognized delegates from Tennessee.[93] Scranton's agitation over the civil rights plank fared no better. The committee recommended to the convention a platform which pledged merely to fully implement the Civil Rights Act but did not endorse it. This was far short of what the moderates wanted, and so when the platform was presented to the convention they tried in vain to block its adoption.[94]

Scranton's bid for the nomination collapsed when the convention adopted the platform without amending the civil rights plank. This cleared the way for Goldwater to be nominated on the first ballot. Watching as state after state voted for the Arizona senator, Scranton stepped up to the platform and asked that Goldwater's nomination be unanimous. Thunderous applause filled San Francisco's Cow Palace as Goldwater accepted the nomination.[95] Shortly thereafter the convention approved William E. Miller, Republican national chairman, as their vice presidential nominee. In his acceptance speech Goldwater taunted moderates and African Americans alike when he declared that "extremism in the defense of liberty is no vice" and condemned "false notions of equality."[96]

While moderates glumly agreed to support their party's nominee, southern conservatives were beside themselves. After Goldwater's address, a thousand southerners poured into the international room of the Jack Tar bar and grill to celebrate Goldwater's nomination. A Dixieland band played loudly as the attendees danced and cut loose with a few rebel yells in honor of their hero's victory.[97] Not all southerners were in the mood to celebrate, however. George W. Lee, embittered by his experiences in San Francisco, returned to Memphis determined to seek revenge on Robert James and Barry Goldwater. In an interview with the *Tri-State Defender* Lee snapped that James had "tried to crucify me and my people upon a cross of racism." He then vowed to do all he could to defeat Goldwater and James, who was running for the ninth congressional district Republican nomination.[98]

In contrast to the GOP, the Democrats embraced African American voters as never before. Officials of the Shelby County Democratic Party appointed labor leader George Holloway to its primary election board, and three African Americans were elected delegates to the Democratic National Convention. A. W. Willis was chosen as an at-large delegate, while Russell Sugarmon and Jesse Turner were selected as alternates.[100] When the convention opened in Atlantic City, it was a foregone conclusion that Lyndon Johnson would receive the party's nomination for president. However, before his nomination could take place, a dispute erupted over the seating of delegates from Mississippi which threatened the unity of the Democratic Party.

Disenfranchised African Americans, along with northern college students of both races who had poured into the Magnolia State during "Freedom Summer," formed the Mississippi Freedom Democratic Party in the spring of 1964 to challenge the selection of an all-white delegation to the national convention. At a rally attended by twenty-five hundred people, sixty-four blacks and four whites were chosen as MFDP delegates to Atlantic City. Arguing that the regular party had discriminated against black citizens by not allowing them to participate in the state convention, the MFDP hoped to challenge the credentials of the all-white delegation much as Lee had done against James. A nervous President Johnson brokered a deal with the credentials committee whereby two members of the MFDP delegation would be recognized as at-large delegates, but both groups refused to accept the compromise. Even though most of the Mississippi attendees were furious with the outcome, Johnson's skillful maneuvering prevented the convention, and consequently the Democratic Party, from tearing itself apart.[101] With Mississippi out of the way, the convention selected Johnson and Minnesota senator Hubert Humphrey as their presidential and vice presidential nominees. On the night of Johnson's and Humphrey's acceptance speeches, convention leaders, in a slight nod to African American Memphians, asked A. W. Willis to lead the delegates in saying the Pledge of Allegiance.[102]

Willis had much more on his mind than the president or the flag as he returned to Memphis. Hoping that their faith in white and black voters was still justified, Willis and Sugarmon announced their candidacies for seats in the Tennessee General Assembly. In their joint platform the two civil rights leaders stressed that "if we are to continue to make progress in elimination of race hatred and discrimination, then the Negro's point of view must be expressed in the councils of government."[103] In the August Democratic primary Willis defeated three other candidates to secure the party's nomination for the district 1 Tennessee House of Representatives seat. Sugarmon was not so fortunate. He came in second in the district 29 Tennessee Senate contest, losing by three thousand votes.[104] Several white Democrats attempted to find a suitable independent candidate to run against Willis, but the movement apparently collapsed after city commissioner and Democratic executive committee member Hunter Lane, Jr., publicly condemned the proposal.[105] As Lane's action reveals, Willis did receive white support for his candidacy, including the endorsement of the *Press-Scimitar* newspaper. In their recommendation, the editors described Willis as "an intelligent, conscientious, and hard-working representative of his race in these times of change."[106]

Willis was not the only African American to seek local office in 1964. In

October former NAACP president H. T. Lockard announced his candidacy for a seat on the Shelby County Quarterly Court. A nonpartisan Citizens for Lockard Committee was formed by several key NAACP leaders, including Jesse Turner, A. Maceo Walker, and Maxine Smith, and his candidacy was endorsed by the Ninth District Democratic League. While Lockard spoke at several African American churches, the committee printed thousands of campaign handbills and distributed them across the city.[107] As we have seen, Lockard was one of the city's leading civil rights attorneys, having defended O. Z. Evers in his suit against the Memphis Transit Authority and initiated legal action against the segregated public libraries on behalf of Jesse Turner. Lockard was born near Ripley, Tennessee, in rural Lauderdale County in 1920. A graduate of LeMoyne College, he earned a law degree from Lincoln University in St. Louis. During World War II he served in the U. S. Army in Italy, France, and Germany, and after the war he returned to Memphis to practice law.[108]

As Willis and Lockard began their campaigns, ninth district congressman Clifford Davis announced his bid for a fourteenth term as a member of the House of Representatives.[109] Despite his age—he turned sixty-seven that year—Davis campaigned vigorously for the post. In mid-July, for example, he toured the rural districts of Shelby County, shaking hands with constituents at several locations, including the Jones Peach Orchard on Highway 51 north near Millington.[110] He was challenged by state senator Frank White and Shelby County squire George Grider. A retired naval officer who commanded a submarine during World War II, Grider was a well-known local attorney with strong African American support. Energetic he might have been, but Davis was unable to grasp how quickly politics were changing. When riots broke out in New York City, the Tennessee congressman declared that the Civil Rights Act was "untimely and the events of Harlem prove it." He defended his vote against the act, boasting that he "would vote the same way tomorrow and the South needs a congressman who knows how to represent the views of the South."[111] Of course, Davis was ignoring the fact that African Americans were southerners, too, and many of them were determined to remind him of that fact.

Like Davis, Robert James continued to do all he could to antagonize black Memphians. In a speech to the junior chamber of commerce promoting his candidacy for the ninth congressional district's Republican nomination, James declared that "unscrupulous carpetbaggers and colored men ran the South during the Reconstruction period. For all the years since then there have been little cadres—mostly colored—scattered throughout the South who had control of the [Republican] party . . . It was very difficult to get control out of the Old Guard hands, but we have done it."[112] James easily defeated the Old Guard candidate Raymond M. Briggs to become the Republican nominee, but Davis was not quite so fortunate. Grider, in a stunning victory, defeated Davis by over 8,000 votes, many of them cast by African Americans. Not surprisingly, Grider's support among African Americans was deep and widespread. In predominately black ward 39, for example, Grider received 358 votes while a mere 55 were cast for Davis.[113]

The campaign between James and Grider quickly became a nasty affair. When the two candidates debated at Southwestern College's Adult Education Center, a raucous crowd of four hundred people subjected both Grider and James to boos and catcalls during their presentations. At one point the crowd became so boisterous that Grider sternly rebuked them: "This is the Adult Education Center but apparently some of you adults didn't understand that." He was no less strident with his opponent. Grider described James as "a lonesome negative voice crying rugged individualism." The Republican nominee, while not mentioning his opponent by name, declared that the 1964 election was "a debate over which kind of world we're going to live in—that of the enterprising individual or that of the regimented socialistic worker."[114] The rancor continued when the two nominees appeared on WREC-TV's *Focus on Memphis* program. James charged the Democratic nominee with supporting programs that would turn America into "a nation of wards of the federal government," while Grider caustically replied that the Republican's "basic campaign has been to call President Johnson soft on Communism and cry out for the good old days of the 19th Century."[115]

In 1964 the city of Memphis remained a small, but vital, presidential battleground for both political parties. As they had in 1960, the candidates planned to campaign vigorously in the Bluff City. The first to arrive was Goldwater, who appeared in Memphis after first visiting Knoxville. While in East Tennessee, the Republican nominee pledged to sell off portions of the Tennessee Valley Authority, but during his appearance in Memphis he avoided the subject entirely. TVA supporters did not let anyone forget where Goldwater stood, however. Throughout his appearance a small plane circled nearby trailing a banner which read "Vote LBJ—Keep TVA." Regardless of his stand on TVA, Memphians enthusiastically welcomed Goldwater to the city. Twenty-five hundred people met him at the airport, and 125,000 swelled downtown Memphis to hear him speak.[116] As might be expected, the crowds were made up predominately of white people. According to newspaper accounts only eighteen African Americans were noticed among the throng. George W. Lee, still smarting over the convention, feigned illness and did not attend.[117]

The crowds were much smaller when Senator Humphrey visited Memphis, at most eight thousand people, but they enthusiastically greeted him and his wife, Muriel, when they arrived on September 26. Speaking at the fairgrounds baseball stadium, the vice presidential nominee praised the Bluff City for "the great strides you have made in providing equal rights and equal opportunities for everyone regardless of race, creed or color." Humphrey also pledged to continue TVA and declared that Lyndon Johnson "has the same sensitivity as [President Andrew] Jackson for the people—all the people." After his speech, Humphrey attended a reception hosted by Mayor Ingram at the auditorium. Humphrey and his wife spent the night in the presidential suite at the Hotel Claridge and the next morning attended church services at St. Luke's Methodist Church on South Highland. Before departing the city, the vice presidential nominee met with former mayor Edmund Orgill and Ray Morton, president of Memphis Light, Gas and Water, presumably to discuss TVA.[118] As Humphrey left, the question on the minds of some Memphians was whether or not President Johnson would visit the Bluff City.

Discouraged by the enormous turnout for Goldwater's visit to Memphis, some Tennessee Democrats were fearful that the Republicans would carry Shelby County as they had in 1956 and 1960. Their hope was that a presidential visit to Memphis would help the Democrats carry Shelby County and, by extension, Tennessee.[119] In early October Johnson visited Nashville and then flew to New Orleans the same evening, which suggested to some that the president planned to bypass the Bluff City. Johnson, aware of Goldwater's inroads into Shelby County as well as local opposition to the Civil Rights Act, phoned the editorial offices of the *Press-Scimitar* to allay Memphians' fears. "I'm definitely coming to Memphis before this campaign is over," the president exclaimed to a delighted member of the fourth estate.[120] Shortly after Johnson's phone call, the White House announced a presidential visit for Thursday, October 24. Thousands of Memphians, buoyed by the news, were determined to catch a glimpse of the nation's thirty-sixth chief executive. One such Memphian was sixty-three-year-old African American Eddie Adams, who arrived at the riverfront, where the president was scheduled to speak, at 6 AM to make sure he got a good seat. As others began to arrive, Adams waved his Social Security card and declared, "Thank God for Mr. Johnson."[121]

Meanwhile fifteen hundred people lined a fence near the runway as Air Force One landed at the airport. When the president appeared, the crowd began to shout, "We want Johnson!" "I hear you," the president replied as he was greeted by Governor Clement. Walking to the fence, Johnson shook hands and handed out LBJ campaign pins to the enthusiastic Memphians.[122] Leaving the airport, Johnson stopped his motorcade several times to shake hands with the thousands lining his route to downtown. At one point the president witnessed two Memphis police officers shoving an African American who was trying to reach his motorcade. "Please don't do that," Johnson shouted. Stunned, the officers complied.[123] A quarter of a million more people surrounded the podium at Riverside Drive to hear the president speak.

As an army helicopter circled above and police snipers peered from downtown rooftops, the president declared, "We are going to wipe away the Mason-Dixon Line across our politics. We are going to wipe away the color line across our opportunity." Feeding off the frenzy of the crowd, Johnson later bellowed, "I want the world to know that campaigns of hate, campaigns of fear, campaigns of smear cannot succeed among the American people."[124] When the president finished speaking, the people, inspired by his rhetoric, broke through a police barricade, smashed into reporters, and swarmed around Johnson's platform. Secret Service agents fearfully grabbed the president to pull him away, but he waved them aside and shook the hands of many.[125] Democratic Party operatives were deeply gratified by Johnson's visit and believed it would make a difference in the upcoming election. Many in the crowd agreed with them. "I think a lot of people who wouldn't have gone LBJ, will, now that he's taken time to come to Memphis," reported East Memphis voter J. W. Coleman.[126]

To the surprise of almost no one, Johnson and the Democrats recaptured both Memphis and Tennessee in a stunning upset over Goldwater and the GOP. In Shelby County, 212,804 citizens went to the polls in the largest voter turnout in local history. The president received 112,306 votes, while 100,495 ballots were cast for Goldwater. The majority of votes cast for Johnson came from African Americans and organized labor, while Goldwater picked up blocs of votes in several large white enclaves, including the upper-middle-class community of Whitehaven and the working-class neighborhood of Frayser.[127] The Democratic tidal wave also upset the Republicans in the ninth district congressional race. Robert James was defeated by George Grider, who, like President Johnson, benefited greatly from the large turnout of black voters. In ward 34-2 the retired naval officer received 1,453 ballots, while a mere 64 votes went to James.[128]

Since 1951 black Memphians had tried, and failed, to elect one of their own to public office. But now, in 1964, their patience and hard work finally resulted in success. Defeating the Republican Garvin Crawford, A. W. Willis received 99,038 votes and was elected to the state house of representatives. H. T. Lockard's margin of victory was far less than Willis's, but nevertheless he was elected a squire, or representative to the Shelby County Quarterly Court. Both men, well aware that many whites viewed them at least with suspicion if not enmity, struck a conciliatory tone when they talked to the press. "We have been working for one America and certainly wouldn't do anything to create two Americas," Willis and Lockard jointly declared.[129]

"The Respectable people have been out-voted," sniffed Robert James when the extent of the Democratic landslide had sunk in. If that was not biased enough, James also predicted that black voting "will build an ever higher wall between the races." His chief rival, George W. Lee, was more sanguine about the future: "The party is not over the hill. Nor has it been deserted permanently by Negroes." Despite his unbending loyalty to the GOP, Lee could not help but be delighted by the outcome of the election. "It was the strange voices and strange tongues and strange people that kidnapped the Republican Party. But they sure didn't kidnap the Republican vote."[130]

Described as "the most absolute political boss in the U.S." by *Time* magazine, Edward Hull Crump is seen here with Fire and Police Commissioner Claude Armour. Photograph courtesy of the E. H. Crump Collection, Memphis Public Library and Information Center.

During the 1952 presidential campaign, Republican nominee Dwight Eisenhower conferred with Memphian Roberta Church on political conditions in Tennessee. Photograph courtesy of the Roberta Church Collection, Memphis Public Library and Information Center.

Edmund Orgill led the initial effort to reform Memphis's government and was elected mayor in 1955. Photograph courtesy of the Memphis and Shelby County Room Photograph Collection, Memphis Public Library and Information Center.

President Eisenhower shakes hands with Gilda Lee, daughter of black-and-tan Republican leader George W. Lee, who is standing second from Eisenhower's left. East Tennessee congressman Carroll Reese is standing next to Lee and behind Gilda. Photograph courtesy of the George W. Lee Collection, Memphis Public Library and Information Center.

A large crowd greeted Dr. Martin Luther King, Jr., when he arrived in Memphis to speak on behalf of the Volunteer Ticket, August 1959. Photograph courtesy of the A. W. Willis Collection, Memphis Public Library and Information Center.

The 1959 "election will give impetus for our whole civil rights struggle to every Negro in the United States," declared Dr. Martin Luther King, Jr., at Mason Temple, August 1959. Photograph courtesy of the Memphis Civil Rights Photograph Collection, Memphis Public Library and Information Center.

Henry Loeb was elected mayor in 1959 as a staunch defender of segregation. Elected to a second term in 1967, Loeb refused to negotiate with striking sanitation workers. That decision had disastrous consequences for Memphis and the United States. Photograph courtesy of the Memphis and Shelby County Room Photograph Collection, Memphis Public Library and Information Center.

African American lawyers A. W. Willis, Benjamin L. Hooks, Ben Jones, Russell Sugarmon, and H. T. Lockard defended the sit-in demonstrators and organized the political campaigns that elected Willis and Sugarmon to the Tennessee House of Representatives and Lockard to the Shelby County Quarterly Court. Photograph courtesy of the A. W. Willis Collection, Memphis Public Library and Information Center.

On October 24, 1964, President Lyndon B. Johnson campaigned in Memphis. From left: Fred Davis, A. W. Willis, Jesse Turner, and President Johnson. Photograph courtesy of the A. W. Willis Collection, Memphis Public Library and Information Center.

State representative A. W. Willis shakes hands with Memphis mayor William Ingram. Tennessee governor Frank Clement is sitting on the far left at Willis's elbow. Photograph courtesy of the A. W. Willis Collection, Memphis Public Library and Information Center.

7

"A Great Movement Here in Memphis"

William Ingram just couldn't keep his promise. Elected mayor on a pledge to bring peace to city government, instead he sowed discord. The city charter stated that the mayor "shall have general supervision of all the officers of the city and see that the ordinances and provisions of the charter are observed."[1] As mayor, Ingram interpreted this passage to mean he had the authority to appoint or dismiss any municipal official regardless of the wishes of the other four commissioners. Shortly after his January 1964 inauguration the mayor dismissed long-time city attorney Frank Gianotti in favor of Patrick Johnson, Sr. Commissioners Lane and Sisson supported Ingram's appointment, but Claude Armour was bitterly opposed.[2] In retaliation, the mayor proposed to rescind the appointment of police chief J. C. McDonald but was rebuffed by the other four commissioners.[3] This discord gave additional credence to those who argued that Memphis was hobbled by an outmoded form of government that seriously needed reform while at the same time having a profound impact on the outcome of the next municipal election.

When Jerrold Moore, director of the Memphis and Shelby County Planning Commission, scheduled a meeting without consulting the mayor, condemnation quickly followed. "This gentleman is going to have to remember that he is just an administrative official and the mayor is the mayor . . . We can't have any subversive activity . . . and if he's not going to cooperate, he's going to have a hard time," Ingram sternly exclaimed during a press conference.[4] Moore was scheduled to be reappointed to his post by the city commission, and Ingram was determined to deny him that position. Describing Moore as an "imported pedigreed propagandist," the mayor tried, and failed, to remove him from the planning commission.[5] Ingram, convinced he had the power to do as he pleased, rejected Commissioner Moore's nominations to the airport commission and instead nominated his own loyalists to the board.[6] In response, the four city commissioners passed an ordinance stripping the mayor of that responsibility.[7] Armour, Lane, Moore, and Sisson, as their actions suggest, were having none of Ingram's notion that all power was vested in the mayor's office. The mayor, however, simply didn't care.

The crisis in city hall grew worse in February when Ingram dismissed personnel director Richard W. Barnes for alleged financial irregularities.[8] Astonished by the mayor's charges, Barnes requested a hearing before the city commission to clear his name.[9] During the contentious meeting, Ingram failed to convince his fellow commissioners that Barnes had done anything improper. Consequently, Armour, Lane, Moore, and Sisson voted to reinstate the personnel director, which prompted Ingram to suspend Barnes a second time. As the hearing dissolved into chaos, Commissioner Moore roared: "Mr. Mayor, you have got to have a reason for suspending people, persecuting people, and in my opinion that man hasn't done a thing that I wouldn't have done, and I know that I am as honorable as you are."[10] This pattern of reinstatement and suspension continued until Barnes filed suit against the mayor in the fall of 1964.[11]

Barnes filed a motion requesting chancery court to issue an injunction barring the mayor from ordering any further suspensions, which was granted by Chancellor Ceylon B. Frazer.[12] Ingram stubbornly refused to back down, appealing the chancellor's decision to the Tennessee Supreme Court. The justices were no more impressed with the mayor's argument, and in December 1965 they ordered Ingram to reinstate Barnes to his post.[13] For the rest of his term the mayor continued to lash out at anyone whom he perceived as an enemy. When, during a press conference, television reporter Norm Brewer started to ask the mayor a question, Ingram interrupted him by saying, "Let's see you smile once, Mr. Brewer. I haven't seen you smile since you were predicting that Mr. [William] Farris was going to win [the mayor's race]." "Mr. Mayor, I've done practically nothing but smile at these city commission meetings," Brewer icily replied.[14] All of this drama took its toll on the mayor's health. In late 1964 Ingram suffered a mild heart attack, which put a temporary end to the gridlock reigning in city hall.[15] The abandonment of consensus by the commission also wore heavily on the citizenry. As we will see, Ingram's acidic style of governance convinced many Memphians it was time to seriously consider changing the city's form of government.

In December 1964 President Johnson invited A. W. Willis and his wife to attend a White House state dinner in honor of the prime minister of England, Harold Wilson. Enjoying a meal of duck, wild rice, and creamed asparagus, Willis exchanged small talk with Johnson and Governor Clement in what was probably a reward for the part he played in Johnson's presidential victory.[16] A few weeks later Willis traveled to Nashville to begin his duties in the Tennessee House of Representatives. To his surprise, he found his white colleagues to be respectful and friendly. "I don't feel like anybody has talked down to me . . . I've felt no strain, no resentment," Willis reported to the press.[17] Conscious of his groundbreaking role, Willis was determined to make good: "I want to do this so Negroes who follow me won't have to have the people vote for or against them just because they are Negroes."[18]

Wasting little time, the freshman representative introduced two pieces of legislation designed to alleviate poverty across the Volunteer State. The first sought to appropriate $3 million to increase the size of the state's antipoverty program. The second was more ambitious. Willis introduced a bill to establish a minimum wage in Tennessee. His proposal called for all non-domestic employees to receive a maximum of $1.25 per hour, while those who worked in homes would be guaranteed 95 cents an hour.[19] In order to build support for the measure, Willis compiled a twenty-five-page report on Tennessee's appalling poverty rate and circulated copies amongst his fellow legislators.[20] Governor Clement was apparently impressed by Willis's argument, for he staked his prestige on its passage. Speaking before a joint session of the house and senate, the governor outlined the desperate economic conditions of many Tennesseans and urged the legislators to pass Willis's measure in order to "put thousands of our fellow citizens and families into the business of better living."[21]

Clement's rhetoric had little effect on conservative and rural legislators. For example, the governor's legislative floor leader, Representative David Givens of Somerville, was strongly opposed to the bill, as were many other loyal Clement supporters. The Tennessee Manufacturers Association lobbied hard against the bill, as did the owners of hotels and restaurants. In the end, their resistance could not be overcome by Clement's and Willis's good intentions, and the bill went down to defeat.[22] The Memphis legislator's proposal to increase antipoverty funding was more successful with $1 million appropriated to combat economic disparity across the state.[23] Defeat may have been handed him over the minimum wage proposal, but Willis nevertheless emerged from that first legislative session as one of the most influential representatives in the general assembly. Because he was so identified with the issue of poverty, Willis was appointed by Mayor Ingram to serve on the city's Community Action Committee, which had been formed to oversee local implementation of the federal government's War on Poverty program. However, when the NAACP criticized Ingram's unwillingness to work with grassroots organizations, he dismissed Willis from the CAC and threatened to appoint a member of the racist white Citizens' Council in his stead.[24]

○ ○ ○

For nearly a decade Memphians had watched helplessly as their city government spiraled into chaos. Since 1956 the city commission had grown increasingly fractious, which often impeded the people's business. Three successive mayors—Orgill, Loeb, and Ingram—had been unable, or unwilling, to build consensus and move the city forward. In the early 1950s, as we have seen, the Civic Research Committee promoted the adoption of the city manager form of government, but the proposal went nowhere. In October 1965 the *Commercial Appeal* newspaper ran a series of articles by reporter Jack Morris. Entitled "Managing the Metropolis," the series of ten articles criticized the commission form of government, explained how Memphis's government could be changed, and described the workings of the mayor-council plan, as well as reporting on the experiences of other municipalities that had reformed their charters.[25] Shortly after the series appeared, Morris met with Lucius Burch, one of the founders of the Civic Research Committee, to discuss reviving the moribund campaign to reform the city's charter.[26]

It was decided that a small group of influential men would be pulled together to form the nucleus of a much larger reform organization. They chose eight men, including Julian Bondurant, the president of Future Memphis, Inc., AFL-CIO Labor Council president Tommy Powell, county court squire Downing Pryor, Dr. Vasco Smith, NAACP vice president, and Republican leader Harry Wellford. Meeting over lunch at the Wolf River Society, Burch and Morris outlined to the group a plan of action to build a community-wide organization.[27] Everyone attending the luncheon was convinced that reform was necessary, so they agreed to create an organization to draft a new city charter and persuade the citizenry of the need for adoption. To that end, several mass meetings were planned to insure widespread participation in the process. The first gathering, attended by four hundred citizens, explained the reasons for a charter change and the steps needed to bring reform about.[28] Many Memphians were intrigued with the possibility of amending the government's structure, and consequently over a thousand of them attended a conference to choose a board of directors to oversee the drafting of charter recommendations.

Despite the ad hoc nature of the proceedings, virtually every major voting bloc in Memphis was represented on the directorate. In addition to organizers Downing Pryor, Vasco Smith, and Tommy Powell, the board included Republicans Gwen Awsumb, Lewis Donelson, and Dan Kuykendall, labor attorney Anthony Sabella, Rabbi James Wax, and local Young Democrats president Cliff Tuck, as well as H. T. Lockard, Russell Sugarmon, Jesse Turner, and A. W. Willis.[29] With the leadership in place, the hard work of drafting a workable charter that would be acceptable to a majority of the electorate began. Adopting the name Program of Progress (POP), the board began by soliciting public input at public meetings held at the Chisca Hotel. Edward Meeman resurrected the 1950s-era city manager form of government, and former Shelby County commissioner Rudolph Jones suggested retaining the five-man commission while also creating a three-position council to carry out the legislative functions; the commission would continue overseeing city departments.[30]

Several conservative directors strongly supported the city manager plan, but they yielded to the African American and labor members who preferred the mayor-council form of government.[31] However, the emerging coalition began to evaporate as the debate turned on how the council would be elected. Many conservative white directors wanted council members to be chosen at large, which would require each winning candidate to receive a majority of votes in a citywide election. Given that whites were in the majority, an at-large city council would make it extremely difficult for black candidates to win electoral office. Unsurprisingly, African Americans objected to the at-large only plan: "No one can adequately represent a Negro unless he is one. I don't see how any city as heterogeneous as our city is becoming can have representative government without the council reflecting this heterogeneity," exclaimed savings and loan manager Lawrence Wade during one POP public hearing. Many whites agreed with Wade, including state representative Jack McNeil, who urged the directorate to "insure representation for all people."[32]

Grudgingly, the conservatives agreed to some district representation but not a majority of the council seats. This was unacceptable to the black directors, but they were unsure of how to proceed. Sugarmon, Turner, and Willis demanded that all seats be chosen by district, while Lockard and Vasco Smith were willing to accept some at-large representation as long as it was in the minority. During a contentious hearing, white director Sam Cooper claimed that "enlightened" whites would be more than willing to vote for "qualified" black candidates. No doubt remembering the 1959 defeat of the Volunteer Ticket, Vasco Smith replied, "We don't stand a ghost of a chance in this town when it comes to running at-large."[33] Despite their feelings, no one wanted to see the Program of Progress fail, so both sides pulled away from the brink of contention. On February 24, the board voted to divide city government into an executive branch headed by an elected mayor and a thirteen-member council to pass laws, approve the budget, and approve the directors of city departments. The directorate also agreed that the majority of council seats, seven, would be chosen from districts, while the six remaining seats would be chosen at large by all voters.[34]

Although the POP board of directors rejected creating a city manager position, the board did debate and approve the creation of an optional chief administrative officer who would act as a mayoral assistant approved by the council. However, the executive would also have the power to dismiss the CAO without legislative consent.[35] Closely related to the CAO issue was the question of which branch would have the power to appoint and dismiss the heads of city departments. Many on the board wanted to give the mayor absolute power to hire and fire departmental leaders, while others wanted this to be strictly a legislative function. After several weeks of contentious debate, the board adopted the measure to require council approval for the appointment and removal of departmental directors.[36] By June 1966 the POP board had completed writing a draft proposal, which was enthusiastically adopted by the membership.[37] The next step was to secure city commission approval, which was required before the charter amendments could be offered to the voters. A copy was sent to each commission member, and Armour, Lane, Moore, and Sisson pledged their support for placing the amendments on the ballot, but Mayor Ingram was less committal. "I'm not going to vote for anything just because it has been proposed," the mayor snapped.[38]

Studying the measure, Ingram came to the conclusion that, as written, the POP gave too much power to the city council at the expense of the mayor. To that end, the mayor proposed several amendments to the charter, including the mayor serving as presiding officer of the council and eliminating the legislature's authority to hire office staff and seek legal advice.[39] The POP board would have none of this, believing that their adoption would enfeeble the checks and balances between the executive and legislative branches. However, they did agree to several of the mayor's other amendments. This did not mollify Ingram in the least, and he did all he could to delay the commission's approval. For example, during one meeting the mayor demanded that the charter amendment be read in its entirety, which took a half hour and strained the nerves of commissioners and citizens alike. When Ingram then began to argue that the POP charter was unconstitutional, Rabbi James Wax strode to the public microphone, and with a raised voice, rebuked the mayor for his truculence: "I respectfully suggest we get on with the business of a public hearing." The four hundred citizens who packed the commission chambers rose to their feet and clapped loudly as Rabbi Wax finished his remarks.[40]

In a last-ditch effort to derail the process, Ingram went on vacation when the commission was scheduled to vote on the charter amendments. Before he left for East Tennessee the mayor vowed to veto the legislation if the commission approved it while he was gone. Anxious to approve the measure so it could be placed on the November ballot, the commission defied the mayor and voted unanimously for the POP charter. After the vote a newspaper reporter noticed that the amendment granting the city council authority to hire staff and seek legal advice had been inadvertently left out. The commission quickly reconvened to add the missing section, but, after a consultation with the city attorney and POP leaders, it was decided not to insert the authority in the final document. It was believed that the council could simply hire staff by appropriating the necessary funds through the budget, and thus it was not necessary to include the language in the charter.[41] Designated Proposition 13 by the election commission, the POP charter amendments were thus placed on the ballot for the November congressional and state elections.

Shortly after returning from his vacation, Ingram formed an anti-POP organization called the Citizens for Good Government to defeat Proposition 13 and prove once and for all that he was the Bluff City's master. Joined by former mayor and congressman Walter Chandler, former commissioner John T. Dwyer, the junior chamber of commerce, and the Citizens' Council, the organization worked assiduously to sway voters against the new charter. Speaking across the city, Ingram charged that Proposition 13 would lead to higher taxes, corruption, and a return to machine-style politics.[42] The mayor's arguments may have had some merit, but they were often obscured by his boorish tactics. For example, he prepared a statement to explain his views but instead of issuing it as a press release or mailing it to the voters he used city funds to purchase advertising space in the two daily newspapers. The fact that he used public money to pay for the advertisement angered many, including the editors of the *Commercial Appeal*, who urged Memphians not to be "conned by the sham of the mayor's tax-paid 'open letter.'"[43]

Ingram's defense of the fifty-six-year-old commission form of government became increasingly shrill as the campaign wore on. Appearing on a local radio call-in program with Russell Sugarmon, the mayor referred to POP as the "program of plunderers" and suggested that only the wealthy stood to gain from the new charter. "I want to thank the mayor for promoting my economic status," Sugarmon dryly retorted. At one point Vasco Smith phoned in to offer his views, and Ingram snapped that he could not understand why African Americans were supporting a plan being promoted by former mayor Loeb. "Sometimes Henry Loeb is better than some of our so-called friends who come around and ask for our support and then double-cross us," Smith snapped back. The mayor argued that the new charter would provide, at most, two black seats on the new council, to which Sugarmon icily replied, "That's better than none out of five."[44]

Advocates for the POP charter far outnumbered its detractors. The broad-based coalition that had been created to draft the proposals not only held, but expanded during the referendum process. As already mentioned, Henry Loeb supported the change, as did his old rivals Claude Armour, William Farris, and Edmund Orgill. The chamber of commerce, Home Builders Association, Interdenominational Ministers Alliance, and several civic and neighborhood clubs, as well as leaders of the local Democratic and Republican parties, endorsed the charter amendments. In addition, Democratic congressman George Grider and his Republican opponent Dan Kuykendall both supported Proposition 13.[45] In newspaper advertisements they answered Ingram's charges in declaring that "these dedicated and proven city leaders would not recommend POP if they thought it would increase taxes, bring back vice and corruption or encourage ward politics."[46] Like Sugarmon and Smith, Loeb debated Ingram on local television, where he described the commission as a "five-headed, headless creature."[47]

By the summer of 1966 many white Americans were disenchanted with Lyndon Johnson and his Great Society programs. The outbreak of civil disturbances in several northern and western cities combined with the militant black power movement and growing dissatisfaction with the Vietnam War convinced thousands that liberal social policies had caused the nation great harm.[48] Republicans, of course, hoped to capitalize on these issues in the 1966 midterm congressional contests. In Memphis, the Shelby GOP nominated business executive Dan Kuykendall to challenge Democratic congressman George Grider in the fall election. Staunchly conservative and a veteran of the Goldwater campaign, Kuykendall opened his campaign by charging that Grider was "rubber-stamping what the federal extremists back in Washington want because it is politically expedient."[49] That Grider was a mere Johnson puppet responsible for the excesses of the federal government was Kuykendall's dominant theme, which he exploited at every opportunity.[50] The first-term congressman, unashamed of his record, emphasized his votes for Johnson's Great Society, particularly the school lunch program, aid to education, Medicare, and the War on Poverty.[51]

Aware of how attractive Kuykendall's anti–big government message was to many of his constituents, Grider invited Louisiana congressman and house majority whip Hale Boggs to speak at the opening of his campaign headquarters. After Boggs praised Grider for his "fine and impressive record," the candidate vowed to "end for all time this combination of ultraconservative and radical Republicanism which has brought so much grief to the South and to the nation."[52] Grider concentrated much of his attention on the black community, visiting several African American neighborhoods, knocking on doors and shaking hands. When he visited the Orange Mound community, for example, children became so excited by his visit that they followed his every move in what became an impromptu parade.[53] Despite the warm welcome he received in some black neighborhoods, Grider was in trouble and he knew it. This was especially apparent when the *Press-Scimitar* newspaper endorsed his Republican opponent for the congressional seat. In explaining why they were withdrawing their support of Grider, the editors echoed Kuykendall's campaign rhetoric. "He [Grider] has been instrumental in getting a number of federally-financed projects for Memphis—true. But this after all is our money which has been detoured by way of Washington—and it comes back discounted and with Big Brother's strings on it."[54] Kuykendall also received help from the national party when House minority leader Gerald R. Ford and Richard Nixon visited the Bluff City on behalf of his candidacy.[55]

As the congressional race began, A.W. Willis announced his reelection campaign for the district 5 seat in the state house of representatives.[56] Not long after Willis's announcement, Russell Sugarmon joined him in seeking the house district 11 position, and attorney J. O. Patterson, Jr., became the third African American candidate when he announced his candidacy for a house seat as well. The three candidates coordinated their campaigns and adopted the same platform, which included a state minimum wage law, abolition of capital punishment, increased funding for the War on Poverty program, and passage of a state civil rights statute.[57] Their candidacies were accepted by white Memphians as a matter of course; Sugarmon and Willis were not even opposed by other candidates, while an unknown African American independent challenged Patterson.[58]

Only twice, in 1880 and 1884, had a Republican been elected to represent Memphis in Congress.[59] The third time came when Kuykendall upset Grider's reelection bid to become the city's first GOP congressman in the twentieth century. The defeat was overwhelming, with Grider receiving 42,716 votes to Kuykendall's 46,578.⁶⁰ The Republicans were successful in marshalling voters in several white sections of the city, including suburban East Memphis, while the turnout in the black Democratic wards was much lighter than expected.⁶¹ Democrats fared better in the Tennessee house races. Eleven of the sixteen seats in the Shelby delegation remained in the hands of the Democrats, including those held by Willis, Sugarmon, and Patterson, who easily won election to the state house of representatives. However, five Republicans were elected to the house from Shelby County for the first time since the nineteenth century. Delighted with the outcome, Lewis Donelson exclaimed to reporters that the local GOP had "proved that Tennessee and Shelby County are two-party territory."⁶² Republicans had been making this declaration since Eisenhower had carried the state a decade before, but this time they were right. For Memphis, the 1966 election was a watershed moment in which the Republicans achieved a kind of political parity with the Democrats, and a two-party system was revealed to have taken root.

In nearly every section of the city Memphians cast ballots in support of Proposition 13. Support was strong in the white neighborhoods of South Memphis and Midtown as well as East Memphis. In one East Memphis precinct, for example, 1,026 votes were cast for POP while a mere 270 ballots were registered against the proposal. African Americans also voted overwhelmingly for Proposition 13. Of the ballots cast in predominately black precincts, 73 percent favored POP. In the end, 57,895 ballots were cast for the new charter, while 39,554 citizens voted against the measure.⁶³ "This is terrific, just terrific," an exhausted Downing Pryor declared to the newspapers. Citizens across the city rejoiced at the adoption of the new charter, and there was much to be happy about.

The overhauled government did separate the legislative and executive functions into two branches and did try to establish checks and balances which had been lacking under the commission. The mayor was granted full authority to dictate the operation of the city by appointing the directors of city departments and members of city regulatory boards and had the power to veto legislation. Citizens were given the power to initiate a referendum to recall the mayor if 10 percent of the voting population signed a petition. The council was granted the power to pass ordinances, approve budgets, establish the tax rate, and approve the mayor's departmental appointments, and it could override the mayor's veto. In addition, city employees were forbidden from participating in political campaigns.⁶⁴ But it was far from perfect. In reality the mayor was granted too much power over city departments and the council too little. The only real oversight given the council was through control of the budget. Perhaps the greatest weakness was the inability of the council to hire its own staff or seek legal counsel. This, in effect, made them dependent on the mayor and prevented them from being a coequal branch of municipal government. As we shall see, this would have grave consequences not only for the Bluff City, but for the entire nation.

Under the newly adopted charter, an election was scheduled for October 1967 to choose the new mayor and city council. Even before Proposition 13 was ratified, Ingram had stated he would run for reelection regardless of the outcome of the charter battle. When, in early June, he made it official, several local leaders scrambled to oppose him.[65] Lane was the first, announcing his candidacy on June 5. Stressing the need for tranquility in government affairs, the public services commissioner declared that "petty discord and personal conflict must not be allowed to characterize city hall in the new administration."[66] Harmony became a main theme in the campaign, echoed by many of the candidates, including Henry Loeb, public works commissioner Pete Sisson, and Shelby County sheriff William N. Morris, each of whom sought the mayoralty.[67] They were eventually joined by a lone female candidate, Mrs. O. E. Oxley, who co-owned the Memphis Flying Service with her husband.[68] With such a crowded field, it was possible that no candidate would receive the required 51 percent of the vote to be declared the winner. If that happened then a runoff election would be held between the two top vote getters, according to the provisions of the new charter.

A. W. Willis was interested in running for mayor as well, and, with five white men in the race, the possibility existed that he could receive far less than a majority of votes but still win in the runoff.[69] After several weeks of deliberation, Willis announced his decision to run at James Lawson's Centenary Methodist Church. Speaking before an overflow crowd, Willis explained that his candidacy was a "declaration of faith in the basic decency of the people of Memphis . . . The mere fact of my election would move Memphis to the forefront among those cities which have shown concern for the betterment of all their people."[70] Willis was strongly supported by Sugarmon, Vasco Smith, and A. Maceo Walker, but his candidacy did not electrify the black community as the 1959 Volunteer Ticket had.[71] In fact the *Tri-State Defender* declined to endorse Willis, recommending Ingram instead.[72] In hopes of compensating for this, Willis reached out to younger voters. In a widely distributed pamphlet Willis declared, "[Y]ou are the hope of the future, you are the leaders of tomorrow . . . We need YOU to canvas your neighborhood. We need YOU to distribute campaign literature. We need YOU to urge voters to go to the polls. We Need YOU to elect A.W. WILLIS!"[73]

Willis's candidacy was crippled, however, when a rumor began circulating that he had received thirty-five thousand dollars from Loeb to run for mayor in order to siphon black support from Ingram and insure the mayor's defeat. "I'm too tight to give money to anybody," said Loeb, making light of the charge.[74] Willis also used humor in dispelling the rumor. At a campaign stop he explained that since he had not yet received the cash Loeb must have "sent it by a blind turtle. While it was wandering around one of Commissioner Lane's inspectors put Mayor Ingram's sticker on his back. Then he fell down one of Commissioner Sisson's potholes. After he escaped he fled to the county with Sheriff Morris' deputies hot on his trail. Mrs. O. E. Oxley is watching the airplanes if he tries to leave town."[75]

Unfortunately for Willis, satire didn't work. Ingram repeated the insinuation, and many came to believe that he was merely a stalking horse for Loeb.[76] For example, the Negro United Baptist Churches Association appealed to Willis to drop out of the race because "it is impossible for you ... to become mayor at this time."[77] In hopes of shoring up black support, Willis invited the powerful African American congressman John Conyers of Detroit to speak at a rally and make television appearances on his behalf.[78] Ingram, meanwhile, continued to make progress with the black electorate. The mayor campaigned heavily in African American neighborhoods and received the endorsement of O. Z. Evers's Unity League organization.[79] This support included the distribution of an offensive pamphlet on behalf of Ingram that pictured Willis sitting on the lap of Henry Loeb. In the crude drawing Loeb asked, "Boy ... do you think you could fool 20,000 negroes to vote for you?" The Willis caricature replied, "Ya-sa. Ya-sar, you know negroes are full of race pride now, and we can easily suck them in, Ya-sa the sell-out would be easy."[80] Angry and frustrated, Willis lashed out at the mayor, accusing him of "slipping into communities under shadow of darkness ... the way it was done in Nazi Germany by Hitler ..."[81]

At the same time the prickly relationship between Armour and Ingram erupted into open warfare when the mayor appointed a special investigator to look into allegations of police brutality. "I'm not going to be harassed by a little would-be dictator who does nothing but mess everything up ...," Armour roared as he announced plans to retire in October.[82] Vowing to defeat Ingram in the upcoming election, Armour apologized for being a part of a "do-nothing administration."[83] The mayor was equally acidic. "The statements attributed to Commissioner Armour sound like the tantrum of a small child," he replied.[84] This war of words did nothing to strengthen Ingram's political position, as it reminded voters of his slash-and-burn style of governing.

As the mayoral candidates began making public appearances and issuing platforms, Memphians read in their newspapers and watched on television as riots erupted in several American cities. During the summer months violent disturbances took place in Tampa, Florida, Cincinnati, Buffalo, New York, Boston, and Newark, New Jersey.[85] The worst riot took place in Detroit, where, during five days of violence, forty-three people were killed and $50 million worth of property damage was done.[86] A sense of dread engulfed the Bluff City as citizens and public officials alike reacted viscerally to what they read and watched. Then, on July 27, Molotov cocktails were thrown at a restaurant and grocery store causing minor fire damage.[87]

Faced with what appeared to be the opening round of a civil disturbance, the mayor and police commissioner set aside their animosity and requested the assistance of Governor Ellington, who ordered three thousand National Guard troops into Memphis.[88] "Let me dispel the rumors that there is imminent danger. We are concerned that rumors of violence might lead to violence," stated Armour as the guardsmen rumbled into Memphis from Mississippi's Camp Shelby. After several days of patrolling the streets of Memphis, the guard units departed the city, but the uneasiness remained.[89] Loeb seized upon the fear of civil unrest and made it the centerpiece of his election bid. At a campaign stop he vowed that Memphis "will have law and order . . . If there is a disturbance, whoever is involved will go to jail."[90] It was not difficult for Loeb to adopt such a hard line because he knew he would receive few, if any, African American votes. Given the understandable fear that many had, Loeb's law-and-order campaign naturally resonated with many Memphians and energized his candidacy.

Confusion reigned as voters went to the polls on October 5. Campaign workers, unaware that the law now required them to stay at least one hundred feet from a polling place, mingled with voters, causing disorder at several precincts. At the Dave Wells Community Center police were called to break up an unruly crowd near the entrance to the polling place, while at another precinct an Ingram worker accosted a Willis supporter.[91] Despite the distractions, 144,888 citizens cast ballots in the city races. The combination of a high turnout and the large number of political aspirants insured that no single candidate won 50 percent of the vote. Henry Loeb received 33 percent while 24.9 percent of the vote went to Ingram. Morris came in third with 30,355 votes, fourth place went to Willis who received 17,575, and Lane came in a distant fifth with a mere 8,439 ballots cast for him. The 46,729 votes cast for Loeb and the 35,852 ballots Ingram received meant that the two front-runners would face each other in the runoff election scheduled for early November.[92]

No one was more devastated by the outcome than A. W. Willis. When the ballots came in and it was clear he had lost, the incumbent legislator expressed profound shock that "the people who could most benefit, the Negro people, could not grasp the problems." In precincts with a black majority, Ingram solidly defeated the incumbent legislator. For example, in ward 24, which had 2,147 black registered voters, the mayor received nearly 200 more votes than Willis. Loeb, meanwhile, received strong support in the white sections of the city. In one East Memphis precinct 645 ballots were cast for Loeb, while the mayor received only 90 votes.[93] The officers and members of the influential Shelby County Democratic Club were equally overwhelmed by the election's outcome. As the runoff campaign began, club president Vasco Smith announced that they would remain neutral in the race between Ingram and Loeb. "The segregationist philosophy of one candidate (Loeb) caused us to look on him with disfavor while the continued obvious lack of respect for the entire Negro community by the other candidate (Ingram) through the dissemination of slanderous rumors and degrading literature makes it impossible for a self-respecting group such as ours to endorse him," Smith explained.[94]

During the month-long campaign Ingram repeatedly emphasized that he was responsible for creating thirty-four thousand new jobs and obtaining twenty-nine new industries for Memphis. In contrast, the mayor argued that Loeb had raised taxes and that his policies had driven several businesses out of the city. "He talks out of both sides of his mouth. He talks of economy yet the number of employees in his department increased one third when he was commissioner." Loeb countered that Ingram wasted taxpayers' money by approving fifty thousand dollars to celebrate the city's 150th anniversary and allowing shoddy construction materials on the new city hall building which had to be replaced. Harking back to the early 1960s, Loeb declared that when he "was mayor, other cities had trouble but Memphis had none. White and Negro worked to keep the peace, the cornerstone of which is law and order."[95]

Voter turnout was slightly higher, 57.3 percent of registered citizens, for the runoff election than it had been the previous month. The vote split almost completely along racial lines, with Loeb receiving a majority of white ballots cast while most of the votes for Ingram came from African Americans. As a result, Loeb defeated Ingram by over 11,000 votes. Despite the acrimony of A. W. Willis and Vasco Smith, of the 66,561 ballots cast for Ingram at least 40,000 of them came from African Americans. For Loeb, the majority of the 78,379 votes he received came from white citizens. Reading the election results made it clear that racial polarization remained deep-seated in Memphis. Loeb seemed to sense this when, on election night, he expressed the need to heal "divisions in the city government" and bring the community together.[96]

Thirteen city council members were also elected in the October regular election and the November runoff. Like the Program of Progress board, the newly elected council was a true cross-section of the community. Downing Pryor was chosen by the voters, as were well-known Republicans Lewis Donelson and Robert James. Several Democrats were also elected, as was one woman, conservative civic leader Gwen Awsumb. Three African Americans were also elected from majority black districts—insurance salesman Fred Davis, Reverend James L. Netters of Mt. Vernon Baptist Church, and state representative J. O. Patterson, Jr.[97]

Shortly after the election, the Memphis novelist and historian Shelby Foote, then at work on the third and final volume of his acclaimed history of the American Civil War, ran into his old friend Ned Cook, who had managed Loeb's successful campaign. During their conversation Foote said he hoped they would "handle this Negro problem well, it is really important." Cook explained that if they came to Henry "with the right kind of attitude" their concerns would be heard. Looking back years later, Foote remembered being dumbfounded by Cook's attitude. "Well, that about knocked me out. In other words, if he's got his hat in his hands we'll give him almost anything we can. Otherwise nothing. And that was a danger flag flying, right there."[98] As the year 1968 began, the celebrated writer had no idea just how right he was.

On a cold and wet February afternoon Echol Cole and Robert Walker, Jr., members of a sanitation crew working in East Memphis, climbed into the back of their garbage truck to make the trip to a city dump. The truck they were riding in was shaped like a barrel; garbage was thrown into the sides and then crushed by a hydraulic press into the back of the vehicle. Purchased by Henry Loeb, who was then public works commissioner, in 1957, the trucks were despised by the workers, who believed them to be unsafe. Cole and Walker positioned themselves between the hydraulic press and the back of the vehicle as the truck rumbled through the streets of East Memphis. When they reached the intersection of Colonial and Quince, a shovel fell onto some wires, shorting the truck's electrical system. All of a sudden the packing unit began moving toward the two men. Hearing the mechanism click on, crew chief Willie Crain slammed on the brakes, jumped out of the vehicle, and hit the stop button. It didn't work. The compressor kept operating and eventually crushed Cole and Walker to death.[99]

For the sanitation department's rank and file, most of whom were African American, the deaths of their fellow workers was the latest in a series of outrages that stretched back a decade to when Loeb was public works commissioner. Terrible working conditions, faulty equipment, and low wages were the standard lot for sanitation workers in Memphis. Most men earned a mere seventy dollars per week, making them the very definition of the working poor. To make matters worse, if it rained in the morning, even briefly, the men would be sent home with only two hours' pay.[100] Tired of this treatment, sanitation workers walked off the job in 1963, but the demonstration ended abruptly when the city fired some of the strikers. Nevertheless, the men organized a union and affiliated with the American Federation of State, County and Municipal Employees (AFSCME). In 1966 members of Local 1733 voted to strike, but the union backed down when the city obtained an injunction making the strike illegal.[101]

Now in the late winter of 1968, with the deaths of Cole and Walker fresh on their minds, the men were not inclined to back down again. Negotiations hastily took place between union president T. O. Jones and public works director Charles Blackburn, but nothing came of them. Faced with official indifference, the workers resolved to fight. A work stoppage was proposed, and the men voted overwhelmingly to stay home until working conditions improved. For years the plight of these oft-abused men had been invisible to most Memphians, white and black. That was about to change.[102]

On Tuesday, February 13, the second day of the strike, eight hundred workers marched downtown to city hall to present their grievances to the mayor and city council. City hall was not big enough to accommodate such a large crowd, so the group reconvened at the nearby city auditorium. As the proceedings began, Loeb couldn't believe his ears. These formerly docile men, who had never dared challenge him before, no longer had the "right kind of attitude." As he made his position known, the men jeered, booed, and laughed at him. "City employees can't strike against their employer ... You are in effect breaking the law!"[103] As the catcalls and laughter increased, Loeb began to lose his temper. "You are putting my back up against the wall, and I am not going to budge." His temper now out of control, the mayor barked, "I promise you the garbage is going to be picked up. Bet on it." He then stormed out of the auditorium.[104]

The majority of white Memphians couldn't believe this was happening either. Most whites, if they thought about it at all, were convinced that the Bluff City had handled the social changes of the past decade rather well. It was hardly a peaceful transition, but compared to Little Rock, Birmingham, Philadelphia, Mississippi, and many other southern localities Memphis had, in their minds, lived up to its image of a racially moderate, progressive city. After all, Memphis had desegregated its public facilities and elected African Americans to public office. Why, some thought, were they not satisfied with this? Of course, black Memphians saw things quite differently. Fully aware that discrimination and inequality still existed in Memphis, many came to feel that the sanitation workers' struggle for higher wages and better working conditions was no different from the war against Jim Crow. Consequently, the NAACP adopted a resolution on February 15 offering "its full support to the sanitation workers in their demands for decent wages, better working conditions, and the type [of] job security offered other city employees . . ."[105] They soon joined with local black ministers and the union in organizing marches and mass meetings to put pressure on Loeb and maintain worker unity.[106]

In the days following his humiliating encounter with the workers, Loeb went through the motions of negotiating with union representatives, but he had no intention of accepting the union's demands, which included a pay increase, a written contract, dues check-off procedure to deduct union fees from the men's paychecks, equal promotion opportunities, and a grievance procedure.[107] The city council, meanwhile, did not know what to do. The newly adopted charter clearly stated that "the mayor shall make all contracts authorized by the city council," which suggested they had a role to play in the negotiations.[108] The council did have a committee on public works chaired by Fred Davis, and it was there that the workers pinned their hopes for a settlement. Ten days into the strike Davis convened a hearing to listen to the men's grievances in hopes a settlement could be found.[109]

The proceedings quickly deteriorated when seven hundred workers jammed the council chambers but were prevented from speaking by their union representatives. The "men are the union and the union is the men," snapped AFSCME president Jerry Wurf. This was not what Davis had in mind, and, when discourse became impossible, he adjourned the meeting. The workers, however, refused to leave. For hours the men lingered in city hall, laughing and clapping as speakers castigated Loeb and the white power structure. At one point volunteers brought food for the workers while nervous council members looked on and debated what to do.[110] Wanting to end the demonstration, committee members James Netters, Lewis Donelson, and Davis decided to adopt a pro-union resolution. "The recommendation of our committee to the council will be that the city recognize the union as the collective bargaining agent and that there be some form of dues check-off," Davis announced to a cheering crowd. A special meeting of the council was hastily scheduled for the next day to vote on the committee's resolution, and this ended the sit-in. Jubilantly the men disbursed, believing that victory would come in a matter of hours.[111]

But it didn't. Prevented by the charter from seeking independent legal and political advice, the majority of council members blithely accepted Loeb's position that only the executive branch could represent the city in contract negotiations. In a closed-door session the morning after the sit-in, the white majority rejected Davis's resolution and substituted a statement that said, in part, that the "council recognizes that the mayor has the sole authority to act in behalf of the city . . ." Later that day at the auditorium, the substitute resolution was read to the men and then adopted by a majority of the council. After the vote was taken, council members skulked out of the building surrounded by a phalanx of police officers. Left behind was an angry group of workers who felt betrayed by both the council's resolution and the cowardly manner in which it was adopted.[112]

Anger spread like wildfire among the workers and leaders who had no visible way of expressing the sense of bitterness they felt. It was quickly decided that the men would march from the auditorium to downtown Memphis's other large gathering place, the Church of God in Christ's Mason Temple, in order to protest the council's action and channel their raw emotions into a constructive direction. When the men poured out of the auditorium they were met by a cordon of police who blocked their way. Warily, strike leaders approached the police and begged to let the men march. After consulting Loeb and police director Frank Holloman, the police allowed the march to go forward. The crowd lurched forward as police squad cars inched towards them to keep them in line and moving.

The marchers ignored these provocative actions until a patrol car ran over the foot of strike sympathizer Gladys Carpenter. Hearing Carpenter scream in pain, several marchers surrounded the car and began rocking it back and forth. Police rushed from their squad cars and began spraying Mace on anyone in their line of sight. As marchers blindly scattered, coughing and gagging, officers began whacking them with nightsticks. Within a few minutes chaos reigned in downtown Memphis.[113] A handful of demonstrators were arrested, but the majority of marchers eventually made their way to Mason Temple. The acrid fumes of Mace dissipated later that day, but the resolve of the strikers never wavered. For many African Americans, the police riot of February 23 was a turning point in their view of the strike. Thousands rushed to support the workers who had not done so before. Wishing to take advantage of this outpouring of goodwill, strike leaders, most notably Reverend James Lawson of Centenary Methodist Church, formed Citizens on the Move for Equality (COME). The new organization coordinated with AFSCME and the NAACP in devising a broad-based strategy to pressure the city into a settlement. In addition to daily marches and evening rallies, a boycott of downtown stores was also organized.[114]

The events of February 22 and 23 also had a profound effect on white Memphians. Dismay hardened into anger as they watched the strikers occupy the seat of government and then, in their eyes, provoke violence in the streets of Memphis. Most refused to either see the strike in racial terms or condemn the police for the disorder. Suddenly the racial line was drawn more starkly than it ever had been before as whites rallied around the mayor as fiercely as their black neighbors did the sanitation workers.[115] On one occasion Loeb waved a handful of letters and declared, "Look here . . . five hundred letters supporting me and five letters against. The people don't want the union." For example, John K. Wood, manager of the White Rose Industrial Laundry, wrote to "commend you on the outstanding job you have done thus far in handling the garbage strike and the gangster type individuals sent down here to stir our citizenry up . . . I'm proud to have helped elect a mayor with such integrity and sticktoitiviness."[116] On February 22, WMC-TV asked its viewers to respond by telephone to the following question: "Would you favor arbitration by a neutral third party to resolve the garbage strike?" Of the 6,882 respondents, 76 percent of them voted no.[117]

As the calls and letters poured into the mayor's office, Loeb sensed an opportunity to revive his long-standing ambition to become governor. It will be remembered that Loeb had briefly run for governor in 1962 only to withdraw his name before the filing deadline. He had done so primarily because his staunch defense of segregation had become irrelevant as schools and public facilities in Memphis were integrated. By taking a hard line with African American workers, Loeb ostensibly believed he was convincing white Memphians and their brethren across the state that he was strong enough to deal with the disorder and civil unrest that seemed to be plaguing the nation in 1968.

Meanwhile the strike continued into March with no real movement on either side. COME's daily marches, nightly mass meetings, and economic boycott continued, but Loeb refused to budge. As the stalemate dragged on, James Lawson invited Martin Luther King, Jr., to Memphis in order to further embolden the strikers, increase pressure on Loeb, and bring national attention to the workers' struggle. King, in the midst of planning massive demonstrations to call attention to American poverty, understood from Lawson's reports that the plight of Memphis sanitation workers was a perfect example of the invisible poverty that he wished to highlight in his upcoming Poor People's Campaign. Consequently, over the vociferous objections of his staff, the civil rights leader agreed to come to Memphis.[118]

Arriving on March 18, King spoke to twenty-five thousand people at Mason Temple, where he had appeared in 1959 on behalf of the Volunteer Ticket. The large and enthusiastic crowd overwhelmed him as it had nine years before: "As I came in tonight, I . . . said . . . they really have a great movement here in Memphis." King urged the assembled crowd to "escalate the struggle" by organizing a "general work stoppage" in the Bluff City. A thunderous roar enveloped the temple as Dr. King ended his speech. Turning away from the podium, King whispered to himself, "I ought to come back and lead a march." James Lawson heard what the civil rights leader said, and he quickly conferred with Andrew Young and several other SCLC aides about the possibility of King leading a demonstration in Memphis. It was agreed that a successful protest would be helpful for both the Memphis movement and the Poor People's Campaign, so it was decided that King would return to the Bluff City.[119] The protest was scheduled for Friday, March 22, but as the city prepared for Dr. King's arrival, the unthinkable happened. Sixteen inches of snow fell on Memphis, paralyzing the city and making a mass demonstration impossible.[120] When the snow melted, organizers settled on Tuesday, March 28, as the day of the mass protest that many hoped would finally end the strike.

It was a warm spring morning when Dr. King's plane landed at the Memphis airport. While the civil rights leader disembarked from his plane, thousands of Memphians poured into downtown, impatiently awaiting his arrival. As King slowly made his way through the city, organizers began losing control of the crowd. The number of people was far more than Lawson and the other leaders had expected. A cadre of volunteer marshals had been recruited to direct the marchers, but they were overwhelmed by the size of the crowd. As protesters milled about, waiting for Dr. King, an unfounded rumor spread amongst them that police had killed a female student during a demonstration at Hamilton High School earlier that morning. Event organizers meanwhile began handing out paper signs stapled to three-foot-long wooden sticks for demonstrators to carry during the march. Volunteers soon noticed that groups of young people were tearing the paper signs off the sticks and brandishing them like weapons. Many grew apprehensive as they mulled over the rumor and watched the students wave their newfound clubs in the air, yelling, "Black power."[121]

Arriving at Clayborn Temple near the intersection of Linden and Hernando, King was dismayed at what he saw. Instead of a disciplined cadre of marchers, he saw only a mob. After a brief discussion with King and his aides, Lawson agreed to start the march while King waited until some semblance of order was established. With great difficulty Lawson got the crowd moving, and soon King and his aides positioned themselves at the head of the march. The crowd snaked down Hernando, turned onto Beale Street, and then shifted toward Main. As the head of the line approached Main Street, King and the others heard the sound of glass breaking. Observers soon reported to King and Lawson that some in the march were throwing bricks, smashing windows, and looting stores. At first King tried to continue the march, but as the violence escalated it was decided to abandon the demonstration. With the help of four police officers on motorcycles, King and several of his aides retreated to a nearby hotel. Lawson then borrowed a police bullhorn and ordered all marchers to return to Clayborn Temple.[122]

As Lawson tried to redirect the march and King motored away from the chaos, police waded into the crowd, beating demonstrators and looters alike. Many began to run, some with stolen goods but many without. One such protester was sixteen-year-old Larry Payne, a Mitchell High School student who fled downtown when the march turned ugly. As he headed back to his residence at the Fowler Homes housing development, police received word that a gang of looters were entering the area. Seeing Payne run into Fowler Homes, police followed him into a darkened basement. Assuming he was a looter, the officers ordered him to come out of the basement. As he did, one of them shot Payne with a shotgun. He died instantly.[123] Meanwhile in Nashville, the general assembly, frightened by the news reports from Memphis, passed a law giving Tennessee mayors the power to impose curfews during civil unrest. Loeb quickly took advantage of the measure, declaring martial law while Governor Ellington sent National Guard troops into the city. Sporadic violence would linger for several days, but the city never experienced anything like Detroit or Newark. The curfew was finally lifted on April 1, and the majority of National Guard troops left the Bluff City.[124]

Memphians, watching their city occupied by soldiers patrolling the streets in armored personnel carriers and brandishing rifles, couldn't believe what was happening. And, of course, they reacted differently based, for the most part, on the color of their skin. To African Americans, it appeared that once again Loeb and the police had overreacted, employing brutal force against strike supporters. They recognized that some unruly elements had disrupted the march and caused property damage, but it was felt by many that the official response went far beyond quelling a minor disturbance. From their perspective the death of Larry Payne was the most egregious example of police brutality. Whites, of course, interpreted the events of March 28 quite differently. For them the disturbance that marred Dr. King's march was a perfect example of the so-called civil rights movement showing its true colors. See, many thought, blacks didn't want equality and justice; they only wanted to destroy white society. As for Larry Payne, it was sad that a young man lost his life, but looters deserved little mercy.

Dr. King, hunkered down in the Holiday Inn Rivermont with his staff, was humiliated by the disturbance. Never before had an SCLC-led protest devolved into a riot, and the media pounced on this fact with gleeful abandon. In newspaper pages and television broadcasts commentators attacked King for fomenting violence and then running away like a coward. Politicians also joined the fray, questioning whether King could control the thousands of demonstrators he planned to bring to Washington for the Poor People's Campaign. The criticism stung King, who, after holding a press conference, left Memphis with no plans to return. But after intensive discussions with his staff in Atlanta, King accepted that he must return to Memphis to salvage the Poor People's Campaign as well as his own reputation. "Either the movement lives or dies in Memphis," King commented to a strike organizer when he returned to Memphis on April 3.[125]

On the same day King landed in Memphis, city attorney Frank Gianotti filed a bill of complaint in federal court requesting a temporary injunction barring King and other out-of-state residents "from organizing in or engaging in a massive parade or march in the City of Memphis." Judge Bailey Brown issued the injunction for a ten-day period but also told the defense he was prepared to hear their motion to lift the injunction.[126] Encouraged by Brown's ruling, Lawson called Lucius Burch and asked him to represent King and COME in oral arguments hastily scheduled for the next day. Reluctantly, Burch agreed, and he met with King shortly after his arrival.[127] As Burch and the rest of the legal team worked through the night preparing to go to court, an exhausted King made his way to Mason Temple to speak to the men whose struggle for dignity had brought him to Memphis in the first place.

The doctor didn't want to go. Worn out and wanting to relax, he initially sent his chief lieutenant, Ralph Abernathy, to the gathering, but the enthusiastic crowd convinced him that they wanted only to hear King. And so he went. A spring thunderstorm was rolling across the Bluff City as Dr. King arrived at Mason Temple. "Something is happening in Memphis," he began. What followed was a brilliant speech in which he reminded the audience that "[n]othing could be more tragic than to stop at this point, in Memphis. We've got to see it through." But then he suggested that "it doesn't really matter to me now. Because I've been to the mountaintop . . . And I've seen the Promised Land. I might not get there with you. But I want you to know tonight that we as a people will get to the Promised Land!" The crowd shouted in joy at King's promise as he turned from the microphone and slumped back in his chair.[128]

On the evening of April 4 police director Frank Holloman was sitting at his desk when the phone rang. Not long before, his intelligence office had reported that Dr. King had been shot while leaning over the balcony of the Lorraine Motel.[129] Picking up the receiver, Holloman cringed at what he heard. Dr. King was dead. As he listened, he nervously recorded the details on a notepad. "Died of a bullet wound—the neck which traveled from the front right to the back and slightly downward."[130] Stunned disbelief mingled with anger as word spread across the Bluff City. Groups of young African Americans flooded the streets of the inner city throwing Molotov cocktails and sniping at the police, but most black Memphians refused to give in to vengeance. Sporadic violence continued through the night, but it never evolved into a full-scale riot. White Memphians, protected from the violence by the police and reactivated National Guard, were also shocked by Dr. King's murder. However, unlike their black neighbors, many were far more disturbed by the fact that the killing had taken place in Memphis than by the actual death of a great American leader.[131]

Ensconced in city hall, Mayor Loeb reacted much the same. As the violence subsided and a nervous calm descended over the city, the mayor was increasingly harassed by almost everyone to settle the damn strike. President Johnson sent a federal mediator to Memphis, while an interracial group of religious leaders marched to Loeb's office and demanded that he end Memphis's nightmare. "What we have come here for this morning, sir, is to appeal to you out of the fervor of our hearts that this city shall be ruled with justice, and justice for all . . . I would remind you most respectfully, sir, that there are laws greater than the laws of Memphis and Tennessee—the laws of God," intoned Rabbi James Wax to an incredulous Henry Loeb.[132]

Pressure increased when, on April 8, the slain civil rights leader's widow, Coretta Scott King, led thousands, including Hollywood celebrities Bill Cosby and Harry Belafonte, on a memorial march through downtown Memphis. Covered extensively by the national media, many in the crowd carried signs proclaiming: "Honor King—End Racism."[133] Substantive negotiations meanwhile continued around the clock at the Hotel Claridge. On April 16 an agreement was finally reached that increased workers' pay, recognized the union, and implemented a dues check-off procedure.[134] It had come at a horrendous cost, but the men had beaten Henry Loeb and the combined forces of the Memphis city government. Mayor Loeb, whose stubbornness and political manipulation had prolonged the strike, was widely blamed for Dr. King's murder, even more than the true assassin. When a reporter from the *Atlantic Monthly* asked the mayor in 1970 how Dr. King's death had affected Memphis, Loeb glared at him and angrily replied, "I don't have any opinion."[135]

The city itself did not escape blame. The national media was often vicious in its descriptions of Memphis, none more so than *Time* magazine. In its coverage of the assassination, the magazine wrote: "In causation and execution, the murder of Martin Luther King was both a symbol and a symptom of the nation's malaise. The proximate cause of his death was, ironically, a minor labor dispute in a Southern backwater: the two-month-old strike of 1,300 predominately Negro garbage collectors in the decaying Mississippi river town of Memphis. The plight of the sanitation workers, caused by the refusal of Memphis' intransigent white Mayor Henry Loeb to meet their modest wage and compensation demands, first attracted and finally eradicated Dr. King, the conqueror of Montgomery, Birmingham and Selma."[136] In other words, it was Memphis, rather than the man who pulled the trigger, that killed Dr. King. These snide comments seeped into the bones of average Memphians, white and black, altering how they saw themselves and their community. A cloak of guilt and failure hung limply over the Bluff City for decades. Economically Memphis was left behind, as much of the rest of the South was transformed into the vibrant "Sunbelt." In 1978 the *Wall Street Journal* described the city as "the Sunbelt's dark spot."[137]

The sanitation strike and Dr. King's murder did more than simply hamstring Memphis's psyche. Suspicion, fear, and even hatred now penetrated into nearly every corner of the city. The relationship between black and white Memphians had hardly been a perfect one before the strike, but at least there had been some semblance of a dialogue and occasional instances of cooperation. This tentative sense of unity evaporated as neither side could quite forgive the other. When the warmth of spring evolved into the heat of summer, a new city began to emerge. Angrier and far more racially polarized, this alternate Memphis began to adjust to its changed circumstances as the rest of the nation began to focus its attention on the upcoming presidential contest.

President Lyndon Johnson was heartsick. His Great Society was in shambles due to a white backlash against civil rights while the nation seemed to be tearing itself apart over Vietnam. In early 1968 Senator Eugene McCarthy, an antiwar Democrat from Minnesota, nearly defeated Johnson in the New Hampshire primary, garnering 42 percent of the vote to the president's 49 percent. Emboldened by McCarthy's upset, New York senator Robert Kennedy also declared his candidacy for the Democratic presidential nomination.[138] Disheartened by these developments, the president made a fateful decision. During a televised speech announcing a bombing halt in Southeast Asia, Johnson announced that he was withdrawing from the 1968 presidential contest. "I shall not seek, and I will not accept, the nomination of my party for another term as your president," he explained to a stunned nation.[139] Most political leaders either ridiculed the president or praised his unselfishness. Former vice president Richard Nixon snidely called Johnson a "dropout," while Tennessee senator Albert Gore declared that "this is the greatest contribution President Johnson could have made toward unity."[140] Arizona senator Barry Goldwater, Johnson's 1964 Republican opponent, sniffed that when he heard the news he "went and had another drink."[141]

Vice President Hubert Humphrey, who was at that moment visiting Mexico on a diplomatic mission, expressed sadness at Johnson's decision but refused to discuss the possibility of his own presidential bid.[142] When Humphrey arrived back in the United States, an enthusiastic crowd greeted him at the airport and urged him to run for president.[143] After mulling over his options for three weeks, Humphrey announced his candidacy on April 27. His decision electrified pro-Vietnam party regulars who were disenchanted with Kennedy's and McCarthy's antiwar insurgencies. Refusing to enter the remaining state primaries, the vice president hoped to stay above the fray and appeal to both wings of the increasingly fractious Democratic Party. Humphrey's chances for the nomination improved when Robert Kennedy was murdered in June after winning the California primary.[144] As Democrats mourned the loss of one of their most dynamic leaders, the Republicans rallied around its most controversial politician.

Since 1966 Richard Nixon had quietly worked to secure the 1968 GOP nomination. By the time the convention opened in Miami, Nixon was the clear front-runner, although Nelson Rockefeller and California governor Ronald Reagan hoped to wrest away enough delegates from the former vice president to become the nominee. Southern delegates in particular were enamored with Reagan, and consequently Nixon courted them assiduously. Meeting with several of them, including Memphians Lewis Donelson, Winfield Dunn, and Dan Kuykendall, Nixon pledged to return authority to local school boards, overturn controversial Supreme Court decisions, curb lawlessness, and restrict the application of the Voting Rights Act by establishing a federal literacy test for voter registration. Impressed with Nixon's promises, many southern delegates abandoned Reagan before the balloting began.[145]

Ultimately the strategy worked. Nixon easily won the GOP nomination, crushing Reagan and Rockefeller on the first ballot.[146] In his acceptance speech Nixon repeated much of what he had said to southern Republicans. "The first civil right of every American is to be free from domestic violence," he declared. He also promised to strengthen law and order throughout the land and excoriated the Supreme Court for weakening "the peace forces against the criminal forces."[147] Meanwhile the Tennessee delegation, along with other southerners, remained enamored with the California governor, and they tried to pressure Nixon into selecting him as his running mate. "I personally find Reagan a highly acceptable choice for the vice presidency," Winfield Dunn explained to the press.[148] Nixon did not agree. Instead he tapped Maryland governor Spiro Agnew, a political unknown with conservative credentials, to be the vice presidential nominee.[149] Despite Nixon's checkered past, most delegates were pleased with his nomination, and this feeling of comity was carried back to their home communities where they began the work of the fall campaign. United in a common effort, most Republicans believed that victory would be theirs in November. The Democrats were not so fortunate.

In the wake of Robert Kennedy's death, delegations from throughout the country were split between supporters of antiwar candidate Eugene MCarthy and administration spokesman Hubert Humphrey. When the Tennessee State Democratic Convention met in June, McCarthy stalwarts attempted to block the nomination of Governor Ellington as the state's favorite son choice for president. Recognizing that this was in effect a vote for Humphrey, McCarthy supporters tried, and failed, to defeat the measure. More ominously for their chances in the fall, the convention elected only one African American delegate, Memphian E. W. Williamson, and two alternates, A. W. Willis and Charles F. Williams, to attend the national convention in Chicago.[150]

The Shelby County Democratic Club was outraged by this situation, and they took their case to the Democratic National Committee. President Vasco Smith sent a scathing letter to chairman John Bailey arguing that since African Americans had given the Johnson-Humphrey ticket 57 percent of the Shelby County votes in the last election, the lack of full representation was "racism and ingratitude at their worst."[151] On the eve of the Chicago convention, Smith appealed to the credentials committee, but their complaint was rejected. Instead the credentials committee agreed with the state party that African Americans received 10 percent of the delegate seats, which adequately reflected the number of black registered voters in the state.[152] The credentials vote was the second defeat for the once-powerful Shelby County Democratic Club, whose candidates, Russell Sugarmon and A. W. Willis, were defeated in the August Democratic primary by two African American political unknowns.[153]

Arriving in Chicago, the Tennessee delegation joined with other southern states in threatening to renominate Johnson unless the convention adopted a pro–Vietnam War platform and chose a southerner as Humphrey's running mate. Leading the revolt was Tennessee governor Buford Ellington, who explained that "we've tried like the devil to avoid sectionalism. Now it comes cropping up again . . . There are some 15 to 20 states which are really dissatisfied."[154] Tennessee, along with several other southern states, held onto its delegates in a vain attempt to pressure Humphrey into choosing a southern vice president. Senator Gore and several other Tennesseans hoped Ellington might be acceptable to Humphrey, but he refused to budge. In the end the southern delegations, including Tennessee, eventually released their delegates and Humphrey was nominated on the first ballot.[155]

African Americans and white southerners were not the only ones dissatisfied with the convention. Thousands of antiwar activists arrived in the city hoping to pressure the Democratic nominee to end the Vietnam conflict. When demonstrators attempted to march on the convention hall, Chicago police savagely clubbed and tear-gassed them. When word reached inside the convention hall several delegates yelled and screamed at Chicago mayor Richard Daley, who had implemented the stringent security measures. One delegate in particular deplored the "Gestapo tactics on the streets of Chicago." By the time Humphrey was formally nominated, millions of Americans had watched on television as the Democratic Party disintegrated before their very eyes.[156] Humphrey tried to rise above the discord in Chicago. In his acceptance speech he declared: "We do not want a police state, but we do need a state of law and order. Neither mob violence nor police brutality have any place in America." But the damage was done. What should have been the greatest moment in Humphrey's political life was instead a dreadfully humiliating affair. Compounding his mortification, the party's vice presidential nominee, Maine senator Edmund Muskie, publicly disagreed with Humphrey's views on Vietnam.[157]

As Nixon and Humphrey were preparing their fall campaigns, both were threatened by the third-party candidacy of Alabama governor George C. Wallace and his running mate, retired air force general Curtis LeMay. Running on an anti-Washington, states' rights platform, Wallace tapped into the growing white working-class obsession with "law and order, welfare cheats, Communists, hippies, and the decline of public education and public morality."[158] Wallace visited Memphis in June 1968, where he raised fifteen thousand dollars at a fund-raising dinner at the Peabody Hotel. At the Mid-South Coliseum, ten thousand people rose to their feet cheering when the Alabaman declared: "If you will elect me president and any anarchists lie down in front of my car that will be the last car they ever lie down in front of."[159] When Nixon's running mate, Spiro Agnew, visited Memphis in October, he echoed Wallace in declaring that the Democrats encouraged "disruptive influences" in America and pledged to never "run from the words law and order . . ."[160]

George W. Lee watched with dismay as his beloved GOP veered again to the far right. When he learned that the Republican state convention had chosen only one African American to serve as an alternate delegate to the Miami gathering, he expressed his "grievous disappointment" and stated that the party was headed down the same "suicidal road" it had walked in 1964.[161] Lee hoped that Nelson Rockefeller could take the GOP down a different road. "We have strayed so far from the philosophy upon which the Party was founded that our backs are to a political wall, and we will die there if the trend continues toward racism . . . I feel that you can stop the retreat of our Party toward racism which is leading us to the borderline of civil war," Lee wrote to the New York governor.[162]

Although he preferred Rockefeller, Lee was not opposed to Nixon, and shortly before the convention he wrote the former vice president praising his plan to expand federal support for African American–owned businesses: "Black America has seen your face and heard your name mentioned a million times, but they have never before had the chance to see your heart. With this blueprint of yours they have the opportunity to see your heart as clearly as if looking into a lighted room."[163] Despite his expressions of confidence in Rockefeller and Nixon, Lee remained critical of the party and had no plans to become directly involved in the campaign. This changed, however, when a voting member of the Tennessee delegation, Louise G. Reece, became ill and could not travel to Miami. One of the alternates would be selected to take her place, and Lee was determined that the lone black alternate delegate, Sarah Moore Greene, be granted voting privileges. Traveling to Miami, Lee successfully convinced his fellow Tennesseans to choose Greene as a voting delegate.[164]

While at the convention, Lee met with Nixon campaign officials who assured him they wanted his support.[165] Not wanting to alienate Lee as Goldwater had done, the Nixon forces asked Howard Baker, Jr., Tennessee's GOP senator, to work closely with the Memphis Republican.[166] Lee worked hard for the campaign, and his most important contribution was securing the endorsement of Dr. J. H. Jackson, president of the National Negro Baptist Convention, for Nixon.[167] Despite his hard work, Lee was discouraged as the contest came to a close. In a letter to Baker, Lee expressed the opinion that "unless this campaign is accelerated . . . Mr. Nixon will get less than 10 percent of the Negro vote . . . Only substantial Negro votes will keep Governor Wallace from carrying the state."[168] Lee wasn't the only one who was unnerved. Alarm spread through the ranks of Shelby County Democrats as they watched Humphrey's inability to shake off the perception that he and his party were responsible for the chaos in Vietnam and the unrest in America's cities. When the vice president scheduled an appearance in Memphis, local party activists asked Humphrey to cancel his visit for fear it would actually hamper efforts on his behalf.[169] County leaders did welcome Edmund Muskie to Memphis, and he, along with Governor Ellington and Senator Gore, spoke to two thousand Democrats six days before the election.[170]

Turnout was heavy in Memphis on election day, with 233,000 voters casting ballots across the city. In neighborhoods with large African American populations, the majority of their ballots were cast for Humphrey, while the white vote was evenly split between Wallace and Nixon. Support for the Republican and Independent candidates hinged, for the most part, on income and class. In the upscale East Memphis and Fox Meadows neighborhoods Nixon won handily, while Wallace took the white working-class sections of Frayser and Parkway Village. The highest totals for Wallace came from white communities that bordered African American neighborhoods. Despite the rejection of white Memphians, Humphrey polled 82,330 votes to win Shelby County. Wallace came in second with 76,669 ballots cast, while Nixon received 72,902 votes to come in third. Nixon, however, won the state of Tennessee and went on to secure the presidency with only 43 percent of the national popular vote.[171] Like Tennessee, the other southern states had cruelly dismissed the party that had dominated its politics for over a century. In addition to the Volunteer State, Nixon won Florida, North Carolina, South Carolina, and Virginia, while Wallace captured Alabama, Arkansas, Georgia, Louisiana, and Mississippi. The only southern state Humphrey won was Texas.[172]

The elections of 1966, 1967, and 1968 fulfilled the hopes of both political minorities in Memphis. A. W. Willis not only won reelection to the Tennessee House of Representatives, but two other African Americans, Russell Sugarmon and J. O. Patterson, Jr., were elected to the general assembly as well. In addition, three black Memphians, Fred Davis, James Netters, and Patterson, secured seats on the newly formed city council. Republicans also had cause for celebration. Conservative Dan Kuykendall defeated Great Society liberal George Grider for the ninth congressional district seat, while Republican stalwarts Lewis Donelson and Robert James were elected to the city council. GOP members could also take heart in Richard Nixon's showing in Shelby County and his securing of Tennessee's electoral votes in the presidential contest.

As 1968 came to a close, both traditional southern minorities, African Americans and Republicans, had been elected to high public office in Memphis. Along the way, both minorities played small but important roles in the presidential elections of Dwight Eisenhower, John Kennedy, Lyndon Johnson, and Richard Nixon. But the political battles that occurred between 1948 and 1968 did far more than elect public officials. A decade before, in 1959, the Volunteer Ticket had adopted the slogan "Crusade for Freedom" to dramatize their struggle to elect African Americans to public office. In many ways that slogan can also be applied to the efforts to erect a two-party political system in the one-party South and alter the Bluff City's form of government. The foot soldiers who carried out these crusades may have defined freedom differently, but most were working to strengthen democratic institutions, and in the main they accomplished their goals. In the end, these three crusades for freedom expanded liberty, reformed local government, and played a role in the political transformation of the American South.

Afterword

In the years following 1968, white Republicans and African American Democrats continued to dominate Memphis government and politics. In 1970 Memphian Winfield Dunn was elected governor, becoming the first Republican chief executive in over fifty years.[1] Lewis Donelson served one term on the city council, and in 1978 he was appointed state commissioner of finance and administration by Republican governor Lamar Alexander.[2] His GOP colleague, Robert James, remained on the city council, serving until his retirement in 1988.[3] In 1974 conservative ninth district congressman Dan Kuykendall was defeated by African American Democrat Harold Ford, Sr., who held the seat for twenty-two years.[4] Meanwhile their nemesis, George W. Lee, refused to abandon the Republican Party despite its lily-white complexion. He advised the Nixon administration on African American issues and campaigned for Dunn in 1970.[5] In 1973 Governor Dunn and the Tennessee General Assembly commissioned a portrait of Lee which was displayed in the state capitol building alongside other notable Tennesseans. Elected a delegate to the 1976 Republican National Convention, Lee supported President Gerald Ford but died in an auto accident shortly before the gathering opened.[6] With Lee's death the last vestiges of black involvement in local Republican politics came to a close.

The three reformers who led the fight to alter local government remained active in civic affairs until their deaths. Edmund Orgill was elected to the Shelby County Quarterly Court in 1966 and served until his retirement in 1972. When he died in 1983, William Farris described the former mayor as "a tremendous force for good in the community."[7] Concentrating on environmental issues after retiring from the *Press-Scimitar* in 1962, Edward J. Meeman was instrumental in the creation of Shelby Forest State Park, which was renamed Meeman-Shelby Forest State Park after his death in 1966. Lucius Burch remained active in legal and civil rights circles but, like Meeman, was also committed to improving the environment. In the 1970s he played a crucial role in the creation of Shelby Farms Park, and before his death in 1996 he worked to preserve the headwaters of the Wolf River.[8]

After his defeat in the August Democratic primary, A. W. Willis concentrated on his mortgage and realty business but remained involved in local politics until his death in 1988.[9] His partner Russell Sugarmon was elected to the Democratic National Committee in 1975 and was appointed a general sessions court judge in 1987.[10] Maxine Smith became the most visible civil rights leader in the years following the sanitation strike. As executive secretary of the local NAACP, she continued to agitate for social change until her retirement in 1995. In addition she was elected to the Memphis school board in 1971 where she served for twenty-four years.[11] Her husband, Dr. Vasco Smith, was elected to the Shelby County Commission in 1973 and served until his retirement in 1994.[12] Smith worked closely with his movement colleague Jesse Turner who, in 1983, was the first African American elected chairman of the commission.[13] In 1967 H. T. Lockard was appointed administrative assistant to Governor Buford Ellington, and in 1975 he was appointed a criminal court judge where he served for nineteen years.[14]

Perhaps the most distinguished member of this extraordinary group of civil rights activists was Benjamin L. Hooks. He became the first African American member of the Tennessee judiciary when Governor Frank Clement appointed him a criminal court judge in 1965.[15] In 1972 President Nixon appointed Hooks to the Federal Communications Commission, and in 1977 he was elected executive director of the NAACP.[16] Retiring from that position in 1992, Hooks remained involved in civil rights issues, and in 2007 President George W. Bush awarded him the Presidential Medal of Freedom for being "a calm yet forceful voice for fairness, opportunity and personal responsibility."[17]

There were no such honors for Henry Loeb. Saddened by the events of 1968 and frustrated with how it defined his political legacy, the mayor did not seek reelection in 1971 and left office at the end of his term. Six years later he left Memphis to open a farm implements business in nearby Forrest City, Arkansas, but he continued to sponsor his Dutch Treat Luncheon and returned often to the Bluff City. Loeb continued his active lifestyle until the spring of 1988, when he suffered a debilitating stroke that made it difficult for him to speak and walk.[18] Despite this, he came to Memphis whenever he could and remained passionately interested in his hometown.

In the fall of 1991 Loeb watched from across the Mississippi River as Memphis elected its first African American mayor. Shortly after the election, mayor-elect W. W. Herenton accepted an invitation to speak at the October Dutch Treat Luncheon. Loeb traveled the forty-seven-mile distance to attend the luncheon despite the difficulty involved. Spotting Loeb in the crowd, Herenton declared that he was "pleased to see Mr. Loeb. I am very pleased to see that God has sustained him the strength to be with us today."[19] When the mayor-elect finished speaking, Loeb slowly shuffled to the podium. The two men clasped hands warmly as the assemblage stood and clapped uproariously. Turning to the crowd, Loeb tried to speak, but his words were so garbled that no one understood what he was saying.[20]

Appendix A

MEMPHIS CITY GOVERNMENT, 1948–1968

Commission Form of Government   1948–1951

James J. Pleasants, Jr.—Mayor and Commissioner of Administration and Health (resigned January 1949)
Watkins Overton—Mayor and Commissioner of Administration and Health (appointed January 1949)
Joseph P. Boyle—Commissioner of Public Safety and Vice Mayor (transferred to Department of Finances and Institutions September 1950)
Claude A. Armour—Commissioner of Public Safety and Vice Mayor (appointed September 1950)
Louis E. Grashot—Commissioner of Finances and Institutions (resigned September 1950)
Joseph P. Boyle—Commissioner of Finances and Institutions (transferred September 1950)
Robert S. Fredericks—Commissioner of Public Services
Oscar P. Williams—Commissioner of Public Works

Commission Form of Government   1952–1955

Watkins Overton—Mayor and Commissioner of Administration and Health (resigned February 1953)
Frank T. Tobey—Mayor and Commissioner of Administration and Health (appointed March 1953, elected August 1954, died September 1955)
Walter C. Chandler—Mayor and Commissioner of Administration and Health (appointed September 1955)
Claude A. Armour—Commissioner of Fire and Police and Vice Mayor
Frank T. Tobey—Commissioner of Finances and Institutions (appointed mayor March 1953)
Joseph P. Boyle—Commissioner of Finances and Institutions (appointed March 1953, elected August 1954)
John T. Dwyer—Commissioner of Public Services
Oscar P. Williams—Commissioner of Public Works

Commission Form of Government   1956–1959

Edmund Orgill—Mayor and Commissioner of Administration and Health
Claude A. Armour—Commissioner of Fire and Police and Vice Mayor
L. Stanley Dillard—Commissioner of Finances and Institutions
John T. Dwyer—Commissioner of Public Services
Henry Loeb—Commissioner of Public Works

Commission Form of Government   1960–1963

Henry Loeb—Mayor and Commissioner of Administration and Health
Claude A. Armour—Commissioner of Fire and Police and Vice Mayor
James W. Moore—Commissioner of Finances and Institutions
John T. Dwyer—Commissioner of Public Services
William W. Farris—Commissioner of Public Works

Commission Form of Government   1964–1967

William B. Ingram—Mayor and Commissioner of Administration and Health
Claude A. Armour—Commissioner of Fire and Police and Vice Mayor
James W. Moore—Commissioner of Finances and Institutions (resigned August 1966)
L. D. "Dutch" Erwin—Commissioner of Finances and Institutions (appointed August 1966)
Hunter Lane, Jr.—Commissioner of Public Services
Pete Sisson—Commissioner of Public Works

Mayor-Council Form of Government   1968

Henry Loeb—Mayor
Gwen Awsumb—City Council Member
Jerred Blanchard—City Council Member
Wyeth Chandler—City Council Member
Fred L. Davis—City Council Member
Lewis R. Donelson—City Council Member
Billy Hyman—City Council Member
Robert B. James—City Council Member
W. T. McAdams—City Council Member
James L. Netters—City Council Member
J. O. Patterson, Jr.—City Council Member
Phillip A. Perel, Sr.—City Council Member
Downing Pryor—City Council Member
Thomas H. Todd—City Council Member

SOURCE: Joe Walk, *A History of African-Americans in Memphis Government* (Memphis, 1996)

Appendix B

ELECTION RETURNS

Memphis Mayor 1948–1968

1954
30,286—Frank T. Tobey
3,669—J. O'Neill Bomar

1955
51,789—Edmund Orgill
33,154—Watkins Overton

1959
85,282—Henry Loeb
32,170—Partee Fleming

1963
57,655—William Ingram
40,830—William W. Farris
14,180—M. A. Hinds

1967
46,729—Henry Loeb
35,852—William Ingram
30,355—William Morris
17,575—A. W. Willis
8,439—Hunter Lane, Jr.

RUNOFF
78,379—Henry Loeb
66,561—William Ingram

Democratic Primary 1948–1968

1948
U. S. SENATE
37,792—John A. Mitchell
27,855—Estes Kefauver

1952
TENNESSEE GOVERNOR
50,863—Frank Clement
30,396—Gordon Browning

1952
U. S. SENATE
47,359—Kenneth McKellar
43,973—Albert Gore

1958
TENNESSEE GOVERNOR
43,996—Andrew "Tip" Taylor
40,809—Edmund Orgill
18,570—Buford Ellington

1962
TENNESSEE GOVERNOR
51,207—William Farris
39,762—Frank Clement
22,034—P. R. Oligiati

Tennessee House of Representatives

1964
DISTRICT FIVE
DEMOCRATIC PRIMARY
24,726—A. W. Willis
19,799—Max D. Lucas, Jr.
17,680—Lawrence Hughes
7,559—Aubrey Fox, Jr.

GENERAL ELECTION
97,373—A. W. Willis
94,668—Garvin Crawford

1966
DISTRICT FIVE
8,140—A. W. Willis
DISTRICT SIX
5,027—J. O. Patterson, Jr.
330—Hugh Wade
DISTRICT ELEVEN
6,417—Russell B. Sugarmon
504—John Lee Jordan

Ninth District U. S. Representative

1964
DEMOCRATIC PRIMARY
43,980—George Grider
35,791—Clifford Davis

1966
GENERAL ELECTION
46,578—Dan Kuykendall
42,716—George Grider

U.S. President

1948
26,246—Strom Thurmond
23,854—Harry S. Truman
13,668—Thomas E. Dewey

1952
71,194—Adlai Stevenson
64,832—Dwight D. Eisenhower

1956
65,999—Dwight D. Eisenhower
62,037—Adlai Stevenson

1960
87,181—Richard M. Nixon
86,265 John F. Kennedy

1964
112,306—Lyndon B. Johnson
100,495—Barry Goldwater

1968
82,330—Hubert H. Humphrey
76,669—George C. Wallace
72,902—Richard M. Nixon

SOURCES: *Memphis Commercial Appeal* and *Memphis Press-Scimitar*

Notes

Chapter 1. "We Are Living in a Different Day"

1. Sally Palmer Thomason, "The Three Ed's: Memphis in 1948," *West Tennessee Historical Society Papers* 52 (1998): 150.
2. Michael R. Gardner, *Harry S. Truman and Civil Rights: Moral Courage and Political Risks* (Carbondale: Southern Illinois University Press, 2002), 16–20.
3. Robert H. Ferrell, *Harry S. Truman: A Life* (Columbia and London: University of Missouri Press, 1994), 293.
4. Gardner, *Harry S. Truman and Civil Rights*, 16–20.
5. Donald R. McCoy, *The Presidency of Harry S. Truman* (Lawrence: University Press of Kansas, 1984), 106–8.
6. Ferrell, *Harry S. Truman: A Life*, 295.
7. Ibid.
8. *Memphis Commercial Appeal*, 3 February 1948.
9. Kari A. Frederickson, *The Dixiecrat Revolt and the End of the Solid South, 1932–1968* (Chapel Hill: University of North Carolina Press, 2001), 78.
10. Ibid., 79; *Memphis Commercial Appeal*, 8 February 1948.
11. *Memphis Commercial Appeal*, 8 February 1948.
12. E. H. Crump to R. M. McKay, 4 March 1948, E. H. Crump Collection, Memphis Public Library and Information Center.
13. Robert H. Ferrell, ed., *Off the Record: The Private Papers of Harry S. Truman* (New York: Harper and Row, 1980), 80.
14. *Memphis Commercial Appeal*, 2 March 1948; *New York Times*, 2 March 1948.
15. E. E. Keller to E. H. Crump, 3 March 1948, Crump Collection.
16. Charles D. Jones to E. H. Crump, 29 April 1948, Crump Collection.
17. E. H. Crump to R. M. McKay, 4 March 1948, Crump Collection.
18. Ibid.
19. Ibid.
20. *Memphis Commercial Appeal*, 10 and 11 May 1948.
21. Ibid.
22. Ibid., 10 May 1948.
23. Evelyn Humphreys to James Roosevelt, 4 July 1948, Crump Collection; *Memphis Commercial Appeal*, 22 June 1948.
24. *Memphis Commercial Appeal*, 11 July 1948.
25. Alonzo L. Hamby, *Man of the People: A Life of Harry S. Truman* (New York: Oxford University Press, 1995), 446.
26. *Memphis Commercial Appeal*, 14 July 1948.
27. Ibid., 15 July 1948.
28. Ibid., 18 July 1948.
29. Gardner, *Harry Truman and Civil Rights*, 105–11.
30. Ibid., 111–21.

31. *Memphis Commercial Appeal*, 23 June 1948.
32. Ibid., 22 and 25 June 1948.
33. Ibid., 2 August 1976; *Memphis Press-Scimitar*, 2 August 1976.
34. G. Wayne Dowdy, *Mayor Crump Don't Like It: Machine Politics in Memphis* (Jackson: University Press of Mississippi, 2006), 49–50.
35. *Memphis Commercial Appeal*, 2 August 1976.
36. Ibid., 22 June 1948.
37. Ibid., 24 June 1948.
38. Ibid., 25 June 1948.
39. William D. Miller, *Mr. Crump of Memphis* (Baton Rouge: Louisiana State University Press, 1964), 323.
40. E. H. Crump to S. J. McCallie, 5 March 1948, Crump Collection.
41. Allen H. Kitchens, "Political Upheavals in Tennessee: Boss Crump and the Senatorial Election of 1948," *West Tennessee Historical Society Papers* 16 (1962): 111.
42. Joseph Bruce Gorman, *Kefauver: A Political Biography* (New York: Oxford University Press, 1971), 37; "Announcement of Candidacy of Estes Kefauver...," n.d., Crump Collection.
43. Gorman, *Kefauver: A Political Biography*, 31–32.
44. Ibid., 38.
45. Clifford Davis to William Gerber, 2 February 1948, Crump Collection.
46. E. H. Crump to S. J. McCallie, 5 March 1948, Crump Collection.
47. Clifford Davis to E. H. Crump, 19 April 1948, Crump Collection.
48. Evelyn Humphries to John A. Mitchell, 31 May 1948, Crump Collection.
49. S. J. McCallie to E. H. Crump, 28 February 1948, Crump Collection.
50. Note on the 1948 Democratic Primary, n. d., Crump Collection.
51. Thomason, "The Three Ed's: Memphis in 1948," 154.
52. *Memphis Commercial Appeal*, 4 June 1948.
53. Ibid.
54. Clark Porteous, "The Two Eds of Memphis—Meeman and Crump," *West Tennessee Historical Society Papers* 45 (1991): 145.
55. E. H. Crump to Edward J. Meeman, 8 December 1943, Crump Collection.
56. Porteous, "The Two Eds of Memphis," 143.
57. Political advertisement, "Liars Will Steal," 1 July 1947, Crump Collection.
58. Porteous, "The Two Eds of Memphis," 143.
59. *Memphis Commercial Appeal*, 5 March 1943.
60. David M. Tucker, *Memphis since Crump: Bossism, Blacks, and Civic Reformers, 1948–1968* (Knoxville: University of Tennessee Press, 1980), 41.
61. Clarence K. Streit, *Union Now: A Proposal for a Federal Union of the Leading Democracies* (New York: Harper and Brothers Publishers, 1938), 6–7.
62. Dowdy, *Mayor Crump Don't Like It*, 93–98.
63. Joe Walk, *A History of African-Americans in Memphis Government* (Memphis, 1996), 12–14, 18–21.
64. Ibid., 27–28.
65. Dowdy, *Mayor Crump Don't Like It*.
66. *Memphis World*, 21 May 1948.

67. Ibid., 2 July 1948.
68. *Memphis Press-Scimitar*, 18 May 1948.
69. Ibid., 2 July 1948.
70. *Memphis World*, 9 July, 1948.
71. Louis O. Swingler to Pleasants, 7 July 1948, Pleasants Papers.
72. *Memphis World*, 16 July 1948.
73. Statement of Mayor James J. Pleasants, Jr., 13 July 1948, Pleasants Papers.
74. Gloria Brown Melton, "Blacks in Memphis, Tennessee, 1920–1955," Ph.D. diss., Washington State University, 1982, 264.
75. *Memphis Commercial Appeal*, 10 June 1948.
76. Ibid., 28 July 1948.
77. *Time*, 16 August 1948.
78. *Memphis World*, 10 August 1948; *Washington Afro-American*, 10 August 1948.
79. *Memphis World*, 24 August 1948; *Memphis Press-Scimitar*, 21 August 1948.
80. *Memphis World*, 7 September 1948.
81. C. M. E. Pastors Alliance Petition, 1948; Henry Pilcher to Pleasants, 25 August 1948, Pleasants Papers; *Memphis World*, 31 August 1948.
82. Memphis Branch NAACP president Utillus R. Phillips to Pleasants, 1 September 1948, Pleasants Papers; *Memphis World*, 7 September 1948.
83. *Memphis Commercial Appeal*, 10 September 1948; statement by Joseph Boyle, n.d., Pleasants Papers.
84. *Memphis Commercial Appeal*, 8 October 1948.
85. Ibid., 3 November 1948.
86. *Memphis Press-Scimitar*, 3 November 1948.
87. Ibid.; Estes Kefauver, "How Boss Crump Was Licked," *Collier's*, 16 October 1948.
88. *Memphis Commercial Appeal*, 1 November 1948.
89. *Memphis Press-Scimitar*, 10 September 1948.
90. Ibid., 11 September 1948.
91. Political circular, "Why You Should Vote the States' Rights Ticket," 1948, Political Advertisements Collection, Memphis Public Library and Information Center.
92. Ibid.
93. *Memphis Commercial Appeal*, 7 October 1948.
94. *Memphis Press-Scimitar*, 3 November 1948; *Memphis Commercial Appeal*, 3 November 1948.
95. *Memphis Press-Scimitar*, 6 November 1940; *Memphis Press-Scimitar*, 8 November 1944.
96. *Memphis Commercial Appeal*, 3 November 1948.
97. Kari Frederickson, *The Dixiecrat Revolt and the End of the Solid South* (Chapel Hill: University of North Carolina Press, 2001), 167–86.
98. *Memphis Commercial Appeal*, 4 November 1948.
99. Ibid.
100. Ibid.

Chapter 2. "My Family Ties in the South"

1. *Memphis Commercial Appeal*, 24 December 1948; Porteous, "The Two Eds of Memphis," 144.
2. Dowdy, *Mayor Crump Don't Like It*, 90–91.
3. Ibid., 104.
4. *Memphis Commercial Appeal*, 24 December 1948.
5. Ibid.; Scott Melton, "Machine Prince or Mayoral Pauper? Watkins Overton's Political Relationship with Ed Crump and the Crump Machine," *West Tennessee Historical Society Papers* 49 (1995): 186.
6. *Memphis Press-Scimitar*, 24 December 1948.
7. *Memphis Commercial Appeal*, 16 January 1949.
8. *Memphis Press-Scimitar*, 27 May 1949; W. M. Barr to E. H. Crump, 10 October 1949, Crump Collection.
9. *Memphis Press-Scimitar*, 28 November 1949.
10. Ibid., 27 May 1949.
11. *Memphis Commercial Appeal*, 27 November 1949.
12. Ibid.
13. Ibid., 28 November 1949.
14. *Memphis Press-Scimitar*, 5 February 1959.
15. *Memphis Commercial Appeal*, 20 January 1951.
16. Ibid., 3 February 1951.
17. Ibid.
18. Ibid., 8 February 1951.
19. Ibid., 10 February 1951.
20. Ibid.
21. Melton, "Machine Prince or Mayoral Pauper?," 188.
22. *Memphis Commercial Appeal*, 11 February 1951.
23. Ibid., 13 February 1951.
24. Ibid., 25 February 1951.
25. Notes of a meeting between E. H. Crump and Watkins Overton, 20 June 1951, Crump Collection.
26. Miller, *Mr. Crump of Memphis*, 342.
27. Statement by Watkins Overton, 12 July 1951, Crump Collection.
28. *Memphis World*, 10 August 1951.
29. Ibid., 14 August 1951.
30. Ibid., 28 September 1951.
31. Ibid., 26 October 1951.
32. Benjamin Hooks, *The March for Civil Rights* (Chicago: American Bar Association, 2003), 50–51; *Memphis World*, 26 October 1951; *Memphis Commercial Appeal*, 7 November 1951.
33. "A Suggested Platform for the Overton-Hale Honest Government Legislative Ticket," 1951, Crump Collection.
34. Statement by Mayor Watkins Overton, 5 November 1951, Crump Collection.
35. *Memphis Commercial Appeal*, 7 November 1951.
36. *Memphis World*, 13 November 1951.

37. Ibid.
38. Ibid.
39. Ibid.; *Memphis Commercial Appeal*, 9 November 1951.
40. *Memphis World*, 13 November 1951.
41. Memorandum on Null Adams, 22 February 1952, Crump Collection.
42. Lee Seifert Greene, *Lead Me On: Frank Goad Clement and Tennessee Politics* (Knoxville: University of Tennessee Press, 1982), 42, 77.
43. Memorandum on Frank Clement, 1951, Crump Collection.
44. *Memphis Commercial Appeal*, 2 March 1952.
45. Ibid., 7 March 1952.
46. Ibid.
47. *Memphis Press-Scimitar*, 27 March 1952.
48. Ibid., 18 April 1952.
49. "Excerpts from Speech, Gordon Browning," 24 May 1952, Crump Collection.
50. Arthur Faquin, Jr., Braxton Gandy, George LaManna, and Greenfield Polk, surveillance report of Governor Browning's speech, 24 May 1952, Crump Collection.
51. *Memphis Commercial Appeal*, 24 July 1952.
52. William R. Majors, *The End of Arcadia: Gordon Browning and Tennessee Politics* (Memphis: Memphis University Press, 1982), 207–12.
53. *Memphis World*, 6 June and 22 July 1952.
54. Ibid., 10 June 1952.
55. *Memphis Press-Scimitar*, 22 July 1952.
56. *Memphis World*, 5 August 1952.
57. Ibid., 29 July 1952.
58. *Memphis Commercial Appeal*, 27 July 1952; Majors, *The End of Arcadia*, 207–12.
59. *Memphis Commercial Appeal*, 26 July 1952.
60. Miller, *Mr. Crump of Memphis*, 305–7; Evelyn Humphreys to D. W. McKellar, 23 July 1945 and D. W. McKellar to Evelyn Humphreys, 25 July 1945, McKellar Collection.
61. E. H. Crump to Kenneth McKellar, 10 January 1952, Kenneth McKellar Collection, Memphis Public Library and Information Center.
62. Kenneth McKellar to E. H. Crump, 14 May 1952, McKellar Collection.
63. *Memphis Commercial Appeal*, 16 June 1951.
64. Crump to McKellar, 10 January 1952, McKellar Collection.
65. Ibid.
66. *Memphis Commercial Appeal*, 3 February 1952.
67. Herbert Walters to Kenneth McKellar, 2 February 1952.
68. Memorandum on the McKellar senatorial campaign, 12 May 1952, Crump Collection.
69. Ibid.
70. Kenneth McKellar to E. H. Crump, 14 May 1952.
71. *Memphis Commercial Appeal*, 3 June 1952.
72. Ibid., 27 July 1952.
73. *Millington Star*, 10 July 1952.

74. *Memphis Commercial Appeal*, 9 August 1952.
75. Ibid.
76. E. H. Crump to Kenneth McKellar, 14 August 1952, Crump Collection.
77. Roger Biles, "Robert R. Church, Jr. of Memphis: Black Republican Leader in the Age of Democratic Ascendancy, 1928–1940," *Tennessee Historical Quarterly* (Winter 1983): 363–65.
78. Ibid., 379.
79. Annette Church and Roberta Church, *The Robert R. Churches of Memphis* (Ann Arbor: Edwards Brothers, 1974), 228–29.
80. Tucker, *Lieutenant Lee of Beale Street*, 157.
81. *Memphis Commercial Appeal*, 18 April 1952; Church and Church, *The Robert R. Churches of Memphis*, 228–29.
82. Church and Church, *The Robert R. Churches of Memphis*, 229–30.
83. Political Circular, "Vote the Eisenhower Ticket," 1952, Roberta Church Collection, Memphis Public Library and Information Center; *Tri-State Defender*, 2 August 1952.
84. *Memphis Commercial Appeal*, 31 July 1952; *Tri-State Defender*, 2 August 1952.
85. Tucker, *Lieutenant Lee of Beale Street*, 158–60.
86. *Memphis Press-Scimitar*, 14 July 1952; Tucker, *Lieutenant Lee of Beale Street*, 161.
87. Dwight D. Eisenhower to George W. Lee, 26 July 1952, reprinted in *Memphis World*, 5 August 1952.
88. Stephen E. Ambrose, *Eisenhower: Soldier, General of the Army and President-Elect, 1890–1952* (New York: Simon and Schuster, 1983), 546; Earl Black and Merle Black, *The Rise of Southern Republicans* (Cambridge: Harvard University Press, 2002), 61–62.
89. Donald J. Lisio, *Hoover, Blacks & Lily-Whites: A Study of Southern Strategies* (Chapel Hill: University of North Carolina Press, 1985), xvi–xvii, 34–39.
90. Remarks at TV Broadcast, August 1952, Roberta Church Collection.
91. *Tri-State Defender*, 16 August 1952.
92. *Memphis Press-Scimitar*, 20 August 1952.
93. Roane Waring, "Statement on the 1952 Presidential Election," n.d., Roane Waring Collection, Memphis Public Library and Information Center.
94. *Memphis Press-Scimitar*, 14 October 1952.
95. Ibid.
96. Citizens for Eisenhower-Nixon Club of Memphis, campaign pamphlet, 1952, Roberta Church Collection.
97. *Memphis Press-Scimitar*, 15 October 1952.
98. Tucker, *Lieutenant Lee of Beale Street*, 162–63; *Memphis World*, 17 October 1952.
99. E. H. Crump to Adlai Stevenson, 19 August 1952; Adlai Stevenson, 29 December 1952, Crump Collection.
100. *Memphis Commercial Appeal*, October 17, 1952.
101. Ibid., November 6, 1952; Phillip Langsdon, *Tennessee: A Political History* (Franklin: Hillsboro Press, 2000), 350.

102. *Memphis Commercial Appeal*, November 6, 1952.
103. Ibid.

Chapter 3. "All the Cooperation We Can Muster"

1. *Memphis Press-Scimitar*, 20 February 1953.
2. Ibid., 5 February 1953.
3. Ibid.
4. *Memphis Commercial Appeal*, 6 February 1953.
5. Ibid., 7 February 1953.
6. Ibid.
7. *Memphis Press-Scimitar*, 20 February 1953.
8. *Memphis Commercial Appeal*, 18 February 1953.
9. *Memphis Press-Scimitar*, 20 February 1953.
10. Ibid.
11. *Memphis Commercial Appeal*, 3 March 1953.
12. Edmund Orgill to Frank Tobey, 9 March 1953, Frank Tobey Papers, Memphis Public Library and Information Center.
13. Frank Tobey to Edmund Orgill, 12 March 1953, Tobey Papers.
14. Clifford Davis to E. H. Crump, 25 March 1953, Crump Collection.
15. *Memphis Commercial Appeal*, 31 March 1953.
16. Transcript of meeting between Mayor Tobey and six Negro men, 12 August 1953, Tobey Papers.
17. Transcript of meeting between Mayor Tobey and five white residents of East Olive Street, Tobey Papers.
18. *Memphis Press-Scimitar*, 29 June 1953.
19. *Tri-State Defender*, 4 July 1953.
20. *Memphis World*, 25 August 1953; *Memphis Press-Scimitar*, 25 August 1953.
21. *Memphis Press-Scimitar*, 25 August 1953.
22. Ibid., 27 August 1953.
23. Ibid., 9 January 1953.
24. William E. Leuchtenburg, *In the Shadow of FDR: From Harry Truman to Bill Clinton* (Ithaca: Cornell University Press, 1993), 54–55.
25. *Memphis Commercial Appeal*, 14 May 1953.
26. Ibid., 15 May 1953.
27. Ibid., 11 July 1953.
28. Robert L. Moon, "Trouble in the Valley: Eisenhower, Dixon-Yates, and Refinancing Tennessee Valley Authority Power Authorizations" (M. A. thesis, University of Alabama in Huntsville, 1995), 22–23.
29. Aaron Wildavsky, *Dixon-Yates: A Study in Power Politics* (New Haven and London: Yale University Press, 1962), 220–23.
30. Memorandum of a meeting between Mayor Tobey and six Mississippi gentleman, 1 December 1954, Tobey Papers.
31. *Memphis Commercial Appeal*, 24 June 1955.
32. Ibid.
33. Ibid., 2 July 1955.

34. Ibid.
35. Ibid., 7 July 1955.
36. Ibid., 7 August 1959.
37. Ibid., 10 January 1963.
38. Gary Hartman, Roy M. Mersky, and Cindy L. Tate, eds., *Landmark Supreme Court Cases* (New York: Facts on File, Inc., 2004), 34–38.
39. *Memphis Commercial Appeal*, 18 May 1954.
40. Ibid.
41. Hartman, Mersky, and Tate, eds., *Landmark Supreme Court Cases*, 38.
42. *Memphis Commercial Appeal*, 6 August 1954.
43. Miller, *Mr. Crump of Memphis*, 350.
44. Ibid.
45. Barbara Mashburn to E. H. Crump, 13 October 1954, Crump Collection.
46. James Richard Howles to E. H. Crump, 13 October 1954, Crump Collection.
47. *Memphis Commercial Appeal*, 16 and 17 October 1954; Miller, *Mr. Crump of Memphis*, 352.
48. *Memphis Commercial Appeal*, 20 October 1954.
49. Ibid., 31 October 1954.
50. Tucker, *Memphis Since Crump*, 70.
51. Ibid., 71–72.
52. *Memphis Commercial Appeal*, 31 October 1954.
53. Ibid.
54. Hazel Faith, *A Dream Come True: The Story of St. Jude Children's Research Hospital and ALSAC* (Dallas: Taylor Publishing, 1983), 16–17.
55. Ibid.
56. State of Tennessee, Certificate of Death, file number 3159, Stillborn Tobey, Shelby County Archives.
57. Danny Thomas to Frank Tobey, 2 February 1955, Tobey Papers.
58. *Memphis Commercial Appeal*, 23 February 1955.
59. Ibid., 2 March 1955.
60. Ibid., 28 February 1955.
61. *Memphis Press-Scimitar*, 3 March 1955.
62. Memphis Junior Chamber of Commerce, resolution of support for St. Jude's Children's Hospital, 19 May 1955, Tobey Papers.
63. *Memphis Press-Scimitar*, 21 March 1955.
64. Sol Rubin to W. W. Scott, 1 April, 1955, Tobey Papers.
65. *Memphis Commercial Appeal*, 20 May 1955.
66. *Memphis Press-Scimitar*, 23 May 1955.
67. Ibid., 26 May 1955.
68. *Memphis Commercial Appeal*, 23 June 1955.
69. Ibid., 28 May 1955.
70. Ibid., 29 October 2006.
71. Ibid.
72. Ibid., 23 December 2007.
73. Ibid., 3 February 1955.
74. Ibid., 6 February 1955.

75. Ibid.
76. Ibid., 4 February 1955.
77. *Memphis Press-Scimitar*, 31 March 1955.
78. Joe Williams to Henry Loeb, 24 May 1955, Tobey Papers.
79. R. M. Child to Henry Loeb, 24 May 1955, Tobey Papers.
80. L. E. Cox to Henry Loeb, 21 May 1955, Tobey Papers.
81. Henry Loeb and Sam Nickey, 25 May 1955, Tobey Papers.
82. Frank Gianotti, Jr., to Frank T. Tobey and the Board of Commissioners, 10 June 1955, Tobey Papers.
83. *Memphis Press-Scimitar*, 8 July 1955.
84. Henry Loeb to Frank Tobey, 30 June 1955.
85. *Memphis Press-Scimitar*, 5 July 1955.
86. *Memphis Commercial Appeal*, 28 July 1955; *Memphis Press-Scimitar*, 30 July 1955.
87. *Memphis Commercial Appeal*, 2 August 1955.
88. Ibid., 3 August 1955.
89. A disgusted law-abiding citizen to Mayor Frank Tobey, 5 August 1955.
90. *Memphis Commercial Appeal*, 8–12 September 1955.
91. Ibid., 13 September 1955.

Chapter 4. "Why Didn't Someone Tell Us This Before?"

1. *Memphis Press-Scimitar*, 16 September 1955.
2. Ibid., 29 August 1955.
3. Ibid., 1 September 1955.
4. Ibid., 7 September 1955.
5. Ibid., 17 September 1955.
6. Ibid., 27 and 28 September 1955.
7. *Memphis Commercial Appeal*, 11 October 1955.
8. *Memphis Press-Scimitar*, 21 October 1955.
9. Ibid.
10. *Tri-State Defender*, 8 October 1955.
11. Ibid., 22 October 1955.
12. Ibid., 29 October 1955.
13. *Memphis Commercial Appeal*, 5 November 1955.
14. *Tri-State Defender*, 5 November 1955.
15. Ibid.,- 29 October 1955.
16. Ibid.
17. *Memphis Press-Scimitar*, 30 September 1955.
18. Ibid., 17 October 1955.
19. Ibid., 19 October 1955.
20. Ibid., 21 October 1955.
21. Ibid., 24 October 1955.
22. *Memphis Commercial Appeal*, 6 November 1955.
23. Ibid., 11 November 1955.
24. Ibid.

25. *Tri-State Defender*, 19 November 1955.
26. Fred A. Bailey, "The Southern Historical Association and the Quest for Racial Justice, 1954–1963," *Journal of Southern History* (November 2005): 833–53.
27. *Memphis Commercial Appeal*, 11 November 1955.
28. William Faulkner, *Essays, Speeches and Public Letters* (New York: Random House, 1966), 151.
29. *Memphis Commercial Appeal*, 27 February 1956.
30. Ibid., 29 February 1956.
31. *Memphis Press-Scimitar*, 22 March 1956; *Memphis Commercial Appeal*, 23 March 1956.
32. "Declaration of Constitutional Principles," from *Congressional Record*, 84th Congress, Second Session. Vol. 102, part 4, March 12, 1956 (Washington, D.C.: Governmental Printing Office, 1956), 4459–4460. Reproduced at http://www.strom.clemson.edu/strom/manifesto.html (accessed June 29, 2007).
33. *Memphis Commercial Appeal*, 27 May 1956.
34. Ibid., 9 June 1956.
35. Ibid., 11 June 1956; Tucker, *Memphis Since Crump*, 87.
36. *Memphis Commercial Appeal*, 27 June 1956.
37. *Tri-State Defender*, 28 July 1956.
38. *Memphis Commercial Appeal*, 18 July 1956.
39. Ibid.
40. Ibid., 20 July 1956.
41. Ibid., 22 July 1956.
42. Ibid.; Tucker, *Memphis Since Crump*, 88.
43. *Tri-State Defender*, 28 July 1956.
44. Ibid.; Tucker, *Lieutenant Lee of Beale Street*, 164–65.
45. *Memphis Commercial Appeal*, 26 July 1956.
46. *Tri-State Defender*, 4 August 1956.
47. *Memphis Commercial Appeal*, 3 August 1956; *Tri-State Defender*, 11 August 1956.
48. *Tri-State Defender*, 18 August 1956.
49. Henry Loeb to Edmund Orgill, 20 June 1957, Henry Loeb Papers, Memphis Public Library and Information Center.
50. Tucker, *Memphis Since Crump*, 90–92.
51. Tucker, *Lieutenant Lee of Beale Street*, 164–65; A. L. Moreland to Clifford Davis, 7 August 1956, Lee Collection.
52. Memphis Citizens Dedication Committee, *Dedication Program of the George W. Lee Post Office*, 29 July 1956, Lee Collection.
53. Church and Church, *The Robert R. Churches of Memphis*, 234.
54. *Memphis Press-Scimitar*, 7 November 1956.
55. George W. Lee, "Stevenson Criticizes a War Master," typewritten editorial, 1956, Lee Collection.
56. *Speech by George W. Lee at Woman Power for Eisenhower Program*, 1956, Lee Collection.
57. Hubert K. Reese to Henry Loeb, 1956, Loeb Papers.
58. *Memphis Commercial Appeal*, 4 August 1956.

59. Ibid., 10 August 1956.
60. Ibid., 10 and 15 August 1956.
61. Ibid., 16 August 1956.
62. Ibid., 17 August 1956.
63. Charles L. Fontenay, *Estes Kefauver: A Biography* (Knoxville: University of Tennessee Press, 1980) 267–70.
64. *Memphis Commercial Appeal*, 17 August 1956.
65. Ibid., 18 August 1956.
66. Ibid., 31 August 1956.
67. Ibid., 27 August 1956.
68. Ibid., 2 and 9 September 1956.
69. Ibid., 7 November 1956.
70. Ibid.
71. Bobby L. Lovett, *The Civil Rights Movement in Tennessee: A Narrative History* (Knoxville: University of Tennessee Press), 42–43.
72. *Memphis Commercial Appeal*, 28 August 1956.
73. Ibid., 30 August 1956.
74. Ibid., 1 September 1956.
75. Ibid., 2 and 3 September 1956.
76. Ibid., 8 January 1957.
77. Ibid., 11 January 1957.
78. The Testimony of O. Z. Evers in the District Court of the United States for the Western District of Tennessee, 6 January 1958, John D. Martin Collection, Memphis Public Library and Information Center.
79. *Memphis Press-Scimitar*, 5 June 1956.
80. Ibid.
81. *Tri-State Defender*, 11 January 1958.
82. Ibid.
83. Order of the United States District Court, Western District of Tennessee, 27 June 1958, Martin Collection; *Memphis Commercial Appeal*, 28 June 1958.
84. *Memphis Commercial Appeal*, 28 June 1958.
85. Ibid., 16 December 1958; H. T. Lockard to John D. Martin, 26 March 1959, Martin Collection.
86. John D. Martin to William E. Miller, August 16, 1960, Martin Collection; Order of the United States District Court, Western District of Tennessee, 1960, Martin Collection.
87. *Memphis Commercial Appeal*, 16 September 1960.
88. Allegra W. Turner with Jini M. Kilgore, *Except by Grace: The Life of Jesse H. Turner* (Jonesboro: FOUR-G Publishers, 2004), 110–11.
89. Ibid., 31.
90. Turner and Kilgore, *Except by Grace*, 8–9, 33–39.
91. *Memphis Press-Scimitar*, 16 July 1957; Minutes of the Board of Directors of the Memphis Public Library, 18 July 1957, Library Collection, Memphis Public Library and Information Center.
92. Wassell Randolph to H. T. Lockard, 2 October 1957, Library Collection.
93. Minutes of the Board of Directors of the Memphis Public Library, 20 June 1958, Library Collection.

94. Ibid., 23 June 1958.
95. Turner and Kilgore, *Except by Grace*, 113–14.
96. Fontenay, *Estes Kefauver: A Biography*, 285–86.
97. Tucker, *Memphis Since Crump*, 96.
98. Roane Waring to Charles Q. Kelley, 26 June and 24 July, 1958, Roane Waring Collection, Memphis Public Library and Information Center.
99. *Memphis Commercial Appeal*, 19 July 1958.
100. Ibid., 16 and 17 July 1958.
101. Ibid., 3 August 1958.
102. *Tri-State Defender*, 26 July 1958.
103. *Memphis Commercial Appeal*, 29 July 1958.
104. Ibid., 5 August 1958.
105. *Tri-State Defender*, 28 June 1958.
106. Ibid., 26 July 1958.
107. Ibid., 9 August 1958.
108. Ibid., 16 August 1958.
109. *Memphis Commercial Appeal*, 9 August 1958.
110. Clayborne Carson, *Civil Rights Chronicle: The African American Struggle for Freedom* (Lincolnwood, IL: Legacy Publications International, 2003), 162, 166.
111. *Tri-State Defender*, 29 October 1955.

Chapter 5. "To Compel the White Race"

1. *Memphis Press-Scimitar*, 20 March 1959; Elizabeth Gritter, "'This Is a Crusade for Freedom': The Volunteer Ticket Campaign in the 1959 City Election in Memphis, Tennessee" (M.A. thesis, University of North Carolina at Chapel Hill, 2005), 19.
2. *Memphis Press-Scimitar*, 20 and 22 May 1959.
3. Ibid., 6 June 1959.
4. Gritter, "'This Is a Crusade for Freedom,'" 20; Sharon D. Wright, *Race, Power, and Political Emergence in Memphis* (New York: J. B. Garland Publishing), 45–46.
5. Gritter, "'This Is a Crusade for Freedom,'" 20.
6. *Memphis Commercial Appeal*, 15 July 1988.
7. *Memphis Press-Scimitar*, 5 June and 18 August 1959.
8. Elizabeth Gritter, "Local Leaders and Community Soldiers: The Memphis Desegregation Movement, 1955–1961" (senior honors thesis, American University, 2001), 35.
9. Wright, *Race, Power, and Political Emergence in Memphis*, 47.
10. *Tri-State Defender*, 11 July and 15 August 1959.
11. Wright, *Race, Power, and Political Emergence in Memphis*, 47.
12. *Tri-State Defender*, 8 August 1959.
13. Ibid.; Gritter, "Local Leaders and Community Soldiers," 35.
14. Wright, *Race, Power, and Political Emergence in Memphis*, 48.
15. *Memphis Press-Scimitar*, 22 May 1959.
16. Mantri Sivananda, "Henry Loeb III as Public Works Commissioner, 1956–1959," *West Tennessee Historical Society Papers* (2000): 68–69, 77.

17. *Tri-State Defender*, 30 May 1959.
18. *Memphis Press-Scimitar*, 9 June 1959.
19. Wright, *Race, Power, and Political Emergence in Memphis*, 48.
20. *Memphis Commercial Appeal*, 12 July 1959.
21. Wright, *Race, Power, and Political Emergence in Memphis*, 48.
22. *Memphis Commercial Appeal*, 13 August 1959.
23. Ibid., 14 August 1959.
24. Wright, *Race, Power, and Political Emergence in Memphis*, 49.
25. Gritter, "Local Leaders and Community Soldiers," 35.
26. *Memphis Press-Scimitar*, 9 July 1959.
27. Ibid., 4 July 1959; *Memphis Commercial Appeal*, 6 July 1959.
28. *Memphis Commercial Appeal*, 6 July 1959.
29. *Memphis Press-Scimitar*, 24 July 1959.
30. Ibid., 3 August 1959.
31. *Memphis Commercial Appeal*, 10 July 1959.
32. Ibid., 7 July 1959.
33. Wright, *Race, Power, and Political Emergence in Memphis*, 49.
34. *Tri-State Defender*, 1 August 1959; *Memphis Press-Scimitar*, 20 August 1959.
35. *Tri-State Defender*, 15 August 1959.
36. *Memphis Press-Scimitar*, 21 August 1959.
37. *Memphis Commercial Appeal*, 21 August 1959.
38. David J. Garrow, *Bearing the Cross: Martin Luther King, Jr., and the Southern Christian Leadership Conference* (New York: Quill William Morrow, 1986), 97.
39. *Tri-State Defender*, 29 August 1959.
40. Gritter, "Local Leaders and Community Soldiers," 38–39; James B. Jalenak, "Beale Street Politics: A Study of Negro Political Activity in Memphis, Tennessee," (honors thesis, Yale University, 1961), 53–54.
41. Jalenak, "Beale Street Politics," 53–55.
42. *Memphis Press-Scimitar*, 5 August 1960.
43. *Memphis Commercial Appeal*, 11 July 1960.
44. Ibid., 11 July 1960; *Memphis Press-Scimitar*, 11 July 1960.
45. *Memphis Commercial Appeal*, 12 July 1960.
46. Ibid.
47. Ibid., 13 July 1960.
48. Ibid.
49. *Memphis Press-Scimitar*, 14 July 1960.
50. *Memphis Commercial Appeal*, 16 July 1960; Robert Dallek, *Lone Star Rising: Lyndon Johnson and His Times, 1908–1960* (New York: Oxford University Press, 1991), 576–82.
51. *Memphis Commercial Appeal*, 18 July 1960.
52. *Memphis Press-Scimitar*, 26 and 27 July 1960.
53. Ibid., 27 July 1960.
54. *Memphis Commercial Appeal*, 18 July 1960.
55. Henry Loeb to Robert F. Kennedy, 21 April 1962, Loeb Collection.

56. *Memphis Press-Scimitar*, 21 September 1960; *Memphis Commercial Appeal*, 22 September 1960.
57. *Memphis Commercial Appeal*, 22 September 1960.
58. Ibid., 21 September 1960.
59. George W. Lee, "Profile of Two Candidates in a Southern Background," Republican National Committee News Release, 5 October, 1960, Lee Collection; *Memphis Press-Scimitar*, 27 September 1960.
60. Ibid.
61. *Memphis Commercial Appeal*, 30 September 1960.
62. *Tri-State Defender*, 15 October 1960.
63. Ibid., 27 October–4 November 1960.
64. Ibid., 5–11 November 1960.
65. Ibid.
66. Minutes of the Board of Directors of the Memphis Public Library, 5 November 1959, Library Collection.
67. David Halberstam, *The Children* (New York: Random House, 1998), 92–94.
68. *Memphis Press-Scimitar*, 19 March 1960; United States Commission on Civil Rights, *Hearings Held in Memphis, Tennessee, June 25–26, 1962* (Washington: U.S. Government Printing Office, 1963), 95.
69. *Memphis Commercial Appeal*, 19 March 1960.
70. *Memphis Press-Scimitar*, 21 March 1960: *Hearings*, 96.
71. *Memphis Press-Scimitar*, 21 March 1960.
72. Ibid.
73. *Hearings*, 96–97.
74. *Tri-State Defender*, 26 March 1960.
75. *Memphis Commercial Appeal*, 21 March 1960.
76. *Memphis Press-Scimitar*, 21 March 1960; *Tri-State Defender*, 26 March 1960.
77. *Memphis Press-Scimitar*, 22 March 1960.
78. Ibid.
79. *Hearings*, 97.
80. *Memphis Commercial Appeal*, 18 May 1960.
81. *Hearings*, 98.
82. *Memphis Commercial Appeal*, 18 May 1960.
83. Report of the Executive Secretary, Memphis Branch, 6 September–3 October 1961, Maxine Smith NAACP Collection, Memphis Public Library and Information Center.
84. *Memphis Press-Scimitar*, 14 October 1960.
85. Board of Trustees Minutes, 31 July 1961.
86. Report of the Executive Secretary, Memphis Branch, 8 November–5 December 1961, Smith NAACP Collection.
87. *Memphis Press-Scimitar*, 4 and 6 September 1958; *Memphis Press-Scimitar*, 31 March 1960.
88. Ibid., 31 March 1960.
89. Ibid.
90. *Memphis Commercial Appeal*, 7 May 1960.
91. *Memphis Press-Scimitar*, 4 February 1961.

92. Ibid., 15 April 1961.
93. Ibid., 30 August 1961.
94. Ibid., 3 October 1961; *Memphis Commercial Appeal*, 3 October 1961.
95. *Hearings*, 85.
96. Joan Turner Beifuss, *At the River I Stand* (Memphis: St. Lukes Press, 1990), 153.
97. *Memphis Press-Scimitar*, 3 October 1961; *Memphis Commercial Appeal*, 4 October 1961; *Hearings*, 84–85.
98. Report of the Executive Secretary, Memphis Branch, 6 September–3 October 1961, Smith Collection.
99. *Tri-State Defender*, 7 October 1961.
100. *Memphis Commercial Appeal*, 4 October 1961.
101. John Branston, *Rowdy Memphis: The South Unscripted* (Nashville: Cold Tree Press, 2004), 122–23.
102. Thea Singer, "How I Did It: When Civil Rights Came to My Box Office," *Inc.*, February 2003.
103. *Memphis Press-Scimitar*, 12 June 1962.
104. *Memphis Commercial Appeal*, 13 June 1962; *Hearings*, 102.
105. *Memphis Press-Scimitar*, 27 May 1963.
106. Henry Loeb to James Peeler, 5 June 1962, Loeb Papers.
107. Statement of Henry Loeb III, 1962, Loeb Papers.
108. Henry Loeb to Gerald A. Bloom, 31 May 1962, Loeb Papers.
109. Jimmy Peeler to Henry Loeb, 5 June 1962, Loeb Papers.
110. Henry Loeb to Patrick T. McGahn, Jr., 2 March 1961, Loeb Papers.
111. Patrick T. McGahn, Jr., to Henry Loeb, 13 April 1961, Loeb Papers.
112. Robert F. Kennedy to Henry Loeb, 19 October 1961, Loeb Papers.
113. Ibid.
114. Henry Loeb to Robert F. Kennedy, 23 October 1961, Loeb Papers.
115. Burke Marshall to Henry Loeb, 6 February 1962, Loeb Papers.

Chapter 6. "Please Don't Do That"

1. *Memphis Press-Scimitar*, 22 March 1961.
2. Oral history interview with A. Maceo Walker by Ronald Anderson Walter and Benjamin Head, 16 September 1976, Everett R. Cook Oral History Collection, Memphis Public Library and Information Center.
3. *Memphis Press-Scimitar*, 22 March 1961.
4. Claude Armour to A. Maceo Walker, 6 July 1961, Russell B. Sugarmon Collection, Rhodes College, Crossroads to Freedom digital archive, http://www.crossroadstofreedom.org/home (accessed 28 December 2007).
5. *Memphis Commercial Appeal*, 26 July 1961.
6. Ibid., 27 and 29 July 1961.
7. Ibid., 27 July 1961.
8. Ibid., 28 July 1961.
9. Ibid., 29 July 1961.
10. Ibid., 31 July 1961.

11. Ibid., 30 July 1961.
12. *Memphis Press-Scimitar*, 31 July 1961.
13. *Memphis Commercial Appeal*, 29, March 1962.
14. *Tri-State Defender*, 19 June 1962.
15. Ibid., 28 July 1962.
16. Ibid., 21 July 1962.
17. Ibid., 28 July 1962.
18. Ibid., 30 June 1962.
19. *Memphis Commercial Appeal*, 31 July 1962.
20. Ibid., 2 August 1962.
21. Ibid., 3 August 1962; *Memphis Press-Scimitar*, 7 August 1962.
22. *Memphis Press-Scimitar*, 3 August 1962.
23. *Tri-State Defender*, 9 June 1962.
24. Lewis L. Gould, *Grand Old Party: A History of the Republicans* (Random House: New York, 2003), 353–55.
25. Tucker, *Lieutenant Lee of Beale Street*, 176.
26. Lisio, *Hoover, Blacks & Lily-Whites*, 37.
27. George W. Lee to Howard Baker, 13 June 1961, Lee Collection.
28. "Biography of Robert B. James" and campaign pamphlet "Shelby County Conservatives Need the Dynamic Leadership of Robert James in the U.S. Congress," 1962, Memphis Information File, Memphis Public Library and Information Center.
29. Policy statement of Robert B. James, 1962, Memphis Information File.
30. *Memphis Press-Scimitar*, 20 June 1962; *Tri-State Defender*, 23 June 1962.
31. Tucker, *Lieutenant Lee of Beale Street*, 180–81.
32. *Tri-State Defender*, 21 June 1962.
33. Ibid., 23 June 1962.
34. Tucker, *Lieutenant Lee of Beale Street*, 180–81.
35. *Memphis Press-Scimitar*, 7 August 1962.
36. Ibid., 3 August 1962.
37. *Memphis Commercial Appeal*, 7 November 1962.
38. Secretary of State Dean Rusk to Russell B. Sugarmon, Jr., 29 August 1962, Crossroads to Freedom digital archive.
39. Vice President Lyndon B. Johnson to George W. Lee, 15 June and 1 July 1963, Lee Collection.
40. *Memphis Press-Scimitar*, 1 January 1963.
41. Ibid., 2 January 1963.
42. *Memphis Commercial Appeal*, 1 January 1963.
43. Ibid., 6 March 1963.
44. *Memphis Press-Scimitar*, 16 September 1964.
45. Mantri Sivananda, "Controversial Memphis Mayor Henry Loeb III, 1920–1992: A Biographical Study" (Ph.D. dissertation, University of Memphis, 2002), 158–59.
46. *Memphis Press-Scimitar*, 17 August 1963.
47. Ibid., 4 January 1963.
48. Campaign brochure for William B. Ingram, Jr., 1963, Memphis Information File, Memphis Public Library and Information Center; *Memphis Press-Scimitar*, 27 August 1963.

49. *Memphis Press-Scimitar*, 17 August 1963.
50. Ibid., 13 September 1963.
51. Ibid., 19 September 1963.
52. Henry Loeb, Statement on Reelection, 21 September 1963, Loeb Papers; *Memphis Press-Scimitar*, 21 September 1963.
53. *Memphis Press-Scimitar*, 23 September 1963.
54. Henry Loeb to Shelby County Election Commission chairman S. Nelson Castle, 3 October 1963, Loeb Papers; *Memphis Press-Scimitar*, 3 October 1963.
55. *Memphis Press-Scimitar*, 12 October 1963.
56. Ibid., 23 September 1963.
57. Ibid., 24 September 1963.
58. Campaign brochure for John Ford Canale, 1963, Memphis Information File, Memphis Public Library and Information Center.
59. *Memphis Press-Scimitar*, 23 September 1963.
60. Ibid., 23 September 1963.
61. *Tri-State Defender*, 19 October 1963.
62. Ibid., 26 October and 2 November 1963.
63. Ibid., 26 October 1963.
64. Volunteer Ticket campaign brochure, 1963, Loeb Papers.
65. A Small Group of Thinking Citizens campaign brochure, 1963, Loeb Papers.
66. *Memphis Press-Scimitar*, 4 November 1963.
67. "Vote and Elect William Farris Mayor," campaign advertisement, Loeb Papers.
68. *Tri-State Defender*, 2 November 1963.
69. *Memphis Press-Scimitar*, 29 October 1963.
70. Ibid., 4 November 1963.
71. Ibid., 8 November 1963.
72. Ibid.
73. *Tri-State Defender*, 16 November 1963.
74. *Public Papers of the Presidents of the United States, John F. Kennedy, 1963* (United States Government Printing Office: Washington, 1964), 469.
75. Ibid., 483–94; Robert Dallek, *An Unfinished Life: John F. Kennedy, 1917–1963* (Boston: Little, Brown and Company, 2003), 603–5.
76. Randall B. Woods, *LBJ: Architect of American Ambition* (Cambridge: Harvard University Press, 2006), 416–17.
77. *Memphis Commercial Appeal*, 23 November 1963.
78. Woods, *LBJ*, 472–78.
79. *Memphis Commercial Appeal*, 3 July 1964.
80. *Tri-State Defender*, 11 July 1964.
81. Woods, *LBJ*, 480.
82. *Memphis Press-Scimitar*, 11 October 1963.
83. *Memphis Commercial Appeal*, 17 March 1964; *Memphis Press-Scimitar*, 17 March 1964.
84. *Memphis Commercial Appeal*, 3 May 1964.
85. Ibid.
86. Tucker, *Lieutenant Lee of Beale Street*, 188; Nelson Rockefeller to George W.

Lee, 4 February 1964, Lee Collection; George W. Lee to Nelson Rockefeller, 23 April and 27 May 1964, Lee Collection.

87. John H. Kessel, *The Goldwater Coalition: Republican Strategies in 1964* (Indianapolis and New York: The Bobbs-Merrill Company, Inc., 1968), 80–89.
88. Tucker, *Lieutenant Lee of Beale Street*, 188–89.
89. *Memphis Commercial Appeal*, 2, 5, 6, 8 July 1964.
90. Tucker, *Lieutenant Lee of Beale Street*, 188–89.
91. *Memphis Commercial Appeal*, 13 July 1964.
92. Tucker, *Lieutenant Lee of Beale Street*, 195–97.
93. *Memphis Commercial Appeal*, 14 July 1964; *New York Times*, 14 July 1964.
94. Tucker, *Lieutenant Lee of Beale Street*, 194–95.
95. *Memphis Commercial Appeal*, 16 July 1964.
96. Ibid., 17 July 1964.
97. Ibid.
98. *Tri-State Defender*, 25 July 1964.
99. *Memphis Press-Scimitar*, 4 May 1964.
100. Ibid., 27 July 1964.
101. Woods, *LBJ*, 534–37.
102. *Memphis Commercial Appeal*, 28 August 1964.
103. Campaign brochure, "Vote for These Courageous, Forthright, Freedom Fighters," 1964, Willis Collection.
104. *Memphis Commercial Appeal*, 7 August 1964.
105. Ibid., 10 August 1964.
106. *Memphis Press-Scimitar*, 27 October 1964.
107. *Tri-State Defender*, 17 October 1964.
108. *Memphis Press-Scimitar*, 24 January 1967; *Memphis Press-Scimitar*, 1 September 1976.
109. *Memphis Commercial Appeal*, 7 June 1964.
110. Ibid., 12 July 1964.
111. Ibid., 24 July 1964.
112. Ibid.
113. Ibid., 7 August 1964.
114. *Memphis Press-Scimitar*, 6 October 1964.
115. Ibid., 15 October 1964.
116. Ibid., 16 September 1964.
117. Ibid.; *Tri-State Defender*, 26 September 1964.
118. *Memphis Commercial Appeal*, 27 and 28 September 1964.
119. *Memphis Press-Scimitar*, 19 October 1964.
120. Ibid., 10 October 1964.
121. *Memphis Commercial Appeal*, 25 October 1964.
122. Ibid.
123. *Memphis Press-Scimitar*, 24 October 1964.
124. Ibid.
125. *Memphis Commercial Appeal*, 25 October 1964.
126. Ibid.
127. Ibid., 4 November 1964.
128. Ibid.

129. *Memphis Press-Scimitar*, 4 November 1964.
130. *Memphis Commercial Appeal*, 5 November 196.

Chapter 7. "A Great Movement Here in Memphis"

1. *The Memphis Digest 1931* (Memphis: 1931), 14.
2. *Memphis Press-Scimitar*, 7 January 1964.
3. Ibid., 11 and 18 January 1964.
4. Ibid., 15 January 1964.
5. Ibid., 17 and 18 January 1964.
6. Ibid., 21 January 1964.
7. Ibid., 22 January 1964.
8. William B. Ingram, Jr., to Richard W. Barnes, 18 February 1964; William B. Ingram, Jr., to Claude Armour, Hunter Lane, James Moore, and Pete Sisson, 25 February 1964, Hunter Lane, Jr., Papers, Memphis Public Library and Information Center; *Memphis Commercial Appeal*, 19 February 1964.
9. Richard W. Barnes to William B. Ingram, Jr., 19 February 1964, Lane Papers.
10. Memphis Board of Commissioners, Transcript of Hearing on Suspension, 31 March 1964, Lane Papers; *Memphis Commercial Appeal*, 1 April 1964.
11. William B. Ingram, Jr., to Claude Armour, Hunter Lane, James Moore, and Pete Sisson, 8 September 1964, Lane Papers; *Memphis Commercial Appeal*, 2 September 1964.
12. Chancery Court of Shelby County, Tennessee, Original Bill for Injunction, 30 September 1964, Lane Papers; *Memphis Commercial Appeal*, 10 December 1964.
13. *Memphis Press-Scimitar*, 16 October 1964.
14. Ibid., 29 January 1964.
15. Ibid., 16 October 1964.
16. Ibid., 9 December 1964.
17. *Memphis Commercial Appeal*, 15 January 1965.
18. Ibid.
19. Ibid., 28 February 1965.
20. *Nashville Tennessean*, 14 March 1965.
21. *Memphis Commercial Appeal*, 12 March 1965.
22. Ibid., 20 March 1965.
23. Ibid.
24. Laurie B. Green, *Battling the Plantation Mentality: Memphis and the Black Freedom Struggle* (Chapel Hill: University of North Carolina Press, 2007), 268–69.
25. Jonathan I. Wax, "Program of Progress: The Recent Change in the Form of Government of Memphis, Part I," *West Tennessee Historical Society Papers* 23 (1969): 89–90.
26. Ibid., 90–91.
27. Ibid., 91–92.
28. Ibid., 93–95.
29. Ibid., 97–98.
30. *Memphis Commercial Appeal*, 9 February 1966.
31. Wax, "Program of Progress, Part I," 103–4.

32. *Memphis Commercial Appeal*, 9 February 1966.
33. Ibid., 18 February 1966.
34. Wax, "Program of Progress, Part I," 106–7.
35. Jonathan I. Wax, "Program of Progress: The Recent Change in the Form of Government of Memphis, Part II," *West Tennessee Historical Society Papers* 24 (1970): 74–76.
36. Wax, "Program of Progress, Part II," 76–80.
37. *Memphis Press-Scimitar*, 28 June 1966.
38. *Memphis Commercial Appeal*, 12 July 1966.
39. Ibid., 27 July and 9 August 1966.
40. Ibid., 10 August 1966.
41. Ibid., 17 August 1966.
42. Ibid., 2 and 6 November 1966.
43. Ibid., 17 October 1966.
44. Ibid., 1 November 1966.
45. Ibid., 6 November 1966.
46. Ibid., 7 November 1966.
47. Ibid.
48. Woods, *LBJ*, 695–98; James T. Patterson, *Grand Expectations: The United States, 1945–1974* (New York: Oxford University Press, 1996), 670–71, 708.
49. *Memphis Commercial Appeal*, 26 June 1966.
50. Ibid., 7 November 1966.
51. *Tri-State Defender*, 5 November 1966.
52. Ibid., 1 and 8 October 1966.
53. *Memphis Commercial Appeal*, 7 November 1966.
54. *Memphis Press-Scimitar*, 7 November 1966.
55. Ibid., 4 November 1966.
56. *Memphis Commercial Appeal*, 8 June 1966.
57. *Tri-State Defender*, 30 July and 6 August 1966; *Memphis Press-Scimitar*, 4 November 1966.
58. *Memphis Press-Scimitar*, 4 November 1966.
59. *Memphis Commercial Appeal*, 10 November 1966.
60. Ibid., 9 November 1966.
61. Ibid., 10 November 1966.
62. Ibid., 9 November 1966.
63. Ibid., 10 November 1966.
64. "Five Minute Digest of P–O–P," 1966, Memphis Information File.
65. *Memphis Press-Scimitar*, 1 June 1967.
66. Ibid., 5 June 1967.
67. Ibid., 17 and 19 July 1967; *Memphis Commercial Appeal*, 2 August 1967.
68. *Memphis Commercial Appeal*, 10 August 1967.
69. *Memphis Press-Scimitar*, 8 June 1967.
70. *Tri-State Defender*, 19 August 1967: *Memphis Press-Scimitar*, 8 August 1967.
71. *Tri-State Defender*, 16 September 1967.
72. Ibid., 30 September 1967.
73. Campaign pamphlet, "The Future Depends on You the Youth of Memphis," 1967, Willis Collection.

74. *Memphis Press-Scimitar*, 11 September 1967.
75. Ibid., 12 September 1967.
76. Ibid., 11 September 1967.
77. Ibid., 3 October 1967.
78. Ibid., 7 September 1967.
79. Ibid., 18 and 27 September 1967.
80. Unity league campaign pamphlet, "A Vote for Willis Will Be a Vote for Loeb," 1967, Willis Collection.
81. *Memphis Press-Scimitar*, 30 September 1967.
82. Ibid., 12 July 1967.
83. *Memphis Commercial Appeal*, 13 July 1967.
84. *Memphis Press-Scimitar*, 12 July 1967.
85. Ibid., 3 June 1967; *Memphis Commercial Appeal*, 13, 14, 29 June, 14 July 1967.
86. Hubert G. Locke, *The Detroit Riot of 1967* (Detroit: Wayne State University Press, 1969), 51.
87. *Memphis Commercial Appeal*, 29 July 1967.
88. Ibid., 29 July 1967.
89. Ibid., 31 July 1967.
90. *Memphis Press-Scimitar*, 9 September 1967.
91. Ibid., 5 October 1967.
92. Ibid., 6 October 1967; *Memphis Commercial Appeal*, 6 October 1967.
93. *Memphis Press-Scimitar*, 6 October 1967.
94. Ibid., 11 October 1967.
95. Ibid.
96. Ibid., 3 November 1967; *Memphis Commercial Appeal*, 3 November 1967.
97. Ibid.; Joan Turner Beifuss, *At the River I Stand: Memphis, the 1968 Strike and Martin Luther King* (Memphis: B&W Books, 1985), 145–55.
98. John Branston, *Rowdy Memphis: The South Unscripted* (Nashville: Cold Tree Press, 2004), 263–64.
99. Beifuss, *At the River I Stand*, 30–31; *Memphis Commercial Appeal*, 2 February 1968; *Tri-State Defender*, 10 February 1968.
100. Beifuss, *At the River I Stand*, 28–29, 32–33; Michael K. Honey, *Going Down Jerico Road: The Memphis Strike, Martin Luther King's Last Campaign* (New York: W. W. Norton & Company, 2007), 35.
101. Green, *Battling the Plantation Mentality*, 277.
102. Honey, *Going Down Jerico Road*, 102–5.
103. Beifuss, *At the River I Stand*, 40–41.
104. Honey, *Going Down Jerico Road*, 118–19.
105. Resolution Unanimously Adopted by the Board of Memphis Branch NAACP, 15 February 1968, Loeb Papers.
106. Ibid., 143–45.
107. Ibid., 118.
108. City of Memphis, *Code of Ordinances* (Memphis: 1967), 74.
109. Beifuss, *At the River I Stand*, 75.
110. Ibid., 78–80.
111. Ibid., 82–83.
112. Ibid., 83–85.

113. Ibid., 86–90.
114. Green, *Battling the Plantation Mentality*, 280.
115. Honey, *Going Down Jerico Road*, 119–21.
116. John K. Wood to Henry Loeb, 12 March 1968, Loeb Papers.
117. M. E. Greiner, Jr., to Henry Loeb, 23 February 1968, Loeb Papers.
118. Honey, *Going Down Jerico Road*, 292.
119. Beifuss, *At the River I Stand*, 193–96; Honey, *Going Down Jerico Road*, 297–308.
120. Beifuss, *At the River I Stand*, 203–5.
121. Ibid., 211–20; E. H. Arkin, "Civil Disorder Memphis, Tennessee" (Memphis Police Department, 1968), housed in the Frank Holloman Collection, Memphis Public Library and Information Center.
122. Honey, *Going Down Jerico Road*, 338–46; Beifuss, *At the River I Stand*, 211–29.
123. *Memphis Commercial Appeal*, 28 March 1998; Honey, *Going Down Jerico Road*, 359–60.
124. Honey, *Going Down Jerico Road*, 382–83; Arkin, "Civil Disorder," 36–39, Holloman Collection.
125. Honey, *Going Down Jerico Road*, 367–81.
126. Beifuss, *At the River I Stand*, 267.
127. Ibid., 267–72.
128. Honey, *Going Down Jerico Road*, 418–20; Beifuss, *At the River I Stand*, 276–81.
129. Arkin, "Civil Disorder," 43, Holloman Collection.
130. Handwritten note on the death of Dr. Martin Luther King, Jr., 4 April 1968, Holloman Collection.
131. Beifuss, *At the River I Stand*, 301–12.
132. Ibid., 319–22, 328–29.
133. Honey, *Going Down Jerico Road*, 474–80.
134. Beifuss, *At the River I Stand*, 345–50.
135. James Conaway, *Memphis Afternoons: A Memoir* (Boston: Houghton Mifflin Company, 1993), 197.
136. *Time*, 12 April 1968.
137. *Wall Street Journal*, 21 August 1978.
138. Woods, *LBJ*, 832–33.
139. *Memphis Commercial Appeal*, 1 April 1968.
140. Ibid.
141. Ibid., 2 April 1968.
142. Ibid., 1 and 2 April 1968.
143. Ibid., 2 April 1968.
144. Theodore H. White, *The Making of the President 1968* (New York: Atheneum Publishers, 1969), 181–87.
145. *Memphis Commercial Appeal*, 7 August 1968.
146. Ibid.
147. Ibid., 9 August 1968.
148. Ibid., 8 August 1968.

149. Ibid., 9 August 1968.
150. *Memphis Press-Scimitar*, 29 June 1968.
151. *Memphis Commercial Appeal*, 20 August 1968.
152. Ibid., 24 August 1968.
153. Ibid., 2 August 1968.
154. Ibid., 25 August 1968.
155. Ibid., 27, 28, 29 August 1968.
156. Ibid., 29, 30 August 1968.
157. Ibid., 30 August 1968.
158. Stephan Lesher, *George Wallace: American Populist* (Reading, Massachusetts: Addison-Wesley Publishing Company, 1994), 389–91.
159. *Memphis Press-Scimitar*, 12 June 1968.
160. *Memphis Commercial Appeal*, 24 October 1968.
161. *Tri-State Defender*, 27 July 1968.
162. George W. Lee to Nelson Rockefeller, 18 March 1968, Lee Collection.
163. George W. Lee to Richard M. Nixon, 3 June 1968, Lee Collection.
164. *Memphis Press-Scimitar*, 12 June 1968.
165. *Nashville Tennessean*, 7 August 1968.
166. George W. Lee to Howard Baker, Jr., 9 August 1968; Howard Baker, Jr., to George W. Lee, 26 September 1968, Lee Collection.
167. George W. Lee to Howard Baker, Jr., 24 October 1968; Howard Baker, Jr., to George W. Lee, 8 November 1968, Lee Collection.
168. George W. Lee to Howard Baker, Jr., 15 October 1968, Lee Collection.
169. *Memphis Commercial Appeal*, 25 September 1968.
170. *Memphis Press-Scimitar*, 31 October 1968.
171. *Memphis Commercial Appeal*, 7 November 1968.
172. Stephen E. Ambrose, *Nixon: The Triumph of a Politician, 1962–1972* (New York: Simon and Schuster, 1989), 220–21; Numan V. Bartley, *The New South, 1945–1980* (Baton Rouge: Louisiana State University Press, 1995), 396–97.

Afterword

1. Michael Rogers, "Dunn, Winfield C.," in *The Tennessee Encyclopedia of History and Culture*, ed. Carroll Van West (Nashville: Tennessee Historical Society, 1998), 266–67; Winfield Dunn, *From a Standing Start: My Tennessee Political Odyssey* (Nashville: Magellan Press, 2007), 321–22.
2. *Memphis Press-Scimitar*, 29 November 1978.
3. *Memphis Commercial Appeal*, 1 May 2004.
4. *Memphis Press-Scimitar*, 7 November 1974; *Memphis Commercial Appeal*, 21 April 1996.
5. George W. Lee to Winfield Dunn, 17 August 1971; Harry W. Wellford to George W. Lee, 8 September 1970; Winfield Dunn to George W. Lee, 30 September 1970, Lee Collection.
6. *Memphis Press-Scimitar*, 2 August 1976; *Memphis Commercial Appeal*, 2 August 1976.

7. *Memphis Commercial Appeal*, 3 February 1983; *Memphis Press-Scimitar*, 2 February 1983.

8. *Memphis Commercial Appeal*, 12 March 1996.

9. Ibid., 15 July 1988.

10. Ibid., 11 May 1975 and 12 May 1987.

11. Ibid., 17 December 1995.

12. Ibid., 8 February 1994.

13. Ibid.; ibid., 13 September 1983.

14. *Memphis Press-Scimitar*, 24 January 1967; *Tri-State Defender*, 27 September 2007.

15. *Memphis Press-Scimitar*, 12 May 1965.

16. *Memphis Commercial Appeal*, 13 April 1972; *Memphis Press-Scimitar*, 1 July 1977.

17. *Memphis Commercial Appeal*, 18 February 1992; *Memphis Commercial Appeal*, 6 November 2007.

18. Mantri Sivananda, "Henry Loeb's Retirement and Last Days," *West Tennessee Historical Society Papers* 56 (2002): 100–103.

19. *Memphis Commercial Appeal*, 13 October 1991.

20. John Harkins, "The Last Time I Saw Henry—a Brief Memoir," *The Best Times*, January 2008.

Bibliography

Manuscript Collections

Roberta Church Collection, Memphis Public Library and Information Center
Everett R. Cook Oral History Collection, Memphis Public Library and Information Center
E. H. Crump Collection, Memphis Public Library and Information Center
Frank Holloman Collection, Memphis Public Library and Information Center
Hunter Lane, Jr., Papers, Memphis Public Library and Information Center
George W. Lee Collection, Memphis Public Library and Information Center
Henry Loeb Papers, Memphis Public Library and Information Center
Kenneth McKellar Collection, Memphis Public Library and Information Center
Edmund Orgill Papers, Memphis Public Library and Information Center
James J. Pleasants, Jr., Papers, Memphis Public Library and Information Center
Political Advertisements Collection, Memphis Public Library and Information Center
Maxine Smith NAACP Collection, Memphis Public Library and Information Center
Frank Tobey Papers, Memphis Public Library and Information Center
Roane Waring Collection, Memphis Public Library and Information Center
A. W. Willis Collection, Memphis Public Library and Information Center

Government Documents

City of Memphis, *Code of Ordinances* (Memphis, 1967)
The Memphis Digest 1931 (Memphis, 1931)
"Declaration of Constitutional Principles," from *Congressional Record*, 84th Congress, Second Session. Vol. 102, part 4, March 12, 1956 (Washington, D.C.: Governmental Printing Office, 1956), 4459–4460. Reproduced at http://www.strom.clemson.edu/strom/manifesto.html
Public Papers of the Presidents of the United States, John F. Kennedy, 1963 (Washington: U.S. Government Printing Office, 1964)
State of Tennessee Constitutional Convention of 1953, *The Journal and Debates of the Constitutional Convention* (Nashville: State of Tennessee, 1954)
State of Tennessee, Certificate of Death, file number 3159, Stillborn Tobey, Shelby County Archives
United States Commission on Civil Rights, *Hearings Held in Memphis, Tennessee, June 25–26, 1962* (Washington: U.S. Government Printing Office, 1963)

Newspapers

Memphis Commercial Appeal
Memphis Press-Scimitar
Memphis World
Millington Star
Nashville Tennessean
New York Times
Tri-State Defender
Wall Street Journal
Washington Afro-American

Articles

Bailey, Fred A. "The Southern Historical Association and the Quest for Racial Justice, 1954–1963." *Journal of Southern History* (November 2005).

Biles, Roger. "Robert R. Church, Jr., of Memphis: Black Republican Leader in the Age of Democratic Ascendancy, 1928–1940." *Tennessee Historical Quarterly* (Winter 1983).

Kefauver, Estes. "How Boss Crump Was Licked." *Collier's*, 16 October 1948.

Kitchens, Allen H. "Political Upheavals in Tennessee: Boss Crump and the Senatorial Election of 1948." *West Tennessee Historical Society Papers* 16 (1962).

Melton, Scott. "Machine Prince or Mayoral Pauper? Watkins Overton's Political Relationship with Ed Crump and the Crump Machine." *West Tennessee Historical Society Papers* 49 (1995).

Porteous, Clark. "The Two Eds of Memphis—Meeman and Crump." *West Tennessee Historical Society Papers* 45 (1991).

Singer, Thea. "How I Did It: When Civil Rights Came to My Box Office." *Inc.*, February 2003.

Sivananda, Mantri. "Henry Loeb III as Public Works Commissioner, 1956–1959." *West Tennessee Historical Quarterly* 54 (2000).

Thomason, Sally Palmer. "The Three Ed's: Memphis in 1948." *West Tennessee Historical Society Papers* 52 (1998).

Walker, Randolph Meade. "The Role of the Black Clergy in Memphis." *West Tennessee Historical Society Papers* 33 (1979).

Wax, Jonathan I. "Program of Progress: The Recent Change in the Form of Government of Memphis, Part I." *West Tennessee Historical Society* 23 (1969).

———. "Program of Progress: The Recent Change in the Form of Government of Memphis, Part II." *West Tennessee Historical Society* 24 (1970).

Books

Ambrose, Stephen E. *Eisenhower: Soldier, General of the Army and President-Elect, 1890–1952*. New York: Simon and Schuster, 1983.

———. *Nixon: The Triumph of a Politician, 1962–1972.* New York: Simon and Schuster, 1989.

Bartley, Numan V. *The New South, 1945–1980.* Baton Rouge: Louisiana State University Press, 1995.

Beifuss, Joan Turner. *At the River I Stand: Memphis, the 1968 Strike and Martin Luther King.* Memphis: B&W Books, 1985.

Black, Earl, and Merle Black. *The Rise of Southern Republicans.* Cambridge: Harvard University Press, 2002.

Branston, John. *Rowdy Memphis: The South Unscripted.* Nashville: Cold Tree Press, 2004.

Church, Annette, and Roberta Church. *The Robert R. Churches of Memphis.* Ann Arbor: Edwards Brothers, 1974.

Conaway, James. *Memphis Afternoons: A Memoir.* Boston: Houghton Mifflin Company, 1993.

Dallek, Robert. *An Unfinished Life: John F. Kennedy, 1917–1963.* Boston: Little, Brown and Company, 2003.

———. *Lone Star Rising: Lyndon Johnson and His Times, 1908–1960.* New York: Oxford University Press, 1991.

Dowdy, G. Wayne. *Mayor Crump Don't Like It: Machine Politics in Memphis.* Jackson: University Press of Mississippi, 2006.

Faith, Hazel. *A Dream Come True: The Story of St. Jude Children's Research Hospital and ALSAC.* Dallas: Taylor Publishing, 1983.

Faulkner, William. *Essays, Speeches and Public Letters.* New York: Random House, 1966.

Ferrell, Robert H. *Harry S. Truman: A Life.* Columbia and London: University of Missouri Press, 1994.

———, ed. *Off the Record: The Private Papers of Harry S. Truman.* New York: Harper and Row, 1980.

Fontenay, Charles L. *Estes Kefauver: A Biography.* Knoxville: University of Tennessee Press, 1980.

Frederickson, Kari A. *The Dixiecrat Revolt and the End of the Solid South, 1932–1968.* Chapel Hill: University of North Carolina Press, 2001.

Gardner, Michael R. *Harry S. Truman and Civil Rights: Moral Courage and Political Risks.* Carbondale: Southern Illinois University Press, 2002.

Gorman, Joseph Bruce. *Kefauver: A Political Biography.* New York: Oxford University Press, 1971.

Gould, Lewis L. *Grand Old Party: A History of the Republicans.* Random House: New York, 2003.

Green, Laurie B. *Battling the Plantation Mentality: Memphis and the Black Freedom Struggle.* Chapel Hill: University of North Carolina Press, 2007.

Greene, Lee Seifert. *Lead Me On: Frank Goad Clement and Tennessee Politics.* Knoxville: University of Tennessee Press, 1982.

Hamby, Alonzo L. *Man of the People: A Life of Harry S. Truman.* New York: Oxford University Press, 1995.

Hartman, Gary, Roy M. Mersky, and Cindy L. Tate, eds. *Landmark Supreme Court Cases.* New York: Facts on File, Inc., 2004.

Honey, Michael K. *Going Down Jerico Road: The Memphis Strike, Martin Luther King's Last Campaign.* New York: W. W. Norton & Company, 2007.
Hooks, Benjamin L. *The March for Civil Rights.* Chicago: American Bar Association, 2003.
Kessel, John H. *The Goldwater Coalition: Republican Strategies in 1964.* Indianapolis and New York: the Bobbs-Merrill Company, Inc., 1968.
Langsdon, Phillip. *Tennessee: A Political History.* Franklin: Hillsboro Press, 2000.
Lesher, Stephan. *George Wallace: American Populist.* Reading, Massachusetts: Addison-Wesley Publishing Company, 1994.
Leuchtenburg, William E. *In the Shadow of FDR: From Harry Truman to Bill Clinton.* Ithaca: Cornell University Press, 1993.
Lisio, Donald J. *Hoover, Blacks & Lily-Whites: A Study of Southern Strategies.* Chapel Hill: University of North Carolina Press, 1985.
Locke, Hubert G. *The Detroit Riot of 1967.* Detroit: Wayne State University Press, 1969.
Lovett, Bobby L. *The Civil Rights Movement in Tennessee: A Narrative History.* Knoxville: University of Tennessee Press, 2005.
McCoy, Donald R. *The Presidency of Harry S. Truman.* Lawrence: University Press of Kansas, 1984.
Majors, William R. *The End of Arcadia: Gordon Browning and Tennessee Politics.* Memphis: Memphis State University Press, 1982.
Miller, William D. *Mr. Crump of Memphis.* Baton Rouge: Louisiana State University Press, 1964.
Patterson, James T. *Grand Expectations: The United States, 1945–1974.* New York: Oxford University Press, 1996.
Perlstein, Rick. *Nixonland: The Rise of a President and the Fracturing of America.* New York: Scribner, 2008.
Streit, Clarence K. *Union Now: A Proposal for a Federal Union of the Leading Democracies.* New York: Harper and Brothers Publishers, 1938.
Tucker, David M. *Lieutenant Lee of Beale Street.* Nashville: Vanderbilt University Press, 1971.
———. *Memphis since Crump: Bossism, Blacks, and Civic Reformers, 1948–1968.* Knoxville: University of Tennessee Press, 1980.
Turner, Allegra W. *Except by Grace: The Life of Jesse H. Turner.* Jonesboro, Arkansas: Four-G Publishers, 2004.
Walk, Joe. *A History of African-Americans in Memphis Government.* Memphis, 1996.
White, Theodore H. *The Making of the President 1968.* New York: Atheneum Publishers, 1969.
Wildavsky, Aaron. *Dixon-Yates: A Study in Power Politics.* New Haven and London, Yale University Press, 1962.
Woods, Randall B. *LBJ: Architect of American Ambition.* Cambridge: Harvard University Press, 2006.
Wright, Sharon D. *Race, Power, and Political Emergence in Memphis.* New York: J. B. Garland Publishing, 2000.

Dissertations and Theses

Gritter, Elizabeth. "Local Leaders and Community Soldiers: The Memphis Desegregation Movement, 1955–1961." Senior honors thesis, American University, 2001.
———."'This Is a Crusade for Freedom': The Volunteer Ticket Campaign in the 1959 City Election in Memphis, Tennessee." M.A. thesis, University of North Carolina at Chapel Hill, 2005.
Jalenak, James B. "Beale Street Politics: A Study of Negro Political Activity in Memphis, Tennessee." Honors thesis, Yale University, 1961.
Melton, Gloria Brown. "Blacks in Memphis, Tennessee, 1920–1955." Ph.D. diss., Washington State University, 1982.
Moon, Robert L. "Trouble in the Valley: Eisenhower, Dixon-Yates, and Refinancing Tennessee Valley Authority Power Authorizations." M. A. thesis, University of Alabama in Huntsville, 1995.
Sivananda, Mantri. "Controversial Memphis Mayor Henry Loeb III, 1920–1992: A Biographical Study." Ph.D. diss., University of Memphis, 2002.

Web Sites

Rhodes College, Crossroads to Freedom Digital Archive (http://www.crossroadstofreedom.org)

Index

Abernathy, Ralph, 130
Acuff, Roy, 16
AFSCME (American Federation of State, County and Municipal Employees), 123–24, 126
Agnew, Spiro, 133, 135
Andrews, Francis, 27
Armour, Claude, 21, 36, 43, 49, 51, 53–55, 57, 64, 70, 78, 82–84, 86–87, 93–95, 97, 108–9, 113, 115, 119–20
Asphalt Plant Controversy, 21–22
Awsumb, Gwen, 111, 122

Baker, Howard, Jr., 136
Barkley, Alben W., 7
Barnes, Richard W., 109
Bates, Daisy, 68
Bates, Guy, 21
Bates, Samuel O., 51, 58
Beale Street, 9, 25, 42, 76, 128
Bell, Joyce Ann, 82
Binghampton Civic League, 67
Blackburn, Charles, 123
Blaine, Ell, 13
Boggs, Hale, 116
Bomar, J. O'Neill, 39
Bondurant, Julian, 111
Boushe, Beverly, 78–80
Boyd, Marion, 81, 83
Boyle, Joseph, 14, 16, 22, 43, 49
Brewer, Norm, 109
Brown, Bailey, 129
Brown v. Board of Education, 38–39, 50
Browning, Gordon, 12, 24–26, 28
Brewster, Herbert W., 79
Bunton, Henry, 67, 71
Burch, Lucius E., Jr., 11, 12, 20–21, 34–35, 52, 129, 139
Bush, George W., 140

Canale, John Ford, 41, 66, 95–96
Chambers, Sam, 69

Chandler, Walter, 47–48, 51, 58, 60, 114
Church, Robert, Jr., 9, 28–29
Church, Roberta, 30, 31, 55
Citizens for Eisenhower-Nixon, 56
Citizens for Eisenhower-Nixon Club, 31
Citizens for Farris and Davis Committee, 89
Citizens for Good Government, 114
Citizens for Progress, 51–55, 58, 63–65
Citizens League for Edmund Orgill, 48
Citizens Non-Partisan Registration Campaign, 64
City Charter, 22, 70, 80, 87, 108, 111–15, 117–18
City Commission, 21–22, 33–34, 37, 43–45, 47, 51, 53, 55, 82, 86–87, 92–94, 96, 108–9, 111, 113
City Council, 124–25
City Manager Form of Government, 20–21, 34–35, 48, 111–13
Civic Research Committee, 20–21, 34, 40, 48, 111
Civil Rights, vii, 3, 29, 38, 65, 68, 71–85, 97, 100–1, 116
Civil Rights Act of 1964, 97–101, 103
Clement, Frank, 24–26, 28, 37, 39, 56, 58–59, 63, 88–89, 109, 110, 140
Clinton, Tennessee, 58–59
Cole, Echol, 122–23
Colored Democrats Club, 14
Colored Methodist Episcopal Church Pastors Alliance, 15
COME (Citizens on the Move for Equality), 126–27, 129
Commission Form of Government, viii, 20, 34, 35, 40, 43, 111, 114
Community Action Committee, 110
Congress of Racial Equality, 83
Conyers, John, 119
Crump, E. H., vii, viii, 3, 5, 6, 8–11, 13–17, 19–22, 24–28, 32–33, 39
Cunningham, Jesse, 62

179

Daley, Richard J., 74, 134
Davis, Clifford, 10, 38, 51–52, 73–74, 88–89, 103
Davis, Fred, 122, 124–25, 137
Dedicated Citizens Committee, 70
Democratic National Convention: 1948, 6–7; 1952, 26; 1956, 57; 1960, 72–74; 1964, 101–2; 1968, 134–35
Democratic Party, vii, viii, 4–6, 10, 17, 31, 58, 85, 92, 101–2, 106, 117, 132–33, 135, 139
Democratic Voters League, 54
DeSapio, Carmine, 74
Dewey, Thomas E., 8, 18
Dilliard, Stanley, 33, 47, 49, 51, 53
Disalle, Michael V., 74
Dixiecrats, 7–8, 17–18, 31
Dixon-Yates Power Plant, 37–38
Donelson, Lewis, 99, 100, 111, 117, 122, 125, 133, 137, 139
Dunn, Winfield, 133, 139
Dutch Treat Luncheon, 93, 140–41
Dwyer, John T. "Buddy," 22, 33, 43, 49, 51, 53, 70, 86–87, 94, 96, 114

East Memphis, 15, 32, 77, 117, 121–23, 136
East Memphis Citizens Club, 15
East Olive Street Bombing, 35–36
Eastland, James O., 17
Eisenhower, Dwight, 28–32, 36, 38, 55–56, 58, 137
Ellington, Buford, 63–64, 73–75, 120, 128, 133–34, 136
Evers, O. Z., 59–61, 67, 103, 119
Executive Order 9980, 7
Executive Order 9981, 7–8

Farris, William W., 66, 69–71, 86–89, 92–97, 109, 115, 139
Faulkner, William, 50
FEPC (Fair Employment Practices Committee), 5, 73
Fitzhugh, Millsaps, 31, 75, 98
Fleming, Partee, 71
Foote, Shelby, 122

Ford, Gerald, 116, 139
Ford, Harold, Jr., 139
Fowler, Will, 66
Fox Meadows, 136
Frayser community, 55, 106, 136
Fredericks, Robert, 22
Freeman, Alvin, 82
Freeman, E. C., 82

Gerber, Will, 14, 47
Gianotti, Frank, Jr., 44–45, 61, 108, 129
Gilliam, H. A., 72
Glenview Civic Club, 67
Goldwater, Barry, 74, 90, 99–101, 104–6, 132
Good Local Government League, 52–54
Gore, Albert, 27–28, 57, 75, 132, 134, 136
Gotten, Henry, 54, 70
Great Society, 115, 132
Grider, George, 52, 103–4, 106, 115–16, 137

Hale, E. W., 27, 39–40, 49
Hayes, Taylor, 23
Heiskill, John, 24, 26, 40, 48–49, 58
Herenton, W. W., 140–41
Hinds, M. A., 93–96
Holloman, Frank, 125, 130
Holt, Deborah Ann, 82
Hooks, Benjamin L., 23, 31, 54, 71, 76, 78–79, 81, 87, 95–97, 99, 140
Hoover, Herbert, 30, 32
Humphrey, Hubert, 7, 102, 105, 132, 134–37
Hunt, Blair T., 64

Ingram, William B., 93–97, 105, 108–11, 113–14, 118–22

Jackson, J. H., 136
Jackson, Mahalia, 67
James, Robert, 90–91, 99–101, 103–4, 106–7, 122, 137–38
John Gaston Hospital, 51
Johnson, Lyndon B., 73–74, 76, 92, 98, 101–2, 105–6, 109, 130, 132, 137

INDEX

Johnson, Patrick, Sr., 108
Jones, T. O., 123
Justice Department, 4, 84–85

Kefauver, Estes, 10–11, 14–16, 26, 57–58, 63
Kennedy, John F., 57, 72–74, 76, 84, 92, 97, 98, 137
Kennedy, Robert F., 75, 84, 132
King, Coretta Scott, 131
King, Martin Luther, Jr., 60, 67–68, 127, 129, 130
Kuykendall, Dan, 111, 115–16, 133, 137, 139
Kyles, Dwania, 82–83
Kyles, Samuel "Billy," 83

Lane, Hunter, Jr., 81, 94–95, 96, 102, 108–9, 111, 120
Laney, Ben, 6–7
Lawrence, David L., 74
Lawson, James, 95, 118, 126, 128–29
Lee, George W., 8–9, 23, 25, 29, 30, 32, 48, 55–56, 58, 67, 71, 74, 76, 87, 90–92, 98, 99–101, 105, 107, 135–36, 139
LeMay, Curtis, 135
LeMoyne College, 78
Lincoln League, 91
Lockard, H. T., 60–63, 88, 103, 107, 111–12, 140
Lodge, Henry Cabot, 75, 100
Loeb, Henry, III, 43–45, 47, 49, 51, 53–55, 66, 68–71, 75, 77, 80–82, 84–87, 92–94, 96, 111, 115, 118–26, 128–31, 140–41
Love, Roy, 48, 67, 71

Malone, Sharon, 82
Malone, Shelia, 82
Marshall, Burke, 85
Marshall, Thurgood, 81
Massive resistance, 51
Mayes, Pamela, 82
Mayor-Council Form of Government, 40–41, 43, 47–48, 111–13, 117–18
Mays, Benjamin, 50

McCarthy, Eugene, 132
McDonald, J. C., 108
McDonald, W. Percy, 58
McKellar, Kenneth, 26–28
Medicare, 115
Meeman, Edward J., 10–11, 112, 139
Memphis and Shelby County Council of Civic Clubs, 87
Memphis and Shelby County Planning Commission, 108
Memphis Committee for Council-Manager Form of Government, 40–41, 47–48
Memphis Light, Gas and Water Division, 53, 86
Memphis Public Library, 61–63, 77
Memphis Street Railway, 59–61
Middlecoff, Cary, 56
Miller, William E., 91, 101
Minimum Wage, Tennessee, 110
Ministers and Citizens League, 48
Mississippi Freedom Democratic Party, 102
Mitchell, John A., 10, 15
Moore, David L., 78
Moore, Jacqueline, 82
Moore, James W., 70, 86–87, 108–9, 113
Moore, Jerrold, 108
Morris, William N., 118, 120
Mosby, James, 15
Motley, Constance Baker, 81
Muskie, Edmund, 135–36

NAACP (National Association for the Advancement of Colored People), vii, 16, 59, 60–61, 78, 81, 83, 124
National Guard, 120, 128–29, 130
Netters, James L., 122, 125, 137
Ninth Congressional District Democrats, 95, 97, 103
Ninth District Democratic League, 97, 103
Nixon, Richard, 30, 72, 74–75, 77, 116, 132, 135–37, 140
Non-Partisan Voters League, 25

Olgiati, P. R., 88, 89
Orange Mound, 116
Orgill, Edmund, 12, 20–21, 23, 34, 48–49, 51–53, 55, 63–66, 68, 70, 86, 105, 111, 115, 139
Overton, Watkins, 13, 19, 20–23, 27, 33–35, 43, 47, 49
Owen Junior College, 78

Park Commission, 43–45, 83–84
Parkway Village, 136
Patterson, J. O., Jr., 116–17, 122, 137
Payne, Larry, 128–29
Personnel Department, 33
Pierce, Clifford, 24
Pleasants, James, 6, 11, 14, 16, 19
Police brutality, 13–15, 119, 125–26, 129
Poor People's Campaign, 127
Powell, Tommy, 111
President's Committee on Civil Rights, 3–4
Price, Hollis, 95, 96–97
Pritchard, Ross, 88–89
Program of Progress, 112–15, 117
Pryor, Downing, 111, 117, 122
Pupil Assignment Law, 59, 80–81

Rayburn, Sam, 74
Reagan, Ronald, 133
Reese, Carroll B., 8, 16, 55
Republican Association, 90
Republican National Convention: 1948, 8–9; 1952, 29–30; 1956, 55; 1960, 74; 1964, 99–101; 1968, 133
Republican Party, vii, viii, 8, 28, 31–32, 58, 85, 90–92, 99, 100–1, 104, 107, 117, 133, 135, 139
Riots: Boston, Massachusetts, 120; Buffalo, New York, 120; Cincinnati, Ohio, 120; Detroit, Michigan, 120; Newark, New Jersey, 120; Tampa, Florida, 120
Rockefeller, Nelson, 99, 135, 136
Roosevelt, Franklin D., 26
Russell, Richard B., 74

Saint Jude Children's Research Hospital, 41–43
Sanitation strike, 122–31
School desegregation, 81–83
School lunch program, 115
Scranton, William, 99, 100
Segregation, 4, 51, 58, 63–65, 68, 71–73, 76–77, 79–81, 83–84, 126
Shelby County Democratic Club, 72, 88–90, 95, 97, 121, 134
Shelby County Quarterly Court, 103, 107
Silver, James W., 50
Sims, Cecil, 6, 50
Single Shot Voting, 23, 66, 69
Sisson, Pete, 95, 96, 108–9, 113
Sit-ins: Greensboro, North Carolina, 77–78; Memphis, Tennessee, 78–80
Smith, Maxine, 82, 103, 140
Smith, Vasco A., Jr., 79, 83, 95–97, 111–12, 114–15, 118, 121–22, 134, 140
South Memphis, 35–36
Southern Declaration of Constitutional Principles, 51–52, 57
Southern Governor's Conference, 5
Southern Historical Association, 49–50
Southern Manifesto, 51–52, 57
Stanback, Elihue, 67
State's Rights Democratic Party, 7–8, 17–18, 31
Stevenson, Adlai, 26, 32, 57–58
Stewart, Tom, 9, 10
Streit, Clarence, 12
Strong Mayor Form of Government, 34, 35
Sugarmon, Russell, 66–67, 69, 78, 81–83, 87–88, 92, 95, 98, 101, 111–12, 114–18, 134, 137, 139

Taft, Robert, 8, 29, 30
Television, 29–30, 37, 40, 49, 51, 54, 67, 89, 93, 104, 109, 115, 119–20, 126, 135
Tennessee Anti-Poverty Program, 109
Tennessee General Assembly, 52, 54, 59, 66, 80, 97, 102, 110, 128, 139

Tennessee House of Representatives, 54, 102, 109–10, 116–17
Tennessee Manifesto, 59
Tennessee Voters Council, 88
Thomas, Danny, 41–43, 45–46
Thurmond, Strom, 5, 7, 17–18, 31
To Secure These Rights, 4
Tobey, Frank, 22, 33–47
Truman, Harry S., 3–8, 17–18, 36, 57
Turner, Jesse H., 61–63, 76–77, 82, 86–88, 101, 103, 111–12, 140
TVA (Tennessee Valley Authority), 32, 36–38

Unity League, 119
Unity Ticket, 70
Union Now, 12
Universal Life Insurance Company, 23, 67, 86

Venson, Ethyl, 23
Venson, R. Q., 55
Vesey, John B., 44–45
Vietnam War, 115, 132, 134, 136
Volunteer Citizens Committee, 95, 97
Volunteer Ticket, 67–69, 71

Walker, A. Maceo, 72, 86–89, 95–96, 118
Walker, J. E., 22–25, 48–49, 51, 54
Walker, James Thomas, 54–55, 88
Walker, Robert, Jr., 122–23
Wallace, George C., 135–37
Wallace, Henry, 8, 18
War on Poverty, 109, 115
Waring, Roane, 6, 31
Watson v. City of Memphis, 84
Wax, James, 111, 113, 130, 131
Wellford, Harry, 111
Whitehaven, 106
Wiggins, Leandrew, 82
Wilbun, S. A., 66
Wiley, Bell I., 50
Williams, Clarence, 82
Williams, Harry, 82
Williams, Nat D., 72, 91

Williams, O. P., 21, 33, 43, 49
Willis, A. W., Jr., 67, 72, 78, 81, 83, 86–88, 96, 101–2, 107, 109–10, 112, 116–22, 134, 137, 139
Willis, Michael, 82–83
Wright, Fielding L., 4–7
Wurf, Jerry, 124

F
444
.M557
D69
2010